Outsiders

FORCED MIGRATION

General Editors: Tom Scott-Smith and Kirsten McConnachie

This series, published in association with the Refugees Studies Centre, University of Oxford, reflects the multidisciplinary nature of the field and includes within its scope international law, anthropology, sociology, politics, international relations, geopolitics, social psychology and economics.

Recent volumes:

For a full volume listing, please see the series page on our website:
https//www.berghahnbooks.com/series/forced-migration

Outsiders

MEMORIES OF MIGRATION TO AND FROM NORTH KOREA

Markus Bell

berghahn

NEW YORK · OXFORD

www.berghahnbooks.com

First published in 2022 by
Berghahn Books
www.berghahnbooks.com

Library of Congress Cataloging-in-Publication Data
Names: Bell, Markus, author.
Title: Outsiders : memories of migration to and from North Korea / Markus
Bell.
Description: New York : Berghahn Books, 2021. | Series: Forced migration ;
Volume 42 | Includes bibliographical references and index.
Identifiers: LCCN 2021026258 (print) | LCCN 2021026259 (ebook) | ISBN
9781800732292 (hardback) | ISBN 9781800732308 (ebook)
Subjects: LCSH: Japanese--Korea (North)--Social conditions. | Korea
(North)--Emigration and immigration. | Japan--Emigration and
immigration.
Classification: LCC DS933.3.J3 B45 2021 (print) | LCC DS933.3.J3 (ebook) |
DDC 305.9/06914095193--dc23
LC record available at https://lccn.loc.gov/2021026258
LC ebook record available at https://lccn.loc.gov/2021026259

British Library Cataloguing in Publication Data
A catalogue record for this book is available from the British Library

ISBN 978-1-80073-229-2 hardback
ISBN 978-1-80073-913-0 paperback
ISBN 978-1-80073-230-8 ebook

https://doi.org/10.3167/9781800732292

Seeds-Time-People by FUNI, you and Genmugi[1]

To seeds over seven seas.
To all my brothers and sisters underground
been feelin' close and yet far–homeland.
Stories to share still in the shade.
We came different routes,
but took roots–same hood.
I dream 'bout a big tree.
It seems like your victory.
And it will set me free.
Set WE free.

蒔きびと
七つの海を越えた種たちよ
近く遠い故郷を憶い
未地の底で踠き苦しむ兄弟姉妹たちよ
語り継がれるべき物語は未だ陰に身を潜めている
我々はそれぞれ別々の未知を辿って
同じ寄るべに根を張った
私は大きな木の夢をみる
あなたの身が蒔かれた時
私の魂も解き放つ
そうして
我々は自由になるだろう

씨앗 뿌리는 사람
일곱 바다를 건넌 씨앗이여
가깝고도 먼 집을 그리워하며
낯선 땅속에서 몸부림치는 언니, 오빠, 누나, 동생이여
이어져 내려와야 할 이야기는 아직도 어둠 속에 드리워져 있디네
우리는 서로 다른 길을 거쳐서
한 동네에 뿌리를 내렸지
나는 커다란 나무의 꿈을 꿔봐
그대 몸의 씨앗이 뿌려질 때
나의 넋도 풀려나는
그렇게
우리는 벗어나게 될 거야

Note

1. FUNI is a Zainichi-Korean rapper, songwriter, poet, and advocate for immigrants in Japan. He debuted in 2004 as part of the group, "KP" (Korean Power, Korean Pride) and released his debut album "KAWASAKI" in 2016.

Contents

Illustrations

Maps

Acknowledgments

This book is the culmination of years of discussions, interviews, dinners, and friendships with people who have risked everything in search of a better life. This book is dedicated to my friends from North Korea, those who welcomed me into their homes and into their lives.

In anthropology circles it is often said that it takes a village to write a book. I have been grateful for my village and its villagers. My sincere thanks go to Sandra Fahy, Mark Caprio, Alex Dukalskis, Andy Kipnis, Philip Taylor, Sonia Ryang, Takeyuki Tsuda, Geoff Fattig and Patricia Bower for reading early versions of this book; to Anne Allison for her advice over wine on a rainy Sheffield evening and to Tessa Morris-Suzuki, Ken George, Kyung-mook Kim, Hyaeweol Choi and Hyang-jin Jung for their tireless support. For assistance during my research in South Korea, Japan, and Switzerland, my thanks go to Jarrod Clyne, Fabrizio Bensi, François Bugnion, Jiro Ishimaru and the team at Asia Press, to Yuseon Lee, Kohong Hiro Im, Fumiaki Yamada, Takahashi sensei, Hiroshi Kato, Susan Menadue-Chun, Marco Milani and Jamie Coates. A further special thanks for advice and support to Anna Vainio, Yuma Osaki, Kyuin Kim, Shinnosuke Yang-Takahashi, Sverre Molland, Kirsty Wissing, Teena Saulo, and Safa Choi.

The many drafts for this book were written across four continents and half a dozen countries. With thanks for coffees and conversation to Deokhyo Choi, Ben Horder, Teodora Gypchanova, Woo-seong Yu, Hyeonseo Lee, Lauren Richardson, Christopher Richardson, Euysuk Kwon, Jenny Hough, Honam Shin, Stephanie Boss, Achim Brueckner, Nick Wilson and Miyako Armytage.

Finally, this project would never have started and certainly would not have lasted without the support of Christine Bell; the guidance of Livingston Armytage during the pandemic months; the love, support, and insights of Rosita; and the love and distraction of Rafael.

Notes on the Text
and Confidentiality

Throughout the text, Korean terms are written in the McCune-Reischauer system of Romanization, except for familiar names and places, such as Kim Il-sung, Syngman Rhee, Pyongyang, and Seoul. Japanese terms, where mentioned, are also Romanized, using romanji. Korean and Japanese names are written with family name first and personal name last. Spellings within quotes are as original.

The names of the participants in this book have been changed to protect the identity of those who kindly gave their time and expertise. In one or two instances the experiences of two or more people have been merged to protect privacy.

All Korean, Japanese, German, and French translations are my own, unless otherwise indicated. All images used throughout the book are my own unless otherwise indicated. Maps have been sourced from the Library of Congress and are labeled using the South Korean Ministry of Culture, Sports and Tourism's Revised Romanization of Korean. All photographs of the repatriations are reproduced with the permission of the International Committee of the Red Cross (ICRC).

Throughout August 2014, 2016, and 2019 I carried out research in the archives of the ICRC, Geneva. The large volume of material in this archive is organized according to the ICRC system. All my references to this material begin with the distinctive "B AG," followed by a reference number. Ethnographic research for this book was transnational in scope, taking place in South Korea and Japan. As such, I have attempted to show a sensitivity to political and cultural frictions that exist between communities in this part of the world. For example, I use both the Korean East Sea and the Japanese/international Sea of Japan to refer to the body of water that lies east of the Korean Peninsula.

An earlier version of chapter 3 was originally published as "Patriotic Revolutionaries and Imperial Sympathizers: Identity and Selfhood of Korean-Japanese Migrants from Japan to North Korea" (Bell 2018). And an earlier version of chapter 5 was originally published as "Making and Breaking Family: North Korea's Zainichi Returnees and 'the Gift'" (Bell 2016).

I presented chapters from this book at Charles University, Czech Republic (2019); the Japan Society, London (2018); the School of Oriental and African Studies (SOAS), University of London (2017); Academy of Korea Studies Europe Conference (2017); Babes-Bolyai University, Romania; National University of Singapore (2016); the Australian Anthropological Society Conference (2015); and the Worldwide Consortium of Korean Studies, Shanghai (2015).

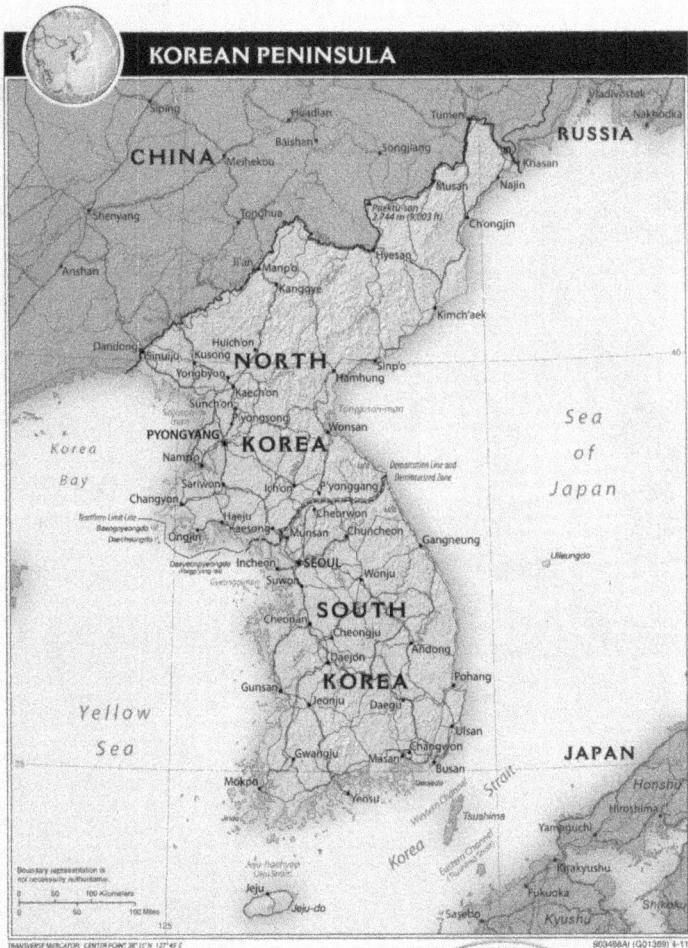

Map 0.1. Map of Korean Peninsula. Library of Congress, Geography and Map Division.

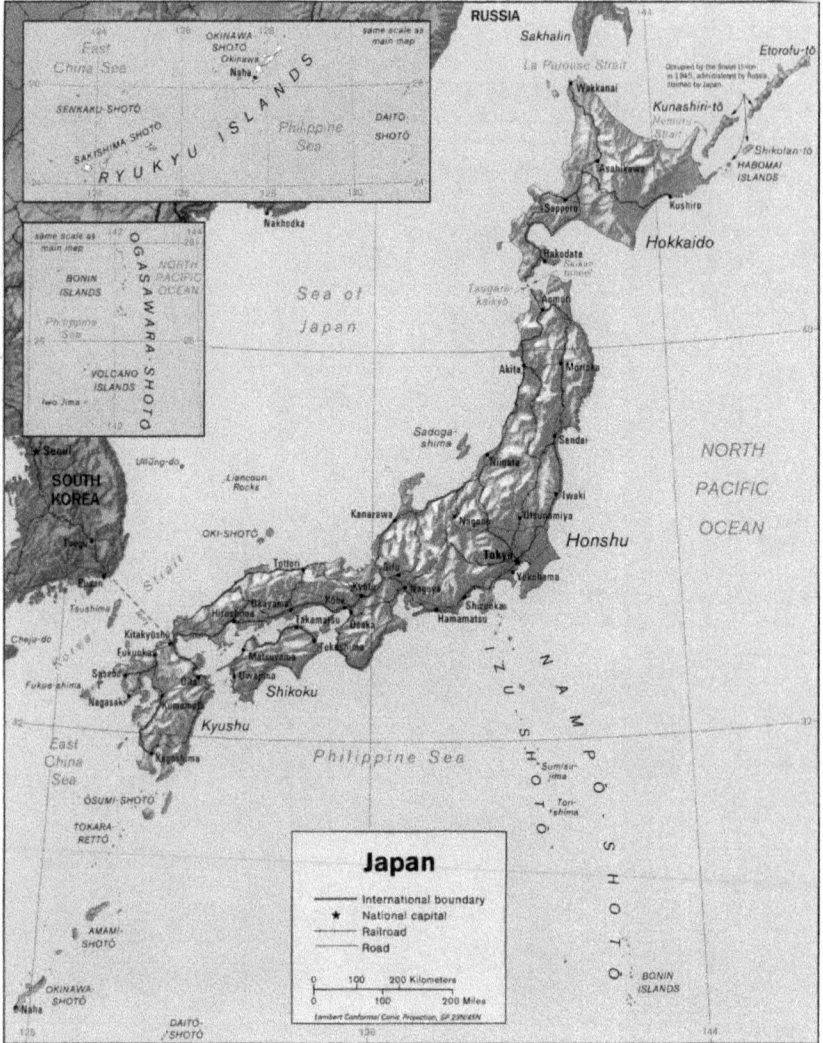

Map 0.2. Map of Japanese Archipelago. Library of Congress, Geography and Map Division.

INTRODUCTION
When There's Nothing Left

One day, Hong Hŭiŭn disappeared. She stuffed a small bag with clothes, Chinese yuan, a few bits of jewelry and ran into the rain. Cutting across fields and avoiding main roads, each step took her farther away from her home and closer to the Yalu River separating North Korea from China. There she met the flimsy boat that was to take her across the flooded waters. Just moments after setting out, Hŭiŭn's guide spotted an armed border patrol and was forced to dock on a small island. It was cold and dark. The pounding rain had retreated to a lazy drizzle. The flickering lights of Dandong seemed so close, but there was nothing to do but wait. Eight hours passed until it was safe to move on. In the soft glow of the early light, tired and scared, Hŭiŭn made it to the Chinese side of the river, where she met a second guide. She changed her clothes, stuffed her wet things into a plastic bag, and followed her companion until they arrived at the home of a *Chosŏnjok* (Korean-Chinese) couple who rented her a room for the night. Hŭiŭn recalled, "The next day I took a bus to Dandong. My relief at reaching China was fleeting. Dandong is dangerous, as it's full of *hwagyo* [ethnic Chinese who live in North Korea] who recognize North Koreans and turn us into the police. The Chinese police have the power to send you back. And if you're sent back, the government punishes you."[1] Realizing the danger, Hŭiŭn had her host buy tickets for a Shenyang-bound train. "I said nothing for the entire ten-hour journey. I was too frightened of someone recognizing me as North Korean." Three days after leaving her home, Hŭiŭn arrived in Shenyang, the capital of China's Liaoning Province. A cousin of the man who had sheltered her outside Dandong met her at the station. "There're so many Koreans in Shenyang, so I felt safer there," she remembered. Hŭiŭn found a place to stay, but she was fast running out of money. "I couldn't find work, because I couldn't speak Mandarin. The owner of the hostel introduced me to another Korean-Chinese woman who agreed to help. She took me to a poor part of the city. From there, I moved into an apartment that was cheap, but had almost no running water or electricity."

In a dilapidated corner of Shenyang city, among poor Chinese and other escapees from North Korea, Hŭiŭn befriended a woman who helped her find a job making noodles in a fast food restaurant. She worked twelve hours a day, every day, returning to a single apartment with one toilet that she shared with eleven other women. "It was so, so hard. But there was nothing left for me in North Korea," she recalled. Hŭiŭn remained in China for three years before she contacted the Japanese consulate in Shenyang with the help of some Japanese activists operating secretly in the city.[2] Several months later, she boarded a plane with a consulate employee and flew to Japan.

Hong Hŭiŭn was born in 1983, in Ryongch'ŏn-gun, in North P'yŏng'an Province, North Korea, to parents who had migrated from Japan in the early 1960s. Now living in Osaka, Japan, she is a survivor of one of the worst famines in modern history, a former member of the North Korean elite, and the fourth generation of her family to move between the Korean Peninsula and Japan.

Hŭiŭn's family was comparatively wealthy in North Korea. They benefitted from the generosity of a well-heeled aunt who owned property in Osaka's gambling industry. Her aunt sent money and clothes to her family. Her mother traded the things that arrived from Osaka and used Japanese yen in the black markets. In the end, it was not hunger that drove Hŭiŭn to leave North Korea, but rather a lack of personal and political freedom. "I was frustrated that I couldn't say or do what I wanted to do. It was suffocating. I thought life would be easier in Japan." Leaving North Korea gave Hŭiŭn some of the freedoms she had imagined, but arriving in Japan without money, status, or belongings brought with it new, unexpected problems.

* * *

Migration is among the greatest challenges confronting the global community in the twenty-first century, as conflict, climate change, and food shortages compel more people to leave their homes than ever before. We need to understand how migration transforms individuals, families, communities, and countries, and how it reconfigures the societies to which migrants relocate.[3]

For refugees—people compelled to leave their home and country when it seems like there is nothing left to stay for—migration offers new hope, as they attempt to start life away from violence and trauma. For receiving societies, the influx of a new and culturally different group might generate social tensions, at least for a time, as the new population attempts to integrate, or simply keep to themselves. But the skills, entrepreneurship, and resilience of these agents of transformation are often regenerative, the presence of these new groups rejuvenates stagnating postindustrial societies, infuses insulated cultures with new life, and presents dynamic solutions to the social instability of ageing societies and declining birth rates.

This book examines displacement and migration. It also explores the strategies used by individuals and families compelled to move at great personal cost, through often deeply hazardous routes, arriving in lands that may or may not bring the better life they seek for themselves and their children. I examine these patterns through the stories of Korean families who, despite experiencing loss, trauma, and dislocation, manage to remake themselves in the process of transplanting their lives. The voices and experiences of the forced migrants in this book and the ways in which their micro transformations are reshaping communities and nations contribute to the argument that migration is not a problem to be solved nor are refugees a threat to the nations that receive them. Instead, the vignettes throughout show that migration is both a strategy and a solution–for the refugees who serve as innovators, entrepreneurs, and agents of social, cultural, economic, and political transformation, and for the societies they socially and demographically transform.

The Age of the Refugee

In the past fifteen years, the volume of people forced to flee from their homes has risen sharply. As of 2020, some 80 million people around the world were displaced within their own country, up from 43 million in 2009. The global COVID-19 pandemic has greatly impacted mobility and migration–with travel restricted, borders closed, labor migration suspended, and assistance to asylum seekers considerably slowed down. Whether migration will soon return to pre-pandemic levels is yet to be seen, but it is likely that people will continue to look to migration as a way of managing the stressors of conflict, climate change, economic immiseration, and political persecution.[4]

The global refugee population has seen alarming growth, doubling in the past decade to around 26 million (UN Office of the High Commissioner for Human Rights [UNHCR] 2018), roughly the current population of Australia. Of the world's refugee population, 68 percent originated in just five countries. Around 1 million are Rohingya fleeing ethnic cleansing by the Myanmar military. Long periods of conflict and instability have compelled a further 2.7 million Afghanis to leave their country, and 2.3 million people are currently displaced outside South Sudan (UN International Organization for Migration [IOM] 2019b, 39). Around 4.2 million people are fleeing political turmoil and socioeconomic instability in Venezuela, and 5.5 million Syrians have fled a horrific civil war. The impacts of people escaping conflict, dwindling resources, extreme weather events, and political persecution are felt on a global scale. Migrants and migration have become foundational issues of debate in domestic politics across the world, such as in the United Kingdom's vote to leave the European Union and the rise to power of far-right governments in Europe and beyond. And yet several million refugees from the Middle East, Africa, South Asia, and Southeast Asia, and another 5 million or so from South America pale in comparison to what we can expect in coming years. Some estimates put the number of people displaced by climate change at more than 140 million by 2050–think everyone in Australia, South Korea, and Thailand combined (World Bank 2018). Less-conservative estimates put the number of people fleeing the effects of a warming planet at around a billion by 2050 (Climate Foresight 2019). A billion human beings displaced by rising sea levels, the extinction of consumable marine life, the salination of arable land, extremes of nature like tsunami, hurricanes and bush fires, and a warming earth that renders large swaths of the planet uninhabitable. A billion people. Migration, in particular the forced movement of people from their homes, is changing the world in unpredictable and unprecedented ways, and what we are seeing now is only the beginning.

Of course, mass migration is not new. Since prehistoric times, individuals, families, communities, and entire ethnic groups have used migration as a strategic response to the effects of changing climate, to conflict, to persecution and to fluctuating resources needed for lives and livelihoods (see Castles and Davidson 2000; Castles and Miller 1998). During the twentieth century, people used migration as a response to stressors of war, famine and ideological division. Globally felt pressures arising from the collapse of empires and the upheaval of global labor markets fractured communities and families, displacing individuals on a massive scale. Such movement tends to be labeled as forced migration. Forced migration is often contrasted with voluntary migration, where people move for marriage, employment, education, or higher salaries. But the binary of forced versus voluntary movement hides more than it reveals. Migration can arise as a response to a combination of negative and positive pressures. For example, long-term economic decline at home (a push factor compelling a person to leave) can arise at the same time as shifting political sands precipitating the emergence of economic opportunities elsewhere (a pull factor directing a person toward a particular destination). Even the way in which we understand a forced migrant is complex and changeable. For instance, extreme hunger may force a person to leave home and become internally displaced within their own country,[5] but subsequent persecution while displaced may compel that same person to travel outside their country, thus rendering them a refugee.[6]

People displaced by seismic, historical changes experience migration in highly personal ways.[7] But even under the most desperate of circumstances, the choices made before, during, and after leaving home–often decisions made by a family–are careful calculations that take into account logistics, such as the amount of food needed to last a journey, the policies of the countries of transit and resettlement, the safety and costs involved in using people smugglers, and the challenges of traveling as a kin group.

In the twenty-first century the growing number of people displaced within and outside of their countries is presenting new and unforeseen challenges to nations around the world. Countries—national communities—have been described as imagined, as comprised of members who think of themselves as sharing particular traits with one another—religious, linguistic, cultural, and political similarities (Anderson [1983] 2006). The idea is that, although you may never meet most of your fellow citizens, they hold similar values that make them more like you than someone, say, in a village just over the river in the neighboring country. Refugees are commonly thought of in opposition to the imagined community, as a provocation to the sovereignty of nation-states and the ability of governments to safeguard their populations. In particular, refugees' alien cultural practices, religions, and languages, and their transnational connections are pointed to as a threat to the safety and imagined singularity of citizens in nation-states (de Haas, Castles, and Miller 2020, 12). A friction between people on the move and those staying put—between the mobile and the sedentary—polarizes public opinion and reshapes political dynamics on a global scale. Even during what Edward Said called, "the age of the refugee, the displaced person, [and] mass immigration" (Said 2000, 174), refugees and displaced people are presented in opposition to the supposedly sedentary nature and timelessness of a country's citizenry, people whose moral bearings are located in their imagined connections both to each other and to the soil of the nation-state (Malkki 1992, 32; Simmel 1971).

The stigma of rootlessness that follows a forced migrant does not simply melt away after arrival in a new country.[8] Displacement and resettlement are messy, overlapping, and emotionally complex processes in which it is difficult to delineate where one ends and the other begins. Physical emplacement, beginning with arrival in the host society, does not mark an end to the experience of being displaced. A refugee may spend years, decades even, experiencing both geographical and emotional transition from the point of initial departure to a time when they are permitted to resettle and are psychologically ready to begin life in their new home (particularly if they are detained while awaiting the results of an asylum claim). Migration, displacement, and the challenges of seeking refuge are thus disorientating experiences, during which time a person never fully occupies one space but exists both here and there concurrently, in a state of being that resembles an in-between or liminal existence (cf. Turner 1967).

The result of living everywhere can be that you belong nowhere. Migrants, forced migrants in particular, do not fit neatly into the ideologies and nationalist imaginaries of nation-states. Hannah Arendt suggested that a loss of home emerges because of the inability of the nation-state to spare a place for the displaced person within its political organization (Arendt 1973,

293–94). Since a refugee does not fit, since they are without place, they instead represent a polluting influence on the ostensible purity of the nation. The host society reads the symbols of the displaced person's pollution—unfamiliar religious, linguistic, political, and cultural practices—as evidence of their failures. The need to purify, to cleanse a person of the more salient aspects of their foreignness, is prevalent with the case of migrants moving to escape conflict, famine, an oppressive government, or other forms of life-threatening crises. A refugee fleeing such hardships becomes the physical manifestation of these struggles—bringing the war, the hunger, the persecution to the doorstep of the host society. In order to manage the symbolic threat posed by such a corrupting influence, the host society may attempt a transformation of the new arrival from polluted to pure—from unknown to known.

Reshaping and reconceptualizing the outsider into a familiar version of humanity means transforming them into a likeness to which a degree of acceptance can be offered. Such a change often takes place under the watchful eye of the state and by means of state-sponsored health, cultural, language, and employment programs (see Ong 2003). In Sweden, for example, as part of a national drive to integrate immigrants who arrived after 2010, municipalities provided free language training; also, immigrants who were more advanced in their Swedish were even paid to keep learning. But simply turning a foreigner into an insider is rarely the intended outcome of these processes, since acceptance of the newcomer is always contingent on his or her behavior. As we will see throughout this book, that acceptance can be rescinded by the host society at any time.

The disciplinary regimes imposed on displaced people reflect public sentiment and policymaking on migration issues in the host society. Refugees seeking asylum in Australia since 2012, for example, have been subject to mandatory offshore incarceration and an average of a year and a half's detention while they await the result of their asylum claims. In the Australian case, rather than attempting a purification of the outsider, the government has pursued a draconian approach to human management that keeps the polluting influence at a distance from the national community—outside the national discourse and outside the national concern. But displaced people are not outside of history, nor they are outside of the territorially rooted logics of the nation-state. Even in a time of global capitalism and national identities, the identities of displaced people and migrant populations are inseparable from nation-states (Basch, Schiller, and Blanc [1994] 2000, 8).

Migration and the experiences of being displaced do not mean that a person is without community or familial networks. Nor does being physically distanced from the homeland mean a person stops thinking about or being connected to home. Migration does not imply a break from the past, "rather the migrant must be understood as inhabiting two worlds simultaneously" (Thapan 2005, 15). With one eye on the past and one on the future, memories and practices of the home left behind subsequently inform an immigrant's resettlement, providing a cognitive scaffolding for their understanding of the social, economic, political, and gender dynamics in the receiving country. These practices are sometimes interpreted as symbols of a failure to assimilate–the continued use of one's mother tongue in public, cooking food unfamiliar to the palates of the host society, unfamiliar ways of celebrating and mourning.

Such cultural expressions are, on the contrary, important demonstrations of belonging and identity. These things almost inevitably continue to reorient a person's sense of home just as they reshape the host society, especially for displaced people and refugees traveling with nothing other than their memories. The 1970s arrival of Vietnamese "boat people," who were refugees fleeing conflict and persecution in Southeast Asia, for example, changed Australian society and transformed the Vietnamese who arrived on its shores. Just a few years after the end of the White Australia policy that restricted immigration to people of European descent, the resettling of tens of thousands of Asian refugees not only changed the cuisine and culture of the land down under, but also provoked a rethinking of what an Australian was "supposed" to look like. Since that time, Australia has come to rely on semi- and high-skilled immigration as a means of economically energizing, upskilling, and diversifying its labor market, while pushing back against the social and economic challenges of an ageing population.

In contrast to the Australian experience, Japan has shown reluctance to using immigration as a means of filling labor gaps and supporting an ageing population. Tokyo's sensitivity with regard to issues of immigration is particularly noticeable in the country's record on asylum seekers. Japan is a generous donor state. In 2019, for example, it contributed more than US$126 million to the UNHCR, the fifth-highest donation behind Sweden, Germany, the European Union, and the United States (UNHCR 2019). But the country's checkbook humanitarianism stands in sharp relief to the reality that it rarely grants requests for asylum. Between 2010 and 2017 the number of refugees who arrived in Japan increased by 1,600 percent, with more than twenty thousand asylum applications received. And yet in 2017 Japan granted refugee status to only 20 people.[9] While the UN has requested that Tokyo help by granting more asylum applications, the government has been loath to do so, citing the ostensible ethnic homogeneity of the country as a reason why the country is unable to accept more refugees.[10]

Home

Displaced people have often experienced major moments of social, political and economic change in heart-wrenching, deeply personal ways. The intergenerational mobility of the families in this book contribute to a better understanding of the complex relationship between an emotional attachment to home(s) and everyday feelings of rootlessness, between the lived reality of belonging to many communities and the imagined experience of belonging nowhere. The idea of home as a place rooted within national borders is often taken as an axiomatic fact: supposedly, if you live in a country for an extended, but undefined period of time, if you adopt the cultural characteristics of the host society well enough to make invisible your differences, speaking, consuming and acting like everyone else, and if you imbibe the symbols and histories of the national community, memorizing national anthems and celebrating patriotic holidays; if you do these things, you are assumed to occupy a place within the community. Rootedness and an attachment to earth, bricks and mortar is equated with normative understandings of belonging. And belonging to a national community is imagined as a timeless, defining human trait. But rootedness is not required for community. Nor does home need to be a material manifestation of belonging.

Migrations reshape connectedness to home, but they do not erase those relationships. Refugees' personal narratives and family stories challenge the idea that stasis within political borders is the only way to create a community. Mobility across time and space has encouraged the people whose stories are described in this book to develop a sense of attachment to multiple places, not just one. Indeed, returning migrants often move back and forth to the homeland on multiple occasions. Each time, their return is accompanied by the realization that their memories of home as it was, do not reflect new realities. Instead, home as it is remembered has become an idealized or exaggerated version of the past. Home—people and places—change during the time away. Migrants also change. A returnee's experience of finding their place in the homeland encourages a reevaluation of their place in the world, in some cases teaching them that a person does not need to be displaced to feel without a place, nor does a person need to be without a home in order to feel without roots.

Families for whom mobility has become central to their self-understanding present alternative, but not uncommon ways of imagining belonging and identity. Belonging not to a single place, but to a multitude of homes in multiple countries at the same time. But at a time when more people are migrating that ever before, militarized borders and high-tech walls reinforce singular modes of belonging by force, when necessary. People on one side of the walls are likely to imagine themselves as immobile, permanent, and unified, while those on the other side are thought of as untrustworthy and parasitic. But the intimate narratives of belonging, displacement and mobility in this book expose the limitations of national identities and nationalist thinking as a means for organizing communities in the modern world and preparing for the future.

The Japanese Underclass: A Window into Migrant Life

There remains in Japan the widely held belief that Japanese society is a homogenous association of likeminded individuals comprising a racially pure collective. This belief is an ideological façade that emboldens both the government to turn away asylum seekers and the public to ignore immigrants who comprise the country's underclass–Nepalis, Vietnamese, Chinese, Filipinos, Koreans. These immigrants work in Japan's factories, fields, and supermarkets; as caregivers for the young, the elderly, and the sick; as meat packers and food vendors; and as service staff in cafés and fast food restaurants. They often live in peri-urban areas of large cities, or in inner-city ethnic neighborhoods that sometimes verge into ghettos. As in so many postindustrial countries, Japan's immigrant communities shore up the economic foundations of society, providing the services Japan needs in roles the Japanese people are reluctant to take, and they are largely invisible to the mainstream society they serve.

The Korean families who form the focus of this historical ethnography comprise a long-marginalized demographic in Japan. In some instances, individuals have managed to transcend the limitations of membership in this underclass common to first generation immigrants: a lack of fluency in speaking the host language, the absence of professional or personal networks from which to engage in lucrative and status providing career options, legal exclusion from the benefits of the nation-state, and the disdain, avoidance, or even misdirected sympathy of the majority society. The experiences of families and individuals in this book, across generations of migration, echo the experiences of migrants everywhere: some try to assimilate; deemphasizing all visible ties to the country they left in an attempt to reform themselves in the image of the good citizen. In such cases, the new arrival throws themselves into a process of reshaping–mastering the nuances of the local language, dressing like a local, actively avoiding coethnics and even fabricating a backstory to hide or reshape the what, where, and why of life before arrival. Others consciously remain in socially segregated ethnic communities, finding comfort in the familiar. Some acquiesce to exploitative work conditions in the hope that it will be a steppingstone to something better; still others engage in entrepreneurship in an attempt to create new opportunities. Sometimes, there seems no other choice than to succumb to their assigned positions, in roles shunned by the host society. In the pages that follow, each of my informants travels one or more of these trajectories, embracing the new opportunities afforded them in some cases, clinging to the identity and memory of a homeland in others, while sometimes slipping into the abyss of despondency and despair, hoping that things will be better for the next generation.

A part of Japan's invisible underclass are the Koreans whose families have moved back and forth between the Korean Peninsula and Japan. Between 1959 and 1984, some 87,000 Koreans and 6,750 Japanese migrated to North Korea from Japan as part of a "repatriation project" organized by the governments of North Korea and Japan, with the oversight of the International Committee of the Red Cross (ICRC). The most telling misnomer with regard to the events discussed in this book is that the mass exodus of Koreans and Japanese to North Korea was a repatriation at all. This expression, "repatriation," suggests that those who left for North Korea were returning home. The reality, as shown in chapters 1 and 2, is that the people who migrated to North Korea, the vast majority of whom were originally from southern areas of the Korean Peninsula, went as a response to untenable social and economic conditions in Japan. My own use of the term reflects both a need to distinguish emigrants to North Korea from Democratic People's Republic of Korea (DPRK, or North Korea)–born Koreans, and an understanding that those who left often felt an ideological affinity for North Korea's ethnonationalism. But even individuals who may have once considered themselves loyal to Kim Il-sung's DPRK were not prepared for what awaited them in the ideological homeland.

The majority of repatriates, including Hŭiŭn's parents and grandparents, whose story opens this book, arrived in North Korea with hopes for better living and working conditions, as promised by Kim Il-sung and the DPRK's apparatchiks in Japan. But since the early 2000s, a small group of around three hundred men, women, and children have returned to Japan, some escaping persecution or poverty, all desiring a new start. This book tells their stories and situates their voices in the broader geopolitical contexts of the time.

The people I refer to as Zainichi returnees commonly resettle in Osaka or Tokyo, in ethnic Korean communities. "Zainichi Korean" is the Japanese label applied to Koreans who initially migrated to Japan from the Korean Peninsula during and in the years immediately following the Japanese colonial period (1910–45). Since that time, the new generations of Koreans resident in Japan–Zainichi Koreans–have, to various degrees, assimilated into mainstream Japanese society. For many Zainichi Koreans, their relationship to their host society, to their homelands and to their Korean/Japanese identity remains complicated (see Ryang 2009, 1–20).[11]

While most returnees I worked with are Korean, a minority are ethnically Japanese, the wives and children of Zainichi Koreans who went to North Korea as part of the repatriations. By returning to Japan, Zainichi returnees and their family complete a migratory loop between the Korean Peninsula and the Japanese archipelago that spans almost a century.

Early Korean Mobility

The story of Koreans on the move is embedded within macrolevel, sociopolitical processes that shaped twentieth century Asia: the rise and fall of imperial Japan, the expansion and collision of US and Soviet geostrategic interests, and the division of the Korean Peninsula into two ideologically antagonistic states on the frontlines of the Cold War. Korean families moving from Japan to the DPRK forged an unusual migratory path at a time when most mass movements traveled away from the communist world, to the Western Bloc. But migration between the Korean Peninsula and Japan and then from Japan to the DPRK is just one of a number of mobility threads that connected and scattered Korean families throughout East Asia and beyond.

There are currently around 7.5 million ethnic Koreans living outside the Korean Peninsula, the result of around 150 years of outward movement propelled by conflict, land reforms, state-directed labor projects, and emerging economic opportunities (Ministry of Foreign Affairs of the Republic of Korea; MOFA-ROK, 2019). Beginning in the 1860s, following the Qing government lifting a ban on non-Manchu migration to Northeast China, a growing number of Koreans moved north of the Tumen and Yalu Rivers, cultivating vast lands for rice cropping. As a result of several waves of migration to China, the Russian Far East, and Japan in the late nineteenth and early twentieth centuries (Kim 2003, 101–27; Ryang 2000b), to South America in the 1960s (Buechler 2004; Park 1999), to the United States following the passing of the 1965 Immigration Reform Act (Light and Bonacich 1988), of forced migrations to Central Asia in 1937 (Yoon 2012, 419–21), and skilled-labor migrations to West Germany and the Middle East from the early 1960s (Light and Bonacich 1988, 102–25), the Korean diaspora is globally dispersed, the greatest numbers concentrated in the United States, China, and Japan (MOFA-ROK 2019). Across a century and a half, Korean families have been compelled to leave their homes as a response to the violent expansion and contraction of imperial and national boundaries in Asia and the shifting of geostrategic and economic influences and alliances in the post–World War II era.

In the past twenty-five years, Koreans from the DPRK have left their country in unprecedented numbers (outside of the large number of refugees generated during the 1950–53 Korean War). The largest out-migration occurred in response to the 1990s nationwide famine that affected all but the country's elite.[12] The famine, often referred to as the Arduous March by North Koreans, emerged in the years following the collapse of the Cold War world order. Specifically, the crumbling of the Soviet Union in 1991 ended the economic assistance the DPRK had hitherto received from its main trading partner and sponsor. Unable to borrow money from the global credit markets and unwilling to press for financial relief elsewhere, North Korea's economy slid further into decline.[13] As North Korea's state food rationing–the Public Distribution System–ground to a halt, chronic shortages emerged across the country.[14] The famine led to the deaths of approximately 600,000 to 1 million people by starvation and malnutrition-related diseases (cf. Goodkind and West 2001; Haggard and Noland 2007; Robinson et al. 1999). During a period of nationwide shortages, widespread unemployment and high rates of mortality, an unknown number of North Koreans were displaced within their country, while others were compelled to cross the Sino-Korean border in search of work, food, and opportunities to trade.[15]

The majority of people crossing into China would later migrate home, their returns reflecting both the difficulty of onward migration from China and the emotional pull back to villages, homes, and family in North Korea. But a small minority continued on to South Korea, Japan, and beyond as refugees. Among the men and women forced to migrate to survive is a small number of people who had been directly or indirectly (children or grandchildren) part of a mass exodus from Japan. This book is the first to explore their stories.

Postwar New Beginnings in Japan

At noon on 15 August 1945 Emperor Hirohito announced the end of the Pacific War. As news of Japan's surrender spread across the country and throughout territories occupied since its 1931 invasion of Manchuria, ordinary Japanese considered their lives as a defeated nation. For millions of newly liberated people working in the coalmines and industrial facilities of the empire, the end of the war prompted new questions on identity, the future, and the sovereignty of Japan's colonies. These questions were perhaps most sharply felt by Koreans living on the Japanese archipelago.

The industrialization and modernization of Japan began with the 1868 Meiji Restoration and included an extended period of economic growth supported by a militarized territorial acquisition.[16] At its peak, Japan controlled territories including Taiwan, the Korean Peninsula, large areas of China, Malaya, the Dutch East Indies, the Philippines, and Burma. The growing Empire of Japan needed a huge pool of labor to work in shipyards, mines, fishing fleets, spinning mills, military posts, and colonial law and order positions. By extending the 1938 National Mobilization Law, Tokyo was able to recruit people from within its territorial acquisitions, particularly from Korea.[17] Japan tightened its control and exploitation of Korea by minimizing the imagined ethnic and cultural differences between themselves and the Koreans, so that Korea's absorption into Japan appeared as a natural stage in the racial and imperial unity of the two peoples.[18] But military defeat ended Japan's imperial experiment.

The surrender of imperial Japan concluded thirty-five years of colonial rule on the Korean Peninsula. During the occupation, millions of Koreans were displaced by Japanese land reforms and in service to the military government. Some people had migrated to such places as Japan or Manchuria by choice; others were compelled to move by unemployment, a loss of arable land, or promises of a better life in service of the emperor. At the time of Japan's capitulation, there were around 2 million Koreans living in Japan.

Following defeat, Japan changed tack, shifting from imperial expansion to strategic alignment with the United States and economic integration within the globalizing free market. Such a dramatic change required the Japanese to withdraw from their shattered conquests and reimagine themselves as bounded by the borders of the archipelago—as a national rather than an imperial community. The shift from empire to nation rendered Japan's huge colonial workforce, the human consequence of an imbalance of power between colonial master and colonized servant, superfluous to requirements. Concerned about the effect that a surplus of labor would have on the struggling postwar economy, the Japanese government, under the supervision of occupying Allied forces, arranged for the repatriation of Koreans in Japan.

By spring of 1946, some 1.4 million Koreans had returned to a homeland that US and Soviet forces had divided at the 38th parallel. American forces moved up the peninsula and occupied the area that in August 1948 became the Republic of Korea (ROK, or South Korea). The Red Army occupied the territory north of the dividing line, land that in September 1948 would become the DPRK. The overwhelming majority of Koreans leaving Japan around this time returned to southern Korea. Only 351 individuals are recorded as having repatriated north of the dividing line prior to 1959.[19]

Once the dust had settled, around 650,000 Koreans remained in Japan. Their reasons for staying varied: some resented the restrictions on the amount of property each person was permitted to take with them back to Korea, and some had made new lives for themselves in the industrial centers of Osaka, Kobe, or Tokyo.[20] Others had nothing to return to, having lost contact with family and friends during the war years. Some Koreans were deterred from returning by rumors that conditions in the homeland were becoming desperate, with poverty and disease widespread, and ideological unrest fomenting. Distance was no protection however, and even Koreans who stayed in Japan would not escape the ideological fissures that divided the homeland.

Divisions in Japan

The Korean community in Japan soon split along ideological lines that mirrored the division of the Korean Peninsula. Although the majority of Koreans in Japan originated from the southern half of the peninsula, most politically supported the DPRK, founding in 1945 the North Korea–sympathizing League of Korean Residents in Japan (Chae'il Chosŏnnin Ryŏnmeang or Choryŏn).[21] Allied occupiers forcibly disbanded Choryŏn in 1949, and it was not until May 1955 that Korean labor activist Han Duk Su founded the organization today known as Ch'ongryŏn.[22] Ch'ongryŏn has since functioned as North Korea's de facto embassy in Japan, responsible for both coordinating informal political relations between the two countries and for managing North Korean business interests in Japan.[23] The organization has been a lightning rod for anti-Korean sentiment in Japan, and has been accused of participating in the abduction of Japanese citizens, of funneling large amounts of money to Pyongyang, and of operating spy networks throughout Japan.[24]

In the same period, anticommunist Zainichi Koreans created the Korean Residents Union in Japan (Chae'il Han'guk'in Koryumindan/Mindan) in 1946. Each side claimed to represent the rights and welfare of Koreans in Japan. But those sympathizing with North Korea were better organized and more capable of rallying support to their cause.

The relationships of the two Koreas to Ch'ongryŏn and Mindan would have a lasting impact on Koreans in Japan. Both organizations claimed to be preparing their members for a return to the homeland, but only the North Korean government was active in providing funding, ethnic education, and employment to Zainichi Korean communities. Amidst the reordering of nationality and citizenship in postwar Japan, Ch'ongryŏn schools fostered an identity as DPRK nationals, and taught North Korean history and language to Zainichi Korean students, many of whom had never seen the homeland (Ryang 1997, 3).[25] Mindan, in contrast, failed to secure funding from Seoul. South Korean president Syngman Rhee regarded Koreans in Japan with suspicion and was loath to support what he imagined as enemies of the fledgling ROK. The DPRK's willingness to provide financial and material assistance meant that North Korea and Ch'ongryŏn enjoyed broad support among Zainichi Koreans. But again, events in the Koreas would prove inescapable to Koreans in Japan.

Following several years of skirmishes, on 25 June 1950 North Korean forces launched a general attack across the 38th parallel. The ensuing conflict, and the destruction and huge loss of life on both sides, made it difficult and undesirable for Zainichi Koreans to return to either side of the divided peninsula. After three years of fighting, during which time some 4 million people were killed including an estimated 2 million civilians (Cumings

2010, 95), the division of the two Koreas solidified into the communist north and the capitalist south. The ideological schism within the Zainichi Korean community was similarly entrenched.

The 1953 armistice between the United States, China, and the DPRK established a ceasefire on the Korean Peninsula and necessitated the lasting presence of US troops in South Korea. The postwar years also saw changes in the United States–Japan relationship. In 1952, for example, the United States ceded control of Japan back to the Japanese government. This period marked the beginnings of Japanese efforts to regulate trade and taxation by shutting down the black markets that had emerged across the country. As a part of Tokyo's efforts to reestablish law and regain control over the economy it moved to legally define who would and would not be included in the new Japan. At the time, fear that the Japanese archipelago was over-populated worked in parallel with a paranoia that the newly distinguished foreigners were a threat to the security and ethnic purity of the nation. Con-sequently, instead of trying to incorporate Zainichi Koreans into Japanese society, the government looked for opportunities to export them.

Tokyo decided that the best way to deal with the human excesses of its imperial decline was to ship it to North Korea. In other words, Japan out-sourced its minority problem as its modernizing trajectory momentarily aligned with North Korea's economic and geostrategic aims. Within just a few years, tens of thousands of Koreans, several thousand Japanese, and even a handful of Chinese had left Japan for North Korea in what was one of the largest mass movements from the capitalist to the communist world. Life in the DPRK for some repatriates offered unexpected opportunities. A few repatriates with membership in Ch'ongryŏn and whose families were relatively wealthy were moved into homes in North Korea's capital, Pyong-yang. Others favored by the regime were allocated housing in cities outside the political center, such as Ch'ŏngjin, Sinŭiju, or Hamhŭng. In urban land-scapes that still bore the scars of American bombing, the state set repatriates to work in industrial, educational, and agricultural positions. But because their propaganda and economic value eroded over time, repatriated Kore-ans soon represented diminishing returns for Pyongyang. For the majority of families who went to North Korea, their new homeland would present a lifetime of challenges.

This book uses declassified archival evidence, ethnographic research, and the voices of returnees from North Korea to show that Japan and North Korea's reordering of national sovereignty created a transient, multi-territorialized community of people with ties reaching across East Asia. The personal accounts in the chapters that follow offer a glimpse into what it means to be displaced in the modern world and to exist as an outsider to the national community, and how, in the age of mass migration, identity and belonging remain highly contested, unstable concepts.

Liberated into Statelessness

Postwar Japan was not the only place experiencing a demographic, economic, and political realignment. Massive population movements took place throughout the United States, Asia, Europe, and Africa as part of an ethnic unmixing (Brubaker 1998) of people following World War II. During this period, colonial administrators, officials, scholars, and bureaucrats moved in the direction of retreating powers (toward the colonial center), while former subjects of predominantly European powers moved toward the colonial periphery, returning to newly independent countries that often faced a long struggle toward economic and governmental stability.

Japan's imperial expansion had mirrored that of European powers in terms of its assimilation practices and an emphasis on modern forms of governance and technological development.[26] In turn, its contraction and subsequent rebirth as a liberal democratic nation presented similar challenges to those experienced by other empires in decline. Following Japan's capitulation, and as bureaucrats and soldiers hurriedly retreated in the face of advancing Soviet and American forces, the Asia-Pacific region experienced a frenetic reordering of people. The withering Japanese imperial order used and subsequently discarded Koreans, Vietnamese, Chinese, and Burmese; these people made up a veritable army of low-skilled workers displaced first by the demands of an expanding militant state and subsequently by shuttered mines, bombed infrastructure, and retreating armies. Many former Japanese subjects found that liberation gave way to statelessness. Statelessness ushered in fears of lost livelihoods and economic precarity. There seemed few options but to leave Japan.

Huge geopolitical ruptures trigger movements in a multitude of directions. For some, unexpected changes prompt a desire to return home. During a migrant's time away, the ethnic homeland may have changed beyond recognition, reshaped and reimagined by economic development and industrialized conflict. Migrants' experiences in the cities and villages to which they return, their feeling of being out of place while surrounded by landscapes of familiarity, is a common feature of diasporic communities. As part of the twentieth century's unmixing of populations, millions of Jewish descendants, for example, "returned" to Israel for the first time (Remennick 2002, 2009), ethnic Hungarian labor migrants relocated from Romania (Fox 2007), *Aussiedler* (ethnic Germans) migrated to Germany from Eastern Europe and the former Soviet Union (Rock and Wolff 2002), and ethnic Spanish "returned" from South America to Southern European countries (Cook-Martin and Viladrich 2009). In some cases, the time between the initial out-migration and the return spans several generations. Ethnic Japanese, for example, initially emigrated to South America in the early twentieth century, with many returning some eighty years later, during Japan's economic boom (de Carvalho 2003; Takenaka 2009; Tsuda 2003, 2009).

In the aforementioned cases, return to the ethnic homeland exacerbated feelings of displacement, but also opened possibilities for the emergence of new ways of being in the world and new understandings of belonging. Most North Koreans who leave their country travel south. Democratic, highly urbanized South Korea is at the polar opposite to what they have previously experienced. North Koreans arriving in South Korea may have high expectations regarding the economic opportunities in their new home. However, South Korean dramas, films, and music smuggled into North Korea on DVDs and USBs shape expectations that are rarely met (Chung 2008, 1–27; Lankov 2006, 120). Instead, North Koreans south of the Korean Demilitarized Zone (DMZ) occupy a socioeconomic position in South Korean society on a par with working-class Korean-Chinese migrant laborers (Hough and Bell 2020; Seol and Skrentny 2009). North Korean refugees are tolerated, but are not regarded as equals within the host society. At best they are regarded as living testament to the political and economic superiority of South Korea. At worst, they represent a threat to the "cocoon of the safe, familiar, established society" (Bauman 2004, 67). North Koreans' incongruous cultural traits contribute to their feelings of marginalization and disorientation, things like unfamiliar accents and vocabulary, understandings of fashion, and consumer habits that differ from cosmopolitan, image-conscious socialites of Seoul, South Korea's capital. These differences, some skin-deep while others cutting to the very core of a politically divided Korean identity, are wrapped up in discourses of nationalism, gender, and modernity that exacerbate points of tension between new arrivals and the host society.

Koreans returning to Japan in the post–Cold War period experience similar feelings of tension and uncertainty in their relationship to both the sending and receiving societies. But among Zainichi returnees, return migration is particularly complicated, as even returnees born in Japan are not ethnic returnees because they are ethnically Korean, not Japanese. As Koreans returning to Japan, they return to a diasporic Korean community in Japan. There are two broad categories of return migrants: people born in Japan and people born in North Korea.[27] With these nuances in mind, the two categories I use are birth returnee, referring to a person born in Japan who returns to the land of their birth; and imagined returnee, a person arriving in a place that was manifested only in family memories and consumables.

Many birth returnees now remaking home in the urban sprawl of Tokyo or Osaka were children when they left for North Korea. Returned to places they left long ago, they experience difficulty feeling at home in Japan, largely because of the significant social, economic, and political changes that have taken place during their absence. Now in their twilight years, birth returnees seek to reconnect with once familiar places and people. For imagined returnees, people born in North Korea to parents of repatriates, migration to Japan is a meeting with the inherited memories of parents and grandparents. But their secondhand memories are slippery recollections of others' experiences, and there is often a significant disparity between an imagined returnee's inherited memories of Japan and the reality of contemporary life in Tokyo or Osaka. For both birth and imagined returnees, memories of Japan rarely prepare them for the challenges that arise following their arrival.

Gateway to a New Life

Osaka has long been both a trading hub and a gateway to the rest of Japan. Made up of many small towns threaded together by the Japanese rail system, the edges of Osaka city spill over into neighboring areas, rapaciously devouring the surrounding suburbs. In the winter, darkness descends around four o'clock in the afternoon and a haze settles under the arches of the low-crouching rail bridges and throughout the undercover malls running south to north across the city. Seeping out of the standing bars and barbecue restaurants located on the periphery of the shopping areas, this fog carries with it a distinctly meaty odor. The haze becomes especially thick in the early evenings, when workers, stopping for a beer and a snack on their way home, provoke the cooking fires to burn with greater intensity.

With its bustling wholesale markets, Korean and Chinese restaurants, and signs written both in Korean and Japanese scripts, Tsuruhashi, Ikuno ward, in the center-east of the city, is a halfway house for newly arrived migrant workers.[28] It is a place where immigrants from neighboring East Asian countries begin life in Japan, while speaking their native languages and engaging with others who understand what it is like to be an outsider in Japan. Tsuruhashi played an important part in Japan's empire building in the late nineteenth and early twentieth centuries.[29] During the colonial era, a direct ferry connected Cheju Island and Osaka, carrying thousands of Koreans looking for work in the factories that sprang up to supply the Japanese military. By the mid-1950s, some 20 percent of Koreans in Japan lived in Osaka city,[30] often working physically demanding jobs in the formal and informal labor markets. Tsuruhashi is less known for being home to two of Japan's more notorious Zainichi Koreans. Ko Yonghŭi, mother to the current leader of North Korea, Kim Jong-un, was born in Tsuruhashi, and migrated to the DPRK as part of the repatriation project. And would-be assassin Mun Segwang also called this corner of Ikuno ward home: On 18 July 1974 Mun stole a Smith & Wesson pistol from a Tsuruhashi police station and attempted to murder South Korean president Pak Chŏnghŭi. Running with his pistol in hand, Mun fired wildly, missing his target and instead killing the president's wife, Yuk Young-soo. He was later hanged in Seoul prison.

Tsuruhashi is now home to an area of commercial and residential buildings that together constitute Osaka's Koreatown. Riding west using the Sennichimae subway line that bisects Osaka, a prerecorded Japanese voice announces the Tsuruhashi stop as "the home of Korean barbecue [*yakiniku*] and offal [*horumon*] restaurants." The doors slide open and the smell of roasting meat fills the nostrils. The sights and sounds of traders selling kimchi, freshly slaughtered animals, and plastic-wrapped clothes resemble markets in South Korea or China more than they do most commercial areas of Japan. Shops on the main street of Koreatown sell South Korean cosmetics, Korean pop music and dramas, imported foodstuffs, alcohol, and locally made fresh food. Following the emergence of the "Korean wave," Ikuno ward has become a hot spot for domestic tourists wanting a taste of Korea, but without the hassle of getting on a plane.

While researching this book, I lived in Osaka, in a dilapidated apartment on Koreatown's main street (figure 0.1). I spent my first months managing a tatami mat flea infestation, carried into the apartment by rats nesting in the walls. Most mornings I awoke to the dull "dunk dunk dunk" sound of knife-hitting-wood, as the elderly women on the other side of the street from my apartment prepared the day's kimchi for sale. Other days I was woken by

Figure 0.1. Tsuruhashi's Koreatown is lined with shops selling Korean products. Photo taken by the author.

the same women, yelling their morning greetings at other shopkeepers in thick Cheju Island Korean.[31]

Older returnees from North Korea talked to me about their experiences in postwar Japan. They also told me of the disappointment they felt in the years following their repatriation to the DPRK. They described cold winters shivering without heating, and ground so hard with frost that nothing would grow. A few recalled lives of privilege among the DPRK's political elite, others spoke of scavenging for food in the mountains and selling their findings in black markets. Returning to Japan after such a long time away comes with its own challenges. Interviewees who had left Japan in the 1960s described returning to a country that had changed beyond recognition. For these people, the sights and sounds of contemporary Osaka, of Tsuruhashi and Koreatown, offer few clues alluding to life as it was a half century earlier.

The Journey

This book examines the lives of families who have moved between Japan and the two Koreas across three generations. In the process they have engaged with five key strategies: intramarriage, identity management, emotionally directed mobility, activist engagement, and imagined belonging.[32] Their memories of strategic movement and resettlement show that, although displacement is often characterized by desperation, refugees are in fact innovators, entrepreneurs, and agents of transformation with the potential to regenerate the societies where they settle.

Each chapter and the strategies described therein highlight the relationship between memory, mobility, belonging, and the reconfiguration of individual identity, of communities, and entire societies. The first chapter explores postwar Japan and the movement of tens of thousands of people to North Korea. I show how migrants create their own powerful retellings of history that exist alongside, and sometimes eclipse, official state narratives. For the migrants in this book, Cold War politics unfolded, writ-small, in Korean communities, tearing families apart and carving a dividing line between Koreans who supported the DPRK and those who supported the ROK. As ideological alliances hardened, a rare moment when the interests of Japan and North Korea overlapped (from the mid-1950s to the mid-1960s) allowed for an exodus of Zainichi Koreans to the DPRK. I argue that what I call the vernacular memories of returnees from North Korea—the micro-histories of families and minority communities—are at odds with official, nationalist histories of modern Japan. The tension that subsequently arises, between vernacular memories and nationalist discourses, unsettles common understandings of Japan as having been victim to North Korean duplicity with regard to the repatriations, suggesting instead that Zainichi

Koreans migrated to North Korea as a response to increasing ethnic discrimination and economic suffocation in Japan.

Chapter 2 examines the strategic use of alliance building through intramarriage between migrant families. Korean families in Japan and those who subsequently emigrated to North Korea created such alliances to survive the painful emotional, economic, and social chaos of displacement. Straddling the boundary of oral history and ethnography, the genealogies of two families in particular reflect the geopolitical upheavals taking place in East Asia at the time. For seemingly powerless migrant families, decisions on who to marry, who to avoid, when to leave and who to send are moments for stabilizing lives and livelihoods threatened by dramatic global disruptions.

In the third chapter, I examine how Zainichi families managed and deployed inner and outer identities as a way to survive the vicissitudes of life in North Korea. Local North Koreans often viewed repatriates as no different from Japanese. Repatriates responded to having their ethnic identity scrutinized in different ways, some by resisting the majority society pressures. I show that resistance took the form not of explicit antistate protest, but rather of "weapons of the weak" (Scott 1985), whereby the ordinary, everyday actions of people ostensibly lacking in power have broader, political implications. Some repatriates, for instance, tried to hide their outsider status, understanding that to survive in North Korea meant obfuscating the peculiarities that set them apart from local North Koreans. Others realized that they would always be outsiders in North Korea, and so mobilized feelings of marginalization to build transnational family connections back to Japan. Such acts of quiet dissidence were materialized through practices such as cooking Japanese food, storytelling in the Japanese language, nostalgic recollections of life before repatriation, and, most importantly, sending and receiving letters and gifts to family who had remained behind. A deepening sense of emotional attachment to the people and places they had left behind in turn incited an unexpected questioning of self-identity and new imaginings of home.

While returning to Japan may reconcile a sense of long-distance yearning, new arrivals' lack of relevant skills, qualifications, and knowledge of the host society create unexpected challenges. Chapter 4 examines the relationship between emotions and mobility, in particular how emotional rather than economic drivers play a crucial part in the strategic choices made before and after leaving North Korea. The families in this book chose to pursue resettlement in Japan, a place where they neither speak the language nor have experience with everyday life, instead of South Korea, a country with which they share cultural and linguistic qualities and are entitled to economic benefits as North Korean defectors. In choosing Japan, they make strategic decisions motivated by highly personal emotional attachments—real and inherited—from family, and by the hope that they will find social support among kin, friends, and other Koreans. Further to these emotionally directed movements, I show how the dramatic socioeconomic changes that took place in 1990s' North Korea have had a ripple effect in the lives of North Koreans in exile. Interviewees' accounts of surviving the North Korean famine reveal how shifting understandings of labor and gender roles in North Korea–in particular, the rise of the female capitalist–shape both returnees' emergent social networks and their understandings of what constitutes success in Japan.

The fifth chapter examines returnees' strategic reliance on, or avoidance of, civic organizations as part of their resettling in Japan. All of the returnees I met had experience with Japanese civic groups; many had found work, accommodations, and the beginnings of a social network through these groups. But returnees' engagement with activist groups emerges within a power dynamic in which activists exercise a moral authority over new arrivals. Specifically, civic groups in Osaka and Tokyo claim possession of new arrivals through gift giving. In a perversion of good intentions and best wishes, the moral economy–an economy of altruism–that has emerged between an already vulnerable group and the people who help them further endangers returnees. Giving, an everyday act that binds families and communities together, obligates returnees to the organizations that help them escape North Korea. The obligation to repay a debt that can never be satisfied subsequently compels returnees to participate in high-profile, high-risk activism. In doing so, Zainichi returnees again put themselves and their family at risk of reprisals from the North Korean government.

Chapter 6 draws on three ethnographic cases to illustrate the fracturing of the self that often arises from multiple migrations, and the lengths to which displaced people go in order to imagine belonging within the host society. The vignettes within this chapter reveal a vulnerability, especially the tendency of displaced people to feel caught between worlds and located outside of time. Some also experience this liminal existence as a time in which to shape new subjectivities by locating one's self among fragments of the past. I highlight returnees' strategic use of remembering and forgetting as a means by which some manage to develop an attachment to Japan. In doing so, I underline the importance of the relationship between memory and displacement, suggesting that, wherever they go, pathologizing refugees' pasts, in particular their relationships to the homeland, makes it even harder for them to find peace in the places they resettle.

People forced to migrate to escape dangerous, restrictive, or economically perilous lives do so at great personal cost. They face isolation, exclusion, poverty, and scorn, and most are integrated–either temporarily or more long term–into the underclass of their host society. To survive the experiences of downward mobility and its limitations–or to escape those experiences–they demonstrate the survival techniques outlined in this book to varying degrees of success. Forced migrants are a self-selecting group; they enter into hardship at great risk, to create a better life. As a result, despite the many hardships they endure, they are survivors. The concluding chapter examines the ways in which the strategies detailed above enable individuals, families, and communities to remake themselves and transform the places in which they settle, shifting the cultural, demographic, economic, and political dynamics of their host society forever.

Notes

1. The term "*hwagyo*" refers to Chinese who have spent time in one or both of the two Koreas.
2. Civic organization members helped Hŭiŭn contact the Japanese consulate general.
3. In this book I use the IOM definition of migrant; "migrant" refers to any person who moves away from his or her place of usual residence, whether within a country or across an international border, temporarily or permanently, and for a variety of reasons (IOM 2019a).
4. For a brief but insightful discussion of how the COVID-19 pandemic could impact global migration, see the UN IOM report, "Migration and Mobility after the 2020 Pandemic" (Gamlen 2020).
5. According to the UN 'Guiding Principles on Internal Displacement', internally displaced persons (IDPs) are people who have been forced or obliged to flee or to leave their homes or places of habitual residence, in particular as a result of or in order to avoid the effects of armed conflict, situations of generalized violence, violations of human rights or natural or human-made disasters, and who have not crossed an internationally recognized border (UN Economic and Social Council 1998).
6. According to the 1951 UN Convention relating to the Status of Refugees and its 1967 Protocol, refugees are persons who flee their country due to well-founded fear of persecution due to reasons of race, religion, nationality, membership of a particular social group, or political opinion, and who are outside their country of nationality or permanent residence and, due to this fear, are unable or unwilling to return to it (UNHCR 1951).
7. In this book I focus on the experiences of IDPs and refugees, but I will use the adjective "displaced" to refer to anyone forced to leave their home and seek shelter elsewhere.
8. I draw on Erving Goffman's understanding of stigma. Goffman explains, "While the stranger is present before us, evidence can arise of his possessing an attribute that makes him different from others in the category of persons available for him to be, and of a less desirable kind—in the extreme, a person who is quite thoroughly bad, or dangerous, or weak. He is thus reduced in our minds from a whole and usual person to a tainted, discounted one. Such an attribute is a stigma, especially when its discrediting effect is very extensive; some-times it is also called a failing, a shortcoming, a handicap. It constitutes a special discrepancy between virtual and actual social identity" (Goffman 1963, 12–13).

9. Japan's low refugee intake is reported in *Business Insider* (Chan 2018).
10. The UN request is also reported in *Business Insider* (Wilson 2017).
11. In Japanese, the word "Zainichi" refers to a foreigner residing in Japan. However, the expression has been appropriated by long-term Koreans in Japan to distinguish them from the Japanese population and from later waves of migrations from South Korea. I use the expression "Zainichi returnee" to refer to ethnic Koreans who migrated to North Korea only to return to Japan in recent years. For a comprehensive account of Koreans' experiences in Japan see Sonia Ryang's *Koreans in Japan: Critical Voices from the Margin* (Ryang 2000b), and Sonia Ryang and John Lie's *Diaspora Without Homeland: Being Korean in Japan* (Ryang and Lie 2009).
12. Although the DPRK Constitution grants citizens the "freedom to reside in and travel to any place," the reality is very different (Haggard and Noland 2007, 169–70). Internal movement and movement beyond the country's sovereign borders requires government permission. Permission is not always granted. Because of the draconian restrictions on movement, citizens who leave the DPRK often do so without government permission and are subsequently vulnerable to punishment if apprehended.
13. For more on the North Korean economic collapse see Smith (2015, 136–64).
14. The Public Distribution System is the rationing system by which the DPRK state distributes food to citizens. Distribution occurs in accordance with a quota system, in which food allocation is determined by age, gender, occupation, and political status.
15. The exact number of North Koreans who left for China is uncertain. Courtland Robinson (2013, 54) estimates that in 1998 there were around 75,000 North Korean refugees in Northeast China, and that by 2009 that figure had dropped to around 10,000.
16. For more on the Meiji Restoration, see Jansen (2002), 333–494.
17. More than 1 million Koreans were brought to Japan as labor and military conscription from 1939 to 1945, according to the Japanese Home Ministry (B AG 232 105-002 "Problème du rapatriement des Coréens du Japon, dossier I: Généralités." 27/02/1953–11/10/1957. Inoue, Masutarô. 1956. "The Repatriation Problem of Certain Koreans Residing in Japan." Japanese Red Cross Society, 1 October 1956, 1).
18. For more on Japan's colonial assimilation policies, see Caprio (2009).
19. Specifically, 233 Koreans went to the north on 15 March 1947 and 118 went on 26 June of that same year (B AG 232 105-002 "Problème du rapatriement des Coréens du Japon, dossier I: Généralités." 27/02/1953–11/10/1957. Inoue, Masutarô. 1956. "The Repatriation Problem of Certain Koreans Residing in Japan." Japanese Red Cross Society, 1 October 1956, 6).
20. Lee notes, "SCAP [Supreme Commander of the Allied Powers] had issued a directive forbidding any repatriate to take with him more than 1,000 yen or objects of equivalent value" (in Lee and De Vos 1981b, 59). Japanese authorities impounded any money or items valued above this limit.
21. Choryŏn was succeeded by a variety of political organizations, of which the most important was the Koreans' United Democratic Front (*Minsen* in Japanese or *Minsŏn* in Korean).

22. The League of Koreans was dissolved on the orders of the Supreme Commander of the Allied Powers (SCAP) on 8 September 1949, ostensibly for carrying out communist activities. (See B AG 232 105-025 15/07/59-15/07/59, p. 31). Furthermore, the Japanese government shut down 350 ethnic Korean schools supported by the League (Shipper 2010, 59–60; Tai 2004, 358).

23. The General Association of Korean Residents in Japan, "Ch'ongryŏn" in Korean and "Chōsen Sōren" using Japanese pronunciation, is one of two main political organisations representing Zainichi Koreans, and has close ties to North Korea.

24. In the 1980s, suspicions arose within Japan that North Korea had kidnapped Japanese citizens from the country's Northwest coastal areas. This came to a head in September 2002, with a meeting between DPRK head of state, Kim Jong-il and Koizumi Junichiro, then Japanese Prime Minister. For reasons still unclear, Kim confessed to Koizumi that North Korean agents, ostensibly operating without his knowledge, had abducted 13 Japanese, five from Europe and eight from Japan.

25. For more on identity, nationalism, and citizenship in postwar Japan and how these things shaped Zainichi Korean identity, see Kashiwazaki (2000, 13–31).

26. For a comparative understanding of Japan's assimilation policies see Caprio (2009, 19–48).

27. These categories are further complicated because a number of returnees to Japan are ethnically Japanese as opposed to Korean. The majority of the individuals I worked with during my research, however, are ethnically Korean.

28. The official website of Ikuno ward states, "The population and density of Ikuno-ku are the sixth largest in Osaka city, but are declining. The number of foreigner registrations is the largest in the city, and one out of four residents here is of foreign nationality. The proportion of senior citizens is also higher than the overall Osaka city average" (Ikuno-Ku website n.d.).

29. For a historical treatment of Osaka city as a site of East Asian modernity, see Cronin (2017).

30. B AG 232 105-002 "Problème du rapatriement des Coréens du Japon, dossier I: Généralités." 27/02/1953–11/10/1957. Inoue, Masutarô. 1956. "Fundamental Conditions of Livelihood of Certain Koreans Residing in Japan." Japanese Red Cross Society, November 1956, p. 4.

31. My research took place in Japan, South Korea, and Switzerland. Multisited research presents particular challenges, in terms of the costs associated with traveling back and forth between sites, and the difficulty of building rapport with interlocutors when you are constantly on the move (cf. Marcus 1995), and the experience of working with findings from multiple sites at the same time. I consciously navigated these challenges by working with North Koreans in South Korea with whom I had previously worked from 2010 to 2012 and, while in Japan, by building relationships with interlocutors over several months before requesting a formal interview. While I was in South Korea, I interviewed North Korean escapees about their relationship to repatriates from Japan. I then moved my research to Japan and began to work with returnees. I realized during my initial research in South Korea that digitally recording interviews changed the dynamic of the experience, sometimes fostering an anxiety in the interviewee. Consequently, I wrote freehand notes and carried out multiple interviews with each interlocutor, documenting the life histories of participants in the repatria-

tion project and those of their children and grandchildren. I complimented oral accounts with ethnographic research into the everyday experiences of migrants from North Korea in Japan.

32. The term "intramarriage" refers to the joining of families with similar ethnic and migratory histories.

1

Remembering the Exodus

Sŏn Donghyŏn was just a skinny thirteen-year-old when he first set foot in North Korea in 1973. He spoke only a smattering of Korean and had shown little interest in returning to the place his parents called "the fatherland." His friends were not planning on leaving Japan, so why should he? But his father was adamant the family would go together. Following their arrival, his family moved into an apartment on the outskirts of Wŏnsan, a port city on North Korea's eastern seaboard. The walk from home, down the valley and into the city, was pleasant enough and gave Donghyŏn a chance to talk with his mother about school, his new classmates, and the difficulties he was having learning Korean.

Summers were the best time to live near the sea. Every year, Zainichi Koreans arrived to visit family who had left Japan for the homeland, spending long afternoons building sandcastles and splashing in the shallows. It was a special beach, the only one Donghyŏn knew of that was not littered with barbed wire and concrete pill boxes. "There's a Young Pioneer Corps[1] park nearby, so the area isn't as heavily defended as others in the country," he explained. A stone's throw away, sheltered by sand dunes that became battlefields to kids reenacting General Kim's attacks on American imperialists, was a laned swimming pool. The pool area, replete with parasols and loungers, had been carefully divided into a section for locals and one for visitors from such places as Japan, Cuba, the Soviet Union, and China. "They wanted to stop foreign visitors from communicating with the locals, so they had an entire separate space built for them," Donghyŏn remembered. Inside the foreigner pool, visitors used Japanese yen and US dollars to buy cold drinks, ice cream, and other snacks.

Donghyŏn studied hard at school and subsequently trained as an engineer. After graduation, he worked six days a week in a Ch'ŏngjin factory, fixing heavy machinery used for construction around Hamgyŏng Province. After being introduced by a repatriate matchmaker, Donghyŏn married a woman whose family had also immigrated from Japan; the couple had two sons. Although considered as a skilled worker in North Korea, he was obligated to take part in regular indoctrination sessions. He told me that he found the state surveillance stifling and resented being forced to attend weekly self-criticism sessions. If nothing else, he recalled, they were tedious and a waste of everyone's time.

Fearing he was being targeted during criticism sessions, and without hope that his family would ever be free from the stigma of being immigrants from Japan, in 2008 Donghyŏn and his family escaped across the border into China. With the help of Japanese activists, Donghyŏn, his wife and two children made it back to Japan, where they settled in Osaka. After thirty-five years in North Korea, he was fortunate that his technical training helped him find work–first on the assembly line in a plastics factory and then as a high school math teacher. In the ethnic Korean school where we both worked, on the outskirts of Osaka, I often saw Donghyŏn walking briskly to class with an oversized mathematics triangle wedged under his arm. Wearing large, gold-framed glasses, with his hair carefully parted and a look of professorial detachment, he gave the impression of a no-nonsense man. "There are only four returnees in Japan with professional jobs," he told me, holding up the same number of fingers. "The rest are working part time or are unemployed." In between teaching classes, we spoke together and Donghyŏn recalled the years before his family moved to North Korea:

> Back in the early-1960s, people went to North Korea with their family in the hope that they'd be able to live well. My family went on board ship number 168. My parents had planned on leaving earlier, but my brother was injured in a car accident and we had to wait until he could travel. By that time, we all knew that things weren't good in North Korea. We knew that Japan was more developed. But we wanted to leave Japan anyway, because of the hatred we faced. It was the prejudice against Koreans that pushed us to leave. Added to this, was the fact that the dictator Pak Chŏnghŭi was in charge of South Korea and people there thought that we [Zainichi Koreans] were spies and such. So, North Korea looked like a better option for us.

Donghyŏn's recollections echoed those of other returnees I met in Osaka and Tokyo. His father had struggled to find work in 1960s Japan and Donghyŏn experienced daily bullying from Japanese children. A growing anti-Korean public sentiment acted as a decisive push factor for his family to leave Japan. Even as a teenager, he knew that his life choices were restricted by his Korean ethnicity. Fear of political persecution ruled out a move to South Korea. However bad things got in Japan, Donghyŏn's parents considered returning south of the DMZ as too great a risk. Instead, the Sŏn family left for North Korea at a time when conditions for repatriates were widely known to be difficult. The North Korean government, it was believed, re-

garded repatriates arriving after the 1960s as opportunists, people who had
not been devoted enough to repatriate during the height of the project. But
the Sŏns were not to be deterred, confident that life in the ethnic homeland
would still be better than living as an unwanted minority in Japan.

Starting in December 1959, thousands of Zainichi Korean families migrated from Japan to North Korea. By the mid-1960s, more than eighty
thousand individuals had made the journey. The question of what motivated
participants is a divisive one, even now. Supporters of Tokyo's position argue that the project was a genuine humanitarian mission, that the Japanese
government was helping displaced people who wished to return home (see
Kawashima 2009; Kikuchi 2009). Others argue that claims of Japanese benevolence fail to account for the complexity of the situation, and that Tokyo
instead regarded repatriation as a way to deport its unwanted ethnic minorities (cf. Lee and De Vos 1981c, 91; Morris-Suzuki 2007, 87; Shipper 2010,
62).

What is clear is that the repatriation project benefitted both Japanese
and DPRK interests, and that each used it for the country's own political
gain. Prime Minister Kishi Nobusuke of Japan (in office 1957–60), for example, regarded the repatriation of Koreans as a way to stave off criticism
of his administration's close relationship with the United States. At the
time, the country's political left wing, spearheaded by the Japan Socialist
Party, was pressuring Kishi over his "pro-Western foreign policy," manifest in the United States–Japan Treaty of Mutual Cooperation and Security
(Lee 1981c, 102–3).[2] Kishi encouraged repatriations to communist Korea as
a way to placate leftist groups while also demonstrating his independence
from Washington, DC. But Kishi's calculations went beyond domestic politicking. The maternal grandfather of Shinzō Abe, who would also become
prime minister of Japan, gambled that even the possibility of opening diplomatic and economic relations with the northern half of Korea would force
South Korean president Syngman Rhee's hand, breaking the deadlock that
had stalled ROK-Japan normalization talks well into the 1960s, and opening
a new chapter between the two US allies in Asia.

Kishi was convinced that focusing the attention of political allies and
adversaries alike on Koreans leaving Japan promised both domestic and
foreign policy gains. Historian Kikuchi Yoshiaki (2009) cites Ministry of
Foreign Affairs of Japan (MOFA-Japan) reports to show that the security
risks believed associated with Zainichi Koreans also featured prominently
in Kishi's planning. In particular, a MOFA-Japan report claims first that the
Zainichi Korean community demonstrated a disproportionately high rate
of criminality and welfare dependence; second, that domestic left-wing parties allegedly working in collaboration with North Korean interests posed
a distinct national security threat; and third, that gains could be made by
removing DPRK-affiliated Koreans, who at the time were thought to be

a hurdle to improving ROK-Japan relations (Kikuchi 2009, 102–5). But claims that reproduce Tokyo's "troublesome Koreans" trope minimize the targeted social and economic impacts of stripping state support from an already underserved and marginalized community, impacts that included pushing struggling Korean families farther into immiseration while denying established Zainichi Korean communities a voice in postwar Japan.

Motivated by security and economic concerns, Kishi correctly calculated that branding the repatriation project as a humanitarian venture allowed Tokyo to claim a moral high ground, no matter what the outcome. Hallam C. Shorrock Jr., Red Cross representative dispatched to support Japan's postwar reconstruction, explained, "Both the Liberal and Socialist Parties in Japan are using the repatriation issue to gain more favor with a [Japanese] public, which will be happy to rid itself of as many Koreans as possible, and with businessmen who see the need of stimulating contacts and future trade with North Korea."[3]

Tokyo's designs aligned conveniently with Pyongyang's. Kim Il-sung similarly welcomed Zainichi Koreans as a way to position the DPRK as a humanitarian actor on the international stage. By accepting Koreans from Japan, Kim's fledgling government hoped to gain de facto recognition in the international community, while at the same time embarrassing the Rhee government. Kim also expected that the repatriation of tens of thousands of capable men and women would provide a boost in worker numbers for his Seven-Year Economic Program (1961–67), while the possibility of opening trade with Japan promised valuable economic gains. It was a rare moment during the Cold War when the interests of two governments in opposing political camps overlapped.

The humanitarian narrative has, over the years, become a dominant explanation in Japan of why the repatriations went ahead. Japanese activists who supported the project echoed such sentiments to me, explaining that they too had in mind the interests of Koreans who longed for a better life (see chapter 5). Activists in Osaka and Tokyo now working to bring back to Japan families repatriated decades earlier told me that they promoted the repatriation project by writing favorable articles for Japanese newspapers, by photographing excited Korean families as they set sail from the Port of Niigata, and through endorsing Kim Il-sung at rallies across Japan. At the time, they believed they were playing a part in history by helping displaced people return to a bright future in their homeland. But time has proven their altruism to have been drastically misguided. Declassified documents in the Red Cross archives and returnees' own memories of the repatriation years are testimony to the turbulent political and social currents that channeled so many families to North Korea. But where do these highly personal, fragmented, family-centric memories fit in the histories and communal memories of modern Japan?

Hegemonic Histories and Vernacular Memory

Within a nation, memories of majority and minority communities each compete for inclusion in the nation's story. Hegemonic histories–the stories of the majority group–are manifest in the erection of monuments, the composition of national anthems, and the creation of textbooks for purposes of public education. Such official memories shape the identity of countries and citizens. In contrast, micro-histories, or what I refer to as vernacular memories, emerge from the peripheries of the majority society. Vernacular memories arise from the local level–from the bottom up–and tend to represent the past not through marble statues, grand narratives, or national anthems, but through fluid, everyday modes of presentation such as speech acts and bodily performances within families and minority communities. These highly personal histories often sit in opposition to and create a friction with state-centric nationalist discourses of the majority group.

The way nation-states manage memory production, building and shaping narratives, elevates particularly significant moments to the level of national folklore. Both George Washington's 1776 crossing of the Delaware River and the Australian and New Zealand Army Corps' doomed 1915 Gallipoli campaign, to take two examples, have acquired almost mythical status, invoked by politicians and patriots to this day. These distinct historical moments have, over time, emerged as founding myths in the United States and Australia/ New Zealand, respectively. Such hegemonic, national memories colonize the past, the present, and the future, squeezing out competing narratives.

In democratic countries it can be challenging to disappear competing events from the national consciousness, due largely to the existence of guardians of communal memory like civic groups, a free press, and an uncensored internet. But where there is a highly centralized, authoritarian exercise of power, erasing unfavorable events and competing memories is a more straightforward task comprised of the destruction of memory, the erasure and suppression of that destruction, and the creation of new, state-approved memories to substitute for those that were eliminated (Buyandelger 2013, 67–68). Societies that have experienced ideological conflict and trauma–the two Koreas and China, for instance–are especially prevalent sites of contested memory and identity. Where a state holds up particular episodes as instructive for young citizens, it treats others as toxic and seeks to hide them from view. The 1947–54 government massacres of civilians on South Korea's Cheju Island, or the 1989 Tiananmen Square massacre are just two examples of historical events regarded as threatening to the state and requiring erasure. In each case, the state's brutal suppression of its citizens has been deliberately obfuscated by state-sponsored nationalist discourses that privilege the South Korean and Chinese governments' perspectives, respectively.[4]

Japanese contemporary history has not been shaped by disappearing or killing its citizenry, but instead by codifying and mapping particular historical events onto a binary of either collective guilt or collective innocence. Categorizing events of the past into one of two historical buckets allowed for the emergence of a victimhood narrative that has subsequently come to characterize historical culture in Japan (Lim 2010, 1). In other words, contemporary Japanese history, as produced and reproduced by the majority society, understands events like the 1910 colonization of the Korean Peninsula, the 1937 Second Sino-Japanese War, the 1945–52 Allied occupation of Japan, and the 2011 Fukushima Daiichi nuclear disaster as either times when ordinary Japanese were misled by incompetent and untrustworthy leaders, or as moments when they collectively suffered under foreign aggression.[5] Either way, Japanese people are represented as victims. In presenting the repatriation project as a humane act that was subsequently coopted by North Korean duplicity, this event is also recognized within a corpus of victimhood narratives that includes both Japanese suffering under a militaristic government in the first half of the twentieth century, and the Japanese being the only people ever to suffer the effects of an atomic bombing (see Buruma 1994).[6]

Returnees from North Korea carry memories of a Japan in transition. Their recollections of economic neglect and racial discrimination in Japan, and their bodies broken through hard labor and state neglect while in North Korea, thrust vernacular memories into the discourse of Japan's victimhood consciousness. My interlocutors' memories oscillated in time and space between the conditions that forced them to leave Japan and those that later convinced them to return. Donghyŏn recalled the poverty of ethnic-minority communities in postwar Japan and racism against Koreans. Other interviewees spoke of Japanese police carrying out public stop-and-searches in Korean neighborhoods, the government's forced closure of ethnic Korean schools, and Zainichi Koreans' fears of being deported to South Korea where they would, at that time, be subject to further state aggression. But historically positioning the micro-histories of families who migrated to North Korea requires a better understanding of the days leading up to the repatriations. What was everyday life like for Koreans in Japan? And how did Cold War geopolitical wrangling play out in Korean communities in Tokyo, Osaka and beyond?

Minority Life in Postwar Japan

Modernization and an accompanying emphasis on economic development drove the postwar production of displaced people. In Japan's case, the state's repositioning in how it procured resources, from colonial exploitation to trade within a United States–led, globalizing market economy, forced a re-think of both borders and national identity.

At the forefront of the state's political and economic realignment was the question of how to manage the country's massive immigrant workforce, a collective largely comprised of foreigners from now-liberated territories. The design of the postwar Japanese state was to be characterized by, among other things, belief in the mythic ethnic homogeneity of the Japanese population. Specifically, an ideology of racial descent and blood ties laid the foundations for Japanese identity and "feelings of ethnic commonality" (Tsuda 1998, 322). This reimagined community constituted denizens of a now much-reduced territory that included Okinawa in the far south of the archipelago and Hokkaido in the north. Former colonial laborers–Koreans, Chinese, and others, however culturally indistinguishable from Japanese they might be, would not be included in the new Japan. Tokyo's commitment to creating a national community along racial lines made difficult the incorporation or "recycling," as Zygmunt Bauman puts it (Bauman 2004, 5), of a glut of unwanted outsiders that subsequently emerged. Consequently, instead of trying to find other uses for Zainichi Koreans, the Japanese government looked for opportunities to distribute its human excess outside of its borders.

Immediately following Japan's capitulation, the majority of Koreans in Japan returned to what had become the Republic of Korea. But some 650,000 Koreans remained in Japan. Koreans who stayed did so for diverse reasons: some had achieved a modicum of success, establishing small businesses, building social networks, and starting families. Others hesitated to move their lives to the instability of the Korean Peninsula. Koreans who had earlier returned to the ROK sent news back to friends and family in Japan, warning them of deteriorating living conditions. Official reports from the time list cholera outbreaks, floods, railroad strikes, and general social disorder as factors making a return less appealing.[7] For many Zainichi Koreans, the risks involved with returning to a country struggling to reabsorb people displaced during the colonial era, and that appeared on the brink of civil war, was less attractive than remaining in Japan.[8]

I met Tanaka Sazuka[9] in Tokyo, on a humid summer's day. Over the course of several hours and many coffees she recalled the chaotic years following liberation. Sazuka was born in Tokyo in 1942. Her parents had migrated separately from colonial Korea–her father from Pusan, in the southeast, when he was seventeen, and her mother from Cheju Island when she was three years old. Sazuka attended a Ch'ongryŏn high school. She studied all the standard subjects–Japanese language, history, geography, math, and biology, as well as Korean language and North Korean history.

Sazuka recalled her neighborhood in Tokyo, surrounded by the sights and smells of open-air butchers, kimchi stalls, and hawkers selling everything from kitchenware to clothes. Her parents encouraged her to go to school, recognizing that the best hope for their daughter to have a better life was to gain an education. But her family struggled to make ends meet on her father's factory wage, and there was mounting pressure on Sazuka to contribute to the family income. In early-1960 a Ch'ongryŏn representative knocked on their door. This was not unusual in itself, since Ch'ongryŏn members often visited Korean neighborhoods, proselytizing on the greatness of Kim Il-sung while soliciting donations to the communist cause. But this time the handsome young man dressed in a dark suit, crisp white shirt, and tie was the bearer of exciting news. Sazuka's mother brewed black tea and the four of them sat on the floor of their two-room wooden home, listening wide-eyed as he described a life free from want—free education and health care, guaranteed white rice from the government, employment, and a future in which Koreans would be building an independent nation for themselves. "Our family was so poor, and North Korea sounded like a good opportunity," she told me. "I started studying harder as I didn't want to miss the chance to go."

Like so many others keen on seizing this opportunity, Sazuka was only a teenager when she left Japan. She traveled alone to North Korea on board the fifteenth ship to leave from Niigata, on the west coast of Honshu Island, to Ch'ŏngjin, in North Korea's northeast. Her parents asked her to go first, both to see what conditions were like and to give the family some temporary financial relief. But soon after she arrived in North Korea Sazuka sent several cryptic messages back to her family, warning them not to follow her. One such message simply ended, "I'll see you when reunification happens." Her parents, she remembered, would understand there was no telling when the two Koreas would again be one. As such, there could be no knowing when her family would be reunited. Alone in her new home, Sazuka had no other option but to try and make the best of it. Not long after arriving, keeping her head down and focusing on her studies, she was given permission to enter university, majoring in mechanics. In spite of what felt like early successes, it was a lonely and disorienting time. Sazuka's teachers scolded her and other young repatriates for using Japanese to speak with one another. Nevertheless, "We ate together, spent time together and, when we were certain there were no native North Koreans around, we spoke Japanese together," she explained, recalling the comfort she felt during such rare moments of intimacy. The tropes that emerge from Sazuka's memories are common to the narratives of other returnees who have escaped from North Korea: poverty and discrimination in Japan and promises of a better life in the DPRK.

Recollections of muddling through under very difficult conditions characterized interviewees' memories of life both in Japan and in North Korea. While Koreans in colonial Japan never enjoyed the same benefits as Japanese nationals, in the postwar period conditions deteriorated for people like Sazuka. The Far Eastern Commission, based in Washington, DC, was designated with overseeing the Allied occupation of Japan. Archival documents show that the commission categorized Koreans who remained in Japan under a "half-Japanese and half-Korean status."[10] This classification was deliberately vague, and Koreans were treated alternately as Japanese or as foreigners, as citizens of a defeated nation or as liberated people, depending on which suited the occupation authorities. Commonly, however, both occupation forces and the Japanese government associated former colonial subjects, especially Koreans, with left-wing political agitation, black-marketeering, and organized violence. In an effort to control Koreans who refused to leave Japan, from May 1947, and under the Alien Registration Regulation, foreigners were required to register their address and to carry a registration certificate with them at all times.[11] People who could not produce their card during police checks were liable to be fined or imprisoned and subsequently deported to South Korea.

In a move to further oversee former colonial subjects, in 1951 the government introduced the Migration Control Ordinance. The law allowed Japan to deport non-Japanese who had committed crimes and received a sentence of more than one year, as well as foreigners deemed unable to economically provide for themselves. To broaden the scope of deportable individuals, the government retroactively applied the ordinance to former colonial subjects who had been convicted on a wide range of charges. As Japan's largest minority, there was a feeling that these laws were specifically designed to target Zainichi Koreans. As the walls closed in, life for Korean families like the Tanakas was becoming increasingly precarious.

On 28 April 1952 the San Francisco Peace Treaty came into effect. The treaty, signed by forty-nine nations and Prime Minister Yoshida Shigeru of Japan, returned control of the country to the Japanese government while securing the presence of US troops that continues to this day. For ethnic minorities in Japan, the treaty signing was a defining moment in their relationship to the government. Previously, as part of the Japanese Greater East Asia Co-prosperity Sphere, minorities in Japan were afforded basic privileges, such as access to public services, social security, and an expectation of legal due process. The reinstated Japanese government immediately rescinded these rights. Almost overnight, Koreans and other former colonial subjects became aliens in Japan. The Social Affairs Bureau in the Ministry of Health and Welfare of Japan announced the termination of support by stating that Koreans in Japan were no longer eligible for assistance under the Daily Life Security Law, as they were not regarded as citizens.[12]

Without the protections and benefits guaranteed by citizenship, former colonial subjects lost access to central government social welfare and occupational and educational opportunities. Pressure continued to build on Korean families as employment opportunities dried up, wages shrank, ethnic Korean schools were forcibly closed, and Korean families seeking to break away from poverty-stricken, high-density inner-city areas were barred from renting in Japanese majority neighborhoods. Some families tried to secure loans as temporary relief, but, outside of the Korean ghettoes, even these were available only at higher rates than the rates for Japanese. As more Koreans turned to the government for assistance, the Yoshida administration in Tokyo became increasingly concerned that Koreans were draining resources at the local level. A report compiled by the Japanese Red Cross Society (JRC) stated that, in terms of employment and welfare, the number of needy Koreans grew in number from 74,911 in September 1952, to 138,972 in December 1955. This marked a rise from 13 percent to 24 percent of the Korean population classified by the government as persons in need of special state economic assistance.[13] JRC staff cited the rise in the number of economically dependent Koreans as evidence that deporting Koreans to their homeland was the only way to solve what they referred to as "the Korean problem." The JRC's report was subsequently dispatched to Red Cross headquarters in Geneva. But the main challenge, if any kind of repatriation were to go ahead, would be ensuring that the North Korean government was willing and able to accept prospective migrants.

During the 18th International Conference of the Red Cross, held in Toronto July–August 1952, JRC representatives met with their counterparts from the Soviet Red Cross and Chinese Red Cross to discuss cooperation on the repatriation of Japanese citizens still in their countries. During discussions, the JRC also inquired about Japanese soldiers and members of the former colonial regime being held in the DPRK. Soviet Red Cross delegates suggested the Japanese contact the DPRK Red Cross directly to negotiate the matter further. In 1954, five years before the beginning of the repatriation project, the JRC sent a dispatch to the DPRK Red Cross in Pyongyang through the ICRC in Geneva. The telegram requested information on Japanese still in North Korea and asked that the North Koreans help with the repatriation of these individuals.[14] In return, "we promised [that if] the North Korean Red Cross help with the repatriation of Japanese, we will help with the repatriation of Koreans to North Korea," Inoue Masutarô, director of the JRC's Foreign Affairs Department, later explained in a 1960 speech to the Meiji Club, Tokyo (Inoue 1960, 3). The proposed exchange planted the seeds for further negotiations on the future of Koreans in Japan.[15]

The question of Japanese wishing to repatriate from North Korea was partially resolved during the 1956 Pyongyang Conference, where participants concluded that some thirty Japanese would return to Japan with North Korean assistance. Koreans in Japan, however, proved a thornier issue, hindered by mutual antagonism between the two Koreas, and territorial disputes between South Korea and Japan.[16] Indeed, Syngman Rhee's awareness of how it would look to the world if tens of thousands of Koreans freely chose the communist DPRK over the supposed free and democratic ROK threatened to undo the repatriation project before it even started.

To strengthen the case for the repatriation of Zainichi Koreans, in 1956 Inoue penned a report for the JRC titled "Fundamental Conditions of Livelihood of Certain Koreans Residing in Japan." In a document calling for an "urgent solution to the question of certain Koreans in Japan," Inoue argued that anti-Korean prejudice aside, rampant unemployment, high rates of crime and less economic ability than Japanese meant that "Koreans can do nothing but go home."[17] Working in close consultation with the Japanese government, Inoue petitioned the ICRC for support in repatriating Zainichi Koreans on what he claimed were "humanitarian grounds."[18] He added to his letter-writing campaign by visiting Geneva as part of two missions to pressure the organization. In Geneva Inoue argued that Japan's exclusion of Zainichi Koreans could not be blamed on the Japanese government, nor on Japanese employers, nor even on racial discrimination, but rather on the "ideological string" that had attached itself to hiring Koreans.[19] Inoue concluded that Koreans were welfare dependents at best and political radicals more broadly. Ultimately, they would never adapt to life in modern Japan. His comments echoed other Japanese officials' comments of the time, in painting struggling Koreans as a natural consequence of a national excess of labor: unable to adapt to a modernizing economy, ideologically subversive, and a threat to Japanese economic and security interests.[20]

Cold War Politics

Some 97 percent of Koreans in Japan had originally come from the southern portion of Korea, territory that in 1948 became the ROK.[21] But home for many Zainichi Koreans was no longer a geographically informed choice. Instead, ideas of home and homelands became inseparable from Cold War politics.

Koreans who did not return to the peninsula following Japan's 1945 capitulation subsequently organized themselves into three loose groups: the League of Korean Residents in Japan (Chae'il Chosŏnnin Ryŏnmeang or *Choryŏn*), formed in October 1945 and affiliated with North Korea; the Korean Residents Union in Japan/Mindan (Chae'il Han'guk'in Koryumindan), established on 3 October 1946 and affiliated with South Korea; and those who were either politically unaligned or who had membership in both organizations. The League of Korean Residents was largely comprised of Koreans sympathetic to the communist cause, but also many non-communists who regarded the league as a means of defending Korean interests in Japan. The league's activities drew the attention of Douglas MacArthur, commander of the Allied occupation forces in Japan. The US general was at the time moving to suppress left-wing political dissent in the country's industrial centers. Concerned with what he regarded as potentially seditious activities, MacArthur ordered the league dissolved on 8 September 1949.[22] Shortly thereafter, in March 1955, the General Association of Korean Residents in Japan, or Ch'ongryŏn (Chae Ilbon Chosŏnin Ch'ongryŏn haphoe or Zai-Nihon Chōsenjin Sōrengōkai/Chōsen Sōren in Japanese), replaced the league.

In the years following the creation of the two competing organizations, Ch'ongryŏn was particularly successful in rousing enthusiasm among Koreans across Japan.[23] Many Zainichi Koreans regarded Kim Il-sung's Soviet-supported government as more politically legitimate than Rhee's American-backed ROK. Realizing the value of having such an organization working on its behalf, the DPRK reached out to Koreans in Japan. From the beginning of January 1958 to the end of June 1959, Pyongyang provided US$1.5 million in Japanese yen to fund individual Koreans and facilities serving Korean communities, such as hospitals, clinics, and schools.[24] With North Korea–funded classrooms and teaching staff, Ch'ongryŏn primary, junior high, and high schools taught a DPRK state–approved curriculum. In a Tsuruhashi café Fukui Miyako, whose uncle, aunt, and cousins went to North Korea in the mid-1970s, recalled her childhood in a Ch'ongryŏn school: "We learnt about the life and deeds of Kim Il-sung. The stories started from his childhood, climbing trees to contemplate the founding of a new Korea, to his time as a partisan fighter, defending the fatherland against the Japanese. We also sang lots of songs about Kim Il-sung and his support for our schools. We learnt that it was his generosity in sending us money that gave us the opportunity to study."

If North Korea was winning the hearts and minds of Zainichi Koreans, in Seoul Syngman Rhee was purging real and imagined communist threats. Rhee's ideological dogmatism worried Zainichi Koreans, many of whom had fled Cheju Island during the unrest that climaxed in the April 1948 Cheju Uprising.[25] Rhee was loath to assist Mindan, an organization that was already hobbled by ineffective leadership and corruption.[26] As such, Mindan was unable to extract financial and material support comparable to its North Korean counterpart.[27] The Rhee administration also made it difficult for Zainichi Koreans to get ROK passports, and offered no promises of employment or stability for those who might consider returning to South Korea.[28]

The ROK government also opposed the movement of Zainichi Koreans to North Korea. Rhee feared that an influx of ideologically motivated, semi-skilled workers would bolster an already strengthening DPRK economy.[29] In late June 1956 South Korea lodged the first in a number of protests with MOFA-Japan, warning that, if Japan continued with plans to send Koreans to the DPRK, Seoul would consider it as an indirect declaration of war

(Morris-Suzuki 2007, 132). Writing at the time, Hallam C. Shorrock Jr. worried that simmering anger within the United States–ROK–Japan alliance would destabilize the region's delicate balance of power: "Another danger [added to the threat of war with the DPRK] implicit in the materialization of the present repatriation plans without the sanction of the ROK government is that though war between South Korea and North Korea may not result, relations between South Korea and Japan would be so strained that it would be years before diplomatic relations could be re-established . . . this would mean a continued break between two of the free world's allies . . . resulting in weakening the free world's stand against communism.[30] As plans for a Korean repatriation gained momentum, Shorrock's fears that the regional US security alliance was straining toward collapse seemed increasingly to be a reality. In early 1959 South Korean protests reached a boiling point. On 14 February 1959, a day after the Japanese government publicly announced its support for the project, the president of the National Red Cross of the ROK, Sohn Chang Whan, wrote to Leopold Boissier, president of the ICRC. In his letter, Sohn referred to the proposed repatriations as "an unprecedented mass deportation, one in which the ICRC has no jurisdiction."[31] Sohn argued that the question of Koreans in Japan was an issue between Seoul and Tokyo, not North Korea. Because Koreans in Japan were neither stateless nor displaced, he explained, the ROK had full authority and obligation to protect them as overseas nationals. Only weeks later, Sohn's letter was followed by another, this time from Cho Chung W., South Korea's minister of foreign affairs. Cho's letter to Boissier attacked the planned repatriations as "a Japanese attempt to expel en masse those Koreans in Japan who are allegedly desirous of going to north Korea."[32] Cho echoed Sohn's vehement opposition, summarizing Seoul's position in three points: First, he argued that the question of Koreans in Japan was a legal and political question and, as such, not within the jurisdiction of any third party. Second, he claimed that the Japanese government was misusing the principle of "freedom of choice of residence," because Koreans who are sent to the DPRK will not be able to exercise these freedoms and DPRK propaganda has "deluded by bribery, false promises, pressures and so on" prospective repatriates. Third, he pointed out that, because Korean residents in Japan were not displaced people, only the government of the ROK, as the legal government in Korea, had the authority to protect them.

In South Korea, government and opposition united in protest against a venture they claimed would "force Koreans into slavery."[33] The *New York Times* reported on government organized rallies during which cabinet ministers denounced the Kishi administration and placard-waving crowds marched through Seoul decrying Japanese support of a "North Korean plot." A rally organized by the "National Committee to Oppose Japan's Deportation of Korean Residents to North Korea" saw more than 130,000 residents of South Korea's capital take to the streets, calling for Tokyo to cancel the repatriations ("Koreans in Protest" 1959). Across the country, South Korean school children mobilized to petition the ICRC, expressing their condemnation of the project. On 24 February 1959, for instance, teachers and students of Ch'ungsong Middle-High School in North Kyŏng-sang Province penned a letter to Leopold Boissier. Over several pages, the young authors reminded Boissier that Japan had once "robbed Koreans of their national sovereignty," and requested that the ICRC "refuse roughly to hand over free men to north-Korea by trade and to condemn the Japanese cruelty."[34] With South Koreans unified against the proposed repatriations, success of the project would depend on how Tokyo presented its case to the watching world.

South Korea was not alone in thinking the repatriations were part of broader Japanese machinations. North of the DMZ, Kim Il-sung was also initially lukewarm to the idea of accepting Zainichi Koreans. With Ch'on-gryŏn acting on Pyongyang's behalf, North Korea's leader thought it prudent to promote improved conditions for overseas Koreans, thereby fostering support and informal trade networks within Japan. In September 1955, for example, Kim announced that the DPRK would try to arrange repatriation if Koreans in Japan wished to return. But his statement was tempered by recommendations that Zainichi Koreans would do better to establish themselves in Japan and work for Korean unification by fostering a closer relationship between Japan and the DPRK (Lee 1981c, 98–99).

Kim's ambivalence toward the fate of Zainichi Koreans shifted again, and on 8 September 1958, during celebrations for the tenth anniversary of the DPRK's founding, the North Korean premier publicly declared, "Our people warmly welcome the aspiration of the compatriots who, having lost the means of living in Japan, are desirous of returning to the bosom of their fatherland" (DPRK 1959, 10). An October message from Pyongyang to Ch'ongryŏn provided further impetus to press forward: "When you leave the shore of an alien land where you roamed in poverty and humiliation without a country of your own," opens the letter, "for your regenerated, prospering homeland, even the raging waves of the East Sea will lower their crest to smooth your way and the lovely seagulls skimming above the sea of the fatherland will wing over your boat rejoicing with you" (DPRK 1959, 109–113).

Kim Il-sung's unexpected announcement signaled the beginning of Ch'ongryŏn's official involvement in promoting a mass migration of Koreans from Japan.[35] The month following Kim's speech, Han Duk Su, chairman of the Central Standing Committee of Ch'ongryŏn, wrote to Prime Minister Kishi. Han reasoned that the Japanese had failed in their moral duty to support Koreans who had been forcibly brought to the country and, since Kim Il-sung had personally guaranteed conditions for Koreans wanting to leave for the DPRK, Kishi should not stand in the way.[36] Han's private communications coincided with Ch'ongryŏn's broader propaganda campaign: "At present our people have been conducting a nation-wide movement to prepare for the stabilization of livelihoods of compatriots in Japan, whose repatriation we welcome with open arms," reads one Ch'ongryŏn proclamation, quoting DPRK vice premier Kim Il. "Factories, firms, farming and fishing villages and organizations relating to science and culture are ready to accept repatriates," North Korea's second-in-command promised, but only if "the Kishi Government should take some appropriate counter-measure for their repatriation."[37]

Locked in an ideological battle with Rhee's South Korea, supporting the repatriations gave Pyongyang a platform for promoting the economic growth ostensibly taking place across the DPRK. "Our country today is not the backward agricultural country of yesterday," Kim Il told reporters from North Korea's Korean Central News Agency. "It is being turned into a strong and prosperous industrial-agricultural country with a developed industry. Modern houses are being built in rural villages as well as in cities, and the material and cultural life of the people is becoming richer and richer."[38] The DPRK leadership hoped for immediate economic gains from the repatriation project. These included the production boost that an influx of workers would bring to an already growing North Korean economy,[39] the propaganda victory of receiving thousands of people fleeing the capitalist world, and a chance to destabilize Japan–ROK relations. In 1959 Shorrock Jr. wrote that the repatriation was an occasion for North Korea to show the world her sympathy toward suffering fellow countrymen who have been persecuted by the imperialist Japanese, and at the same time who have been neglected by their own country and place of birth, South Korea; to establish trade ties with Japan, contribute toward the eventual recognition of North Korea by Japan, cause the complete breakdown in normalization of relations between Japan and South Korea, weaken the dignity and reputation of the Rhee government, and establish a more effective system of Communist influence in Japan and throughout Asia.[40] Pyongyang began energetically promoting the repatriation of comrades desirous to "see their dreams realized in the northern part of the DPRK" (DPRK 1959, 3). A 1959 book published by the DPRK titled *On the Question of 600,000 Koreans in Japan* reflects this new sense of purpose. *On the Question* underlines the "consistent concern the Government of the Republic [DPRK] has directed toward Korean nationals in Japan" (DPRK 1959, 1). Replete with monochrome photos of North Korean mechanized agriculture and collective farmers "rejoicing over their big shares" (DPRK 1959, 150), the book lays the blame for the failure of Zainichi Koreans to "realize their cherished dream" at the feet of "US imperialists, the Syngman Rhee clique and the Japanese authorities" (DPRK 1959, 1). The publication denigrates South Korea as a living hell, quoting a select few Zainichi Koreans as insisting that it would be better to die than to go to South Korea. The DPRK, on the other hand, welcomed Korean comrades:

> Not only will Korean youth and students who come to the northern part of the Republic from Japan to study be welcomed, but also schooling and living expenses, such as stipend, clothing, footwear, stationary etc., will be provided free of charge. Furthermore, each will be given 20,000 won (in old currency) on his or her arrival in the North, plus the monthly stipend that was established in honor of the tenth anniversary of the founding of the Korean Democratic Youth League. . . . Korean nationals from Japan will be ensured rest and employment. Moreover, necessary funds for farming and establishing oneself in business will be loaned, in addition to a guarantee for housing and education of their children. (DPRK 1959, 3)

For a now stateless minority in Japan, Kim Il-sung promised full, unconditional citizenship–a country to which to belong–for those who made the journey, and a sumptuous-sounding care package on arrival. As citizens of the DPRK, repatriates would enjoy free education, employment, housing, and opportunities for social advancement. These were possibilities that many Koreans felt unlikely to be forthcoming in Japan. With Pyongyang's approval, Ch'ongryŏn organized sit-down strikes demanding repatriation in front of the JRC headquarters, and disseminated North Korean propaganda at public rallies throughout the country.[41] North Korea's diplomatic arm in Japan also printed fliers and pamphlets calling on Korean compatriots to return to the homeland, and Ch'ongryŏn members canvassed Korean populated areas of Osaka, Kobe, Nagoya, and Tokyo, projecting greetings from Premier Kim Il-sung promising a better life across the sea.[42] Constant messaging from powerful sources fostered an imagining of North Korea as a place in which patriotic Koreans would live free from the marginalizing practices they experienced in Japan.

Yamamoto Hiroko, in her early seventies when we met in Osaka, emigrated from her native Japan to North Korea in 1961 only to escape the DPRK in early 2000. She explained how Ch'ongryŏn went door to door, extolling the benefits of life in the DPRK. In a blend of Japanese and Korean she recalled, "Ch'ongryŏn representatives came to my husband's house and talked to him and his family about going to North Korea. I'm actually Japanese, so I didn't need to leave. But my husband's father, a Zainichi Korean, decided to go and I had to go with the family. Ch'ongryŏn officials told me that I'd be able to return after three years. This is what gave my parents comfort and why they gave me permission to leave. Of course, they lied."

Japanese spouses were permitted to go with their husbands to North Korea (discussed in chapter 3). If emigration from Japan to North Korea was imagined as a chance for Zainichi Koreans to live without the insecurity that marked life in Japan, then for Japanese women like Hiroko it was likely framed as the dutiful act of a good wife. Hiroko spoke no Korean and had little understanding of the local customs when she arrived in her new home. She recalled her years in North Korea as the time "when I stopped speaking."

Japanese authorities agreed to assist Koreans' emigration, organizing tax-payer-funded transportation from around Japan to the Niigata docks, and enticing Korean convicts with commuted sentences if they would leave and promise not to return. Yi Si-nae, a prominent Osaka-based activist for the rights of Zainichi Koreans, recalled to me her mother's experiences in 1950s Japan. At the time, there was a strong anti-Korean war movement within the Zainichi Korean community, she explained. One day, Japanese police arrested Si-nae's stepfather for protesting against the munitions factories that operated in the industrial areas of Osaka, around which many Zainichi Koreans lived. While in detention, her stepfather was given the choice of either expulsion to South Korea, which risked punishment as a communist sympathizer, or deportation to the DPRK. Si-nae explained, "In Tsuruhashi at that time, there were many factories making cluster bombs. My mother's ex-husband was strongly opposed to the production of these weapons. He tried to disrupt the manufacturing process, but Japanese secret police arrested him. While the Japanese government hesitated to send him to South Korea where he might have been executed, they didn't want him to stay in Japan, either. So, when the chance came up, they sent him to North Korea."

Although Pyongyang was far from keen to receive convicts and others whom it regarded as elements of the Japanese criminal underworld, there was little they could do to screen for such people. As such, when offered a choice that was framed as either time in a South Korean prison or a new start in the prosperous DPRK, people like Si-nae's stepfather opted to join the exodus.[43]

Belonging and Exclusion

The Japanese government would have struggled to justify its claims that the repatriation project was a humanitarian venture without the involvement of the ICRC. On 14 February 1959, Foreign Minister Fujiyama Aiichiro and Welfare Minister Sakata Michita approached the president of the JRC, Shimazu Tadatsugu, requesting the ICRC cooperate with Tokyo in facilitating the repatriation of Zainichi Koreans, including screening applicants and providing a transport ship. That same day, the *New York Times* speculated that, by bringing in a neutral organization to oversee the project, the Japanese were attempting to avoid direct governmental responsibility ("Japan Asks Red Cross Help" 1959). Indeed, ICRC involvement lent legitimacy to the mass migration and also stifled South Korean protests that the project was a coordinated attempt to undermine the Rhee regime. Furthermore, having the ICRC as a guarantor to the humanitarian aims of the project was a means to avoid US intervention on what was to be one of the largest movements of people to the communist world during the Cold War.

A Humanitarian Venture

The repatriation of Koreans presented the Red Cross with an opportunity to establish an intermediary role between the capitalist and communist blocs. The early years of the Cold War had fostered a sense of pessimism within the ICRC, and the urgency of developing cross-ideological lines of communication grew out of fears of an impending third world war. Many in the organization were convinced that open warfare between the two ideological blocs was inevitable. In such a case, the immediate concern was how to communicate with communist forces for situations of prisoner exchange and negotiations. There was concern within the Red Cross that little had changed since World War II, when the organization had failed to protect German troops captured by the Soviet Union. The Germans had subsequently used Soviet abuses to justify their own ill-treatment of Russian prisoners. Before the outbreak of another global conflict, the ICRC had to find more-effective ways to protect combatants and civilians against the effects of conventional and nuclear war.[44] The challenge was to win the trust of the Soviet Union and convince the Kremlin of the need for a third-party facilitating communication between the two blocs.

As a means for the ICRC to include the Soviet Union while guaranteeing the safety of passengers headed to North Korea, the organization requested the Soviet Union provide transport vessels. It was calculated that South Korea would be less likely to attack a vessel provided by Moscow and guarded by Soviet troops. As expected, Soviet Union premier Nikita Khrushchev welcomed the opportunity to promote his image on the world stage, and speculated that the Soviet Union would also benefit from worsening Japan–ROK relations. Khrushchev thus provided two transport ships, the *Kyl'ion* and the *Tobol'sk,* and a naval escort to defend them.[45] Once passage was secured and the threat of South Korean military intervention diminished, attention turned to the ICRC's role in establishing the free will of applicants for repatriation. An agreement between the Red Cross and the Kishi government required that prospective repatriates pass through an assessment to ensure each person was migrating of his or her own free will. An official screening would also placate those within the ICRC who had reservations regarding the project. Over lunch in a restaurant adjoining Geneva's Red Cross headquarters, François Bugnion, former director for international law and cooperation of the ICRC, clarified, "The job of the ICRC was to screen

Koreans wishing to leave for North Korea to ensure they were leaving of their own volition. What wasn't obvious to the representatives of the ICRC was that, behind the process, there was a web of tension and pressure reflecting the geo-political strains of the Cold War."[46]

Beyond a simple confirmation of free will, several additional reasons existed for checking the motives of repatriates. First, requiring a confirmation of free will unencumbered the ICRC of responsibility for any misadventure that might occur, both during the journey to North Korea and after resettlement. While the threat of South Korean naval attacks had largely been resolved, there remained a possibility that repatriations would trigger a broader regional conflict. Furthermore, a fair screening of individuals wishing to migrate to a communist country also demonstrated the ICRC's sincerity in acting as a neutral party between the two blocs.[47] A letter from the director of the Central Counter-measure Headquarters of Japan to the head of the JRC Niigata Center underlined what was at stake for the ICRC: "Confirmation of will at the Niigata Center is made so that the International Committee of the Red Cross can confirm the fact that there is none that has gone back against his or her will." The author emphasizes, "If it should be found in future that even only one [person] has returned against his or her will, what the Japan Red Cross Society and the International Committee of the Red Cross have done so far will be totally damaged."[48]

With securing free will a guiding principle of the predeparture process, new arrivals to Niigata's Red Cross Center prepared themselves to pass through four stages prior to leaving for North Korea.[49] During the first stage, each prospective repatriate met individually with a Red Cross representative and an interpreter. This first meeting, according to a JRC guidebook distributed at the time, confirmed a person's independent desire to go to North Korea. At a second meeting, an official of the Immigration Control Bureau of MOFA-Japan directed prospective repatriates to sign a report of exit, confirming that each person understood the process that awaited them in the coming days. Following the report's submission—Stage 3—a customs official inspected the luggage of each person to ensure that he or she was not carrying items prohibited for travel by the Japanese authorities. The final stage comprised a meeting with an official who was charged with changing a prospective repatriate's Japanese currency into a pound sterling check for travel to North Korea.[50]

At first, those awaiting repatriation in the center were not permitted to meet with relatives, friends, or outsiders. Isolation was another way that the Red Cross tried to guarantee each person acted of his or her own volition. But guaranteeing the free will of prospective repatriates would be a complex task. Amendments later made to the guidebook permitted prospective repatriates to meet with visitors to the center while awaiting departure.[51] Reports subsequently emerged from the Niigata Center of Ch'ongryŏn members

Figure 1.1. Ueno train station, Tokyo. Koreans leaving for Niigata bid farewell to friends and family. © Photothèque CICR (DR)/ (Photograph by Elsa Casal, confidentiality level: public). Date: sometime between 1959 and 1963.

pressuring individuals who were wavering on their decision to leave Japan. Since the center was open to all, there was little that could be done to prevent such interference.[52] Consequently, Red Cross officials struggled to ensure repatriates were not subject to political influence.

The Red Cross employed translators, speaking Korean and Japanese, to interview prospective repatriates. For some, the interview offered a final moment of reflection. Kin Hanako, for example, arrived in the interview room with her two sons on 11 January 1961 from Ube city, Yamaguchi. When the Korean translator asked her if it was her will to go to North Korea, Kin replied that she did not in fact wish to go, as she was unable to support her two children without her husband, from whom she had recently separated. Kin told Red Cross employees that she now wanted to return to her husband in Kobe, but was scared of how Ch'ongryŏn representatives would respond to her decision. A Red Cross representative reassured Kin that nobody has the right to force her to repatriate, and instead encouraged her to reconcile with her husband. She departed that afternoon with her children for Kobe.[53]

Similarly, sixteen-year-old Yi Midori from Yamaguchi Prefecture entered the Red Cross Center on 18 December with her parents and three siblings,

Figure 1.2. Niigata, Japan. Arrival at Niigata train station. Repatriation toward North Korea of Koreans living in Japan. © Photothèque CICR (DR)/ (Photograph by Elsa Casal, confidentiality level: public). Date: sometime between 1959 and 1963.

along with 972 other prospective repatriates. Telling the interviewer that she preferred to leave at a later date, she refused to accompany her family on board the ship to North Korea. Seemingly, Yi was a determined young woman, and she is recorded as having returned to Osaka and her factory job two days later.[54]

At other times, however, behind the fabric screen that officials drew across the doorway of the interview room, there was little guarantee of a fair assessment. Inside the room, whole families sat in front of ICRC and JRC staff. The conversation, including interviewees' responses to the question of whether each and every one of them desired to go to North Korea, was audible outside the Special Room.[55] Yamamoto Hiroko remembered her time spent waiting in the Niigata screening center. On the day she was due to be interviewed, ICRC staff invited her whole family into the room and asked them, as a group, if they wanted to leave for North Korea. "The only person that could answer, however, was my father-in-law. He replied, 'Yes, we want to go.' He was the head of the family, so we had to follow him."

The issue of free will was further complicated for people detained by the Japanese police, including several hundred Koreans awaiting punishment for various criminal offenses. As was the case for Yi Si-nae's stepfather,

Japanese officials told them that they were not allowed to stay in Japan, but instead had to choose between the DPRK and the ROK. The ICRC's difficulty in effectively screening prospective migrants, the Japanese government's use of the project as a means of deporting unwanted Koreans, and the patriarchal practices of Korean families each contributed in its own way to the failure of the project as a voluntary, humanitarian mission.

Repatriations Begin

On 14 December 1959, following several years of negotiations that culminated in the signing of the Calcutta Accord between the JRC and the DPRK Red Cross, the repatriations went ahead.[56] Prospective repatriates traveled to Niigata from around the country, on trains arranged by the Kishi government. Men, women, and children met with ICRC staff and, after completing the required four-step process, boarded the ferry to the DPRK amid singing and flag-waving crowds organized by Ch'ongryŏn.[57]

Mindan, in a last-ditch effort to oppose the repatriations, directed its local and prefectural chapters to rouse public opposition to the project with nationwide demonstrations and a Preventative Month Against Forced Labor Recruitment (Lee 1981c, 105). When it became clear that the project would go ahead regardless of opposition, rumors surfaced of South Korean agents sabotaging railway lines to prevent repatriates from reaching Niigata. In a politically divisive atmosphere, it became difficult to distinguish the truth from propaganda. In 1959, for example, the Mindan newspaper *Minshu Shimbun* reported growing confusion surrounding preparations for repatriations:

> Officials of the Kanagawa Prefectural Branch of Sōren [Ch'ongryŏn] forced 23 persons of five households to come to the [Red Cross] Window of the Takamatsu City Office and finish their application for return [to North Korea] at about 10am on November 5. Later, the applicants expressed their wish to cancel the application, because they applied for repatriation to North Korea not of their own free will and want to stay in Japan. Knowing this, the officials of the Sōren came to their houses almost every day and threatened them and sold their furniture and effects against their will. Such incidents are happening everywhere in this country and complaints and requests for help are coming into the Headquarters of Mindan day after day.[58]

Mindan's report is followed by another, this one from the Kanagawa Prefectural Chapter of the JRC to Kasai Yoshisuke, the JRC's vice-president.[59] This second report refutes Mindan's claims that Ch'ongryŏn was forcing Koreans to migrate, pointing to South Korean propaganda as the source of the fabrications:

With regard to your letter dated December 17, we made careful study, in secret, about the issue of application for repatriation of Koreans in Japan and
wish to inform you as follows:
1. On November 5, 1959 . . . staff members of the Kanagawa Prefectural
Branch of the Sōren . . . appeared at the Red Cross Window . . . accompanying
23 Koreans . . . who had long expressed their strong wish for repatriation.
2. Such being the situation, we think that the source of the information in
question was some anonymous notice obtained from the Mindan side. The
December 8 article in the Minshu Shimbun, organ of Mindan, mentioned that
Kim Yoo Ryong was forced to sell all of his furniture and effects, but he has
not sold them yet.[60]

South Korean protests, political squabbling, and alleged sabotage attempts had little impact on proceedings, and more than forty-nine thousand
people left for North Korea in 1960. Instead of migrating to North Korea
all at once, some families tried to spread the risk of relocating by sending
only one or two family members. For those uncertain of what awaited them,
dividing family was often a financial gambit based on an expectation widespread within Japan's Korean communities at the time, that the two Koreas
would soon reunify, and a hope that Zainichi Koreans would benefit from
the trade that they imagined would emerge once Japan and a unified Korea
had normalized diplomatic relations. In such cases, selected family stayed
in Japan and waited to hear about conditions before deciding whether to
follow.

Initially, reports coming out of North Korea were largely positive. DPRK
government sources boasted that Pyongyang was providing repatriates with
"jobs suitable for their wish and qualifications" and modern housing.[61] Ageing comrades were reportedly well looked after, provided with employment,
and, when required, accommodation in elderly care homes. The *Chōsen Nip-
pon,* a pro-DPRK newspaper printed in Tokyo, declared that all repatriates
had been awarded employment in fields such as construction, heavy and
light industries, agriculture, science, and education. Young repatriates, in
particular, were thriving, the report further explained; they were enjoying a
free education under the loving care of Kim Il-sung, while almost nine hundred returned comrades had been elected to local government positions.[62] If
these reports were an accurate barometer of life for Zainichi Koreans in the
DPRK, then it appeared the repatriation project—and Kim Il-sung's North
Korea—had lived up to the highest hopes of those in Tokyo and Geneva.

Each time a Soviet ferry returned to Japan, it carried on board Korean
Workers' Party members—members of the DPRK's political elite. Wary of
the security threat posed by North Korean officials, the Immigration Control Bureau of MOFA-Japan refused to issue special temporary visas that
would have allowed Korean Workers' Party cadres to disembark. Instead,
party members summoned Ch'ongryŏn officials from around the country to

Figure 1.3. Niigata, Japan. A Soviet ship embarking for the DPRK. Passengers wave to friends and family. The ICRC supervised the movement of Koreans from Japan to North Korea, beginning in December 1959. © Photothèque CICR (DR)/ (Photograph by Elsa Casal, confidentiality level: public). Date: sometime between 1959 and 1963.

meet with them onboard the vessel. On 18 December 1967, for example, the repatriation ship docked in Niigata and 3,140 visitors boarded the vessel before it returned to North Korea four days later. Among the visitors, which included 2,207 Korean high school students, high-ranking officials Kim Hei Shoku and Boku Zai Ro visited the ship for up to sixteen hours each day.[63] During these meetings, according to interviewees, Ch'ongryŏn officials relayed to party members developments in the Zainichi Korean community, including membership numbers and political attitudes at the regional and local levels. Party cadres in turn issued instructions that included demands for specific items to be sourced and shipped to North Korea, and directives for the recruitment of more repatriates. But even with such close coordination between Pyongyang and its Japanese political arm, it was clear as early as 1961 that not all Zainichi Koreans longed for the warm bosom of Kim's socialist paradise.

After just eighteen months the repatriations started to falter, troubled by a downturn in the number of people registering for return. From May 1961, the ferries between Japan and North Korea were suspended intermittently.[64]

As of the closing months of 1962, departures dropped from an average of three to four times a month to once a month. The average number of passengers making the trip also fell, from an average of a thousand to around four hundred on each trip.[65] Perhaps many of the people who had initially wanted to go to North Korea had already left. What is clear is that unofficial reports coming out of North Korea told a story that was very different from DPRK propaganda. In stark contrast to Pyongyang's glowing assessment, repatriates' letters home detailed dire living conditions, inedible food rations, and tensions with local North Koreans. Interviewees told me of secret messages, composed on the back of stamps or encoded into the text of letters home, warning family not to follow. Secret communications were one of the few ways for repatriates to safely communicate with family, since it was common knowledge that state censors examined letters bound for Japan. Some people used personal knowledge to communicate that conditions in North Korea were not suitable for family to follow. "I let my parents know I was well and that I would see them when my brother was ready to get married. But my brother was a still a child, so they understood that I was actually warning them not to follow me to North Korea," one interviewee told me. Cryptic messages were less likely to raise the suspicions of the cadres tasked with monitoring information leaving the country.

Reported difficulties in North Korea were at odds with what was happening in Japan at the time. Shifting gear from postwar recovery to high-level production and consumption, Japan's economic boom was evident in the living standards of Japanese and, to a lesser extent, Zainichi Koreans. The benefits of Japan's economic gains made it further challenging for Ch'ongryŏn to recruit people willing to try their luck in North Korea. The drying up of candidates for repatriation now raised troubling questions for Ch'ongryŏn. In particular, if North Korea was such a promising place, if it was indeed paradise on earth as DPRK propaganda claimed, why were fewer and fewer people opting to go? To halt the repatriations would be a tacit concession that Ch'ongryŏn had been wrong about North Korea. While there was initially plenty of support for the project from the Japanese government, the Communist Party, the Labor Party, and the JRC, to name a few, as time went on repatriates' warnings became common knowledge in Japan, and support for continued repatriations waned.

Further complicating matters, Tokyo now appeared increasingly concerned that its ongoing involvement in the project would hamper negotiations for the normalization of relations with South Korea. Suggesting that the falling number of Koreans requiring repatriation indicated there was no further need for a vessel moving between the two countries, the Japanese government requested Ch'ongryŏn terminate the ferry. Ch'ongryŏn vehemently opposed the request, claiming that Tokyo was again discriminating against Koreans.

Across Japan, Ch'ongryŏn launched petitions and mobilized its members in public displays of outrage. The organization claimed that even if fewer Koreans desired to repatriate, the ferry offered a means for divided families to visit one another.[66] Responding to Tokyo's threats to terminate the ferry link, Han Duk Su lobbied the ICRC for free travel between the two countries, something he described as a "lofty cause of humanity. . . . The Japanese Government is going to use the question of Korean residents in Japan as an unfair political bait in its dealings with the South Korean 'regime,' which cannot be regarded as representing any Korean people," Han seethed.[67]

The debate over free movement threatened to spill over into a diplomatic embarrassment for Tokyo. Pyongyang called for protecting what it claimed was a human right of Koreans to travel between the two countries, rallying international support to its cause. In 1963 the chairman of the Central Committee of the DPRK's Red Cross Society, Pak Shin Duk, wrote to Sir Adetokunbo Ademola, president of the Nigerian Red Cross Society. Pak requested that Ademola support free travel to and from the homeland, a principle he described as "a question of elementary human rights, a sacred right that no one should impinge upon."[68] The following year, in August 1964, Ro Zai Ho, president of Ch'ongryŏn's English language newspaper, *The People's Korea*, requested that the Palang Merah Indonesia (Indonesian Red Cross Society) pressure the Japanese government to permit free travel to the DPRK.[69] North Korean pleas were again couched in the language of humanitarianism for oppressed people, since doing so united support for keeping the ships moving across the Sea of Japan/East Sea.

Reflecting Tokyo's shifting stance on the repatriations, Pyongyang's calls for the protection of human rights and a guarantee of free travel were met with skepticism in Japan. The conservative newspaper *Yomiuri Shimbun*, for example, voiced concerns within the Ikeda administration that Pyongyang was motived by political and not humanitarian goals.[70] According to the article, Japanese government officials were nervous that free travel would permit North Korea to de facto normalize Japan-DPRK relations, thus driving a wedge between Japan and South Korea. If granted, the report predicted, free travel would allow North Korea to use Japan as a launching point for clandestine operations inside South Korea, and to obtain materials and technology needed to boost the DPRK's economy. In a final conciliatory act, Tokyo opened an investigation into the possibility of both visitations to gravesites in North Korea and visits to Japan of North Korean industrialists.[71] Not long after, however, the government upheld its decision to refuse free movement between the two countries, citing again the associated security risks posed to both national security and the much-anticipated normalization of Japan-ROK relations.

Tokyo's waning support for continuing repatriations positioned it well to progress talks with Seoul, and on 22 June 1965 Japanese foreign minister

Shiina Etsusaburo and ROK foreign minister Lee Dong Won signed the Treaty on Basic Relations. During the ceremony, Japanese prime minister Satō Eisaku looked on as agreements were penned that normalized diplomatic ties between the two countries, guaranteed future economic cooperation and economic assistance for the ROK, and confirmed the legal status of Koreans living in Japan ("Japan, South Korea Sign Normalization Treaty" 1965). Of particular significance for relations between Japan and the two Koreas at the time, Article 3 of the treaty confirmed the government of the ROK as the only lawful government in Korea, as per UN General Assembly Resolution 195. For Zainichi Koreans, the treaty and its related agreements also presented opportunities to apply for ROK citizenship while living permanently in Japan, albeit without the same political rights as Japanese. Zainichi Koreans who did not register as overseas South Korean citizens remained stateless in Japan.[72]

Once the settlement with Seoul was completed, the Satō administration moved to conclude all involvement with the repatriations. On 20 April 1967, following a meeting of vice ministers of the cabinet, Tokyo announced that it was ending support for the project. Citing a considerable decrease in the number of Koreans leaving, the government set the deadline for final applications for 12 August of that year ("Gov't to End Repat Pact" 1967). Anyone wishing to go to North Korea after this date would have to apply for an exit visa and travel as a tourist to North Korea using Soviet vessels.[73] North Korea responded swiftly, with Foreign Minister Nam Il declaring null and void the Japanese attempt to unilaterally abrogate the repatriation agreement. "This is also an open manifestation of its consistent hostile policy against the Democratic People's Republic of Korea," Nam Il declared.[74] The Japan Socialist Party, the Japan Communist Party, and the Japan-Korea Association each publicly added to the chorus of condemnation, but to no avail. Tokyo terminated its support of the repatriation project on 12 November 1967. On 29 February of the following year, the doors of the Niigata Red Cross Center were permanently shuttered, and the Red Cross ships confined to port. The following month, the ICRC withdrew its representative delegates from Japan. The project was frozen until May 1971.[75] From 1971 onwards, following an agreement between the JRC and DPRK Red Cross societies, the repatriations restarted using North Korean vessels, but with neither Japanese financial support nor ICRC involvement. A one-way movement of Zainichi Koreans and some Japanese continued, with occasional pause, until the early 1980s.

* * *

Years of negotiations between state and nonstate actors culminated in a mass movement that saw tens of thousands of Koreans, several thousand Japanese, and even a handful of Chinese leave for North Korea. The project was a bipartisan endeavor in Japan, and drew strong commitment from the Japanese Diet and the general public. The Japanese government and JRC, in collaboration with their North Korean counterparts, played pivotal roles in coordinating the repatriations, pressuring the ICRC into legitimizing the project, and disseminating propaganda that induced Zainichi Koreans to leave Japan for a country they had never before seen.

Returnees' vernacular memories of the repatriation years unsettle a nationalist discourse in which Japan is the victim and North Korea the victimizer. The nationalist narrative frames Japan's role in the repatriations as one of benevolence, a moment when the state offered a helping hand to its minority population and tried to move beyond its imperial past. The reappearance of people like Donghyŏn and Sazuka–their memories of poverty and racial exclusion–drags long-buried fragments of Japan's past into the light. The micro-histories of a seemingly powerless group of people have the power to antagonize fissures in the Japanese nationalist discourse, as returnees' intimate recollections of everyday life in postwar Japan provoke a questioning of the both the country's past and its racially based identity.

In the next chapter I delve deeper into the experiences of families who went to North Korea. Although seemingly pushed along by the weight of historical events, people like Donghyŏn and his family make choices at each step of their journey in terms of when to migrate, where to go, and with whom to build strategic alliances. Such decisions, embedded in family-centric narratives, are part of a refugee's strategy for survival.

Notes

1. The Young Pioneer Corps is a political youth organization for children ages six to fifteen.
2. Also known as the Treaty of Mutual Cooperation and Security between the United States and Japan.
3. B AG 232 105-025 "An Analysis and Appraisal of the Problems of Koreans in Japan and the Role of the International Committee of the Red Cross and Other Agencies in their Solution." Hallam C. Shorrock Jr. 15 July 1959, Seoul, Korea 15/07/59-15/07/59.
4. For more on how Cheju Islanders' victim-centric memories of the massacres interact with nationalist discourses see Wright (2015).
5. The Yasukuni Shrine, in Tokyo, serves as a further example of how official histories are presented in Japan. The shrine, said to house souls of the country's war dead, including some 1,000 convicted war criminals, has long been a diplomatic flash point for Japan and its neighbors, in particular China and the two Koreas.
6. For a thorough treatment of the victim consciousness that has emerged in Japan, see Orr (2001).

7. B AG 232 105-002 "Problème du rapatriement des Coréens du Japon, dossier I: Généralités." 27/02/1953–11/10/1957. Inoue, Masutarô. 1956. "The Repatriation Problem of Certain Koreans Residing in Japan." Japanese Red Cross Society, 1 October 1956, 9).

8. The status of Koreans in Japan has long been characterized by a friction between acquiring the rights of citizenship on the one hand and maintaining a distinct Korean identity on the other. Koreans who remained in Japan after 1945 would eventually be allowed to choose to either naturalize as Japanese, which meant assimilation and a loss of Korean identity (Tai 2004, 355), or remaining as Korean nationals, but without the benefits of citizenship. In the 1990s all Koreans who could prove their residential origins to the colonial period and their descendants residing in Japan were made special permanent residents. Although special permanent residency offered an improvement in status (Ryang 2009, 11), it was not a path to Japanese citizenship. According to the Ministry of Justice of Japan, a little under 500,000 Korean special permanent residents currently live in Japan.

9. Sazuka and her family members now living in Japan use the Japanese family name Tanaka.

10. B AG 232 105-025 "An Analysis and Appraisal of the Problems of Koreans in Japan and the Role of the International Committee of the Red Cross and Other Agencies in their Solution." Hallam C. Shorrock Jr. 15 July 1959, Seoul, Korea 15/07/59-15/07/59, p. 24

11. Changsoo Lee reasons that both the 1947 Alien Registration Law and the 1951 Immigration Control Law were "undoubtedly aimed at Koreans, since Koreans comprised almost 90 percent of all aliens in Japan" (Lee 1981c, 94–95).

12. B AG 232 105-002 "Problème du rapatriement des Coréens du Japon, dossier I: Généralités," 27/02/1953–11/10/1957. "Fundamental Conditions of Livelihood of Certain Koreans Residing in Japan." Written by Masutarô Inoue, JRC, November 1956.

13. B AG 232 105-002 "Problème du rapatriement des Coréens du Japon, dossier I: Généralités," 27/02/1953–11/10/1957. "Fundamental Conditions of Livelihood of Certain Koreans Residing in Japan." Written by Masutarô Inoue, JRC, November 1956.

14. Jung Jin Park suggests that the telegram, sent on 6 January 1954, was more than a promise for a like-for-like trade of displaced Japanese and Koreans. Park writes, "Behind the Japan Red Cross Society's 1954 offer to repatriate the Zainichi Koreans, in other words, was a subtly expressed intention to expel all Korean residents from Japan" (2016, 207).

15. In an addendum to the "Report on the Phyongyang Conference," dated 17 March 1956, Inoue explained to Leopold Boissier, president of the ICRC, that, after the conference and in the car to the airport, Inoue asked Mr. Shin, foreign liaison director of the DPRK Red Cross, his opinion of the conference. It appears that Shin offered a lukewarm response, to which Inoue recalls, "I sympathized with Shin and said to him: The solution of the question of Koreans in Japan should be carried out resolutely, as a last resort, by the exclusive hands of both Japanese and North Korean Red Crosses." Inoue continued, "Therefore, after my return to Tokyo, I will contrive all reasonable plans for the solution of the question of Koreans in Japan." Shin replied: "Please try every reasonable means for the

solution, after your return to Japan" (B AG 232 105 006-007, "Report of the Phyongyang Conference: held by Japanese and North Korean Red Cross Societies" (27 January–28 February 1956, postscript, 17 March 1956).

16. Specifically, the maritime border between Japan and the ROK was an issue. In January 1952 President Rhee announced the establishment of a Peace Line (or the Syngman Rhee Line, as it is still referred to by the Japanese government) around the Korean Peninsula and banned all non-Korean fishing vessels from crossing into the territory. Japanese fishing vessels that crossed over the boundary were seized and the fishers arrested. Masutarô Inoue said that because Japanese fishers were being indefinitely detained by the South Korean government, the Japanese government did not deem it appropriate to continue with plans for repatriation until the detention of Japanese fishers had been resolved. For more on the issue of Japanese fishers detained in Pusan and Koreans detained by the Japanese government in Ōmura detention center, see Morris-Suzuki (2007, 124–39).

17. B AG 232 105-002 "Problème du rapatriement des Coréens du Japon, dossier I: Généralités," 27/02/1953–11/10/1957. "Fundamental Conditions of Livelihood of Certain Koreans Residing in Japan." Written by Masutarô Inoue, JRC, November 1956, p. 37.

18. According to Morris-Suzuki, the relationship of the JRC to the Japanese government was as a "shadow foreign ministry." Specifically, the JRC's Foreign Affairs Department, Morris-Suzuki notes, had the reputation of being a "second Ministry of Foreign Affairs" (Morris-Suzuki 2007, 74).

19. B AG 232 105-002 "Problème du rapatriement des Coréens du Japon, dossier I: Généralités," 27/02/1953–11/10/1957. "Fundamental Conditions of Livelihood of Certain Koreans Residing in Japan." Written by Masutarô Inoue, JRC, November 1956, p. 25.

20. B AG 232 105-002 "Problème du rapatriement des Coréens du Japon, dossier I: Généralités," 27/02/1953–11/10/1957. "Fundamental Conditions of Livelihood of Certain Koreans Residing in Japan." Written by Masutarô Inoue, JRC, November 1956, pp. 35–36. Lee and De Vos highlight the case of Shiikuma Saburo, a Progressive party member of the House of Representatives from Hokkaido. In his speech in the House plenary meeting of 17 August 1946, Shiikuma blamed Koreans and Taiwanese for the postwar black-market operation and associated violence. He is quoted as declaring, "Gentlemen, these acts, committed by Koreans and Taiwanese, which we can hardly bear to watch, make us, who have gone through all ordeals of the defeat, feel as if our blood flows the wrong way" (Lee and De Vos 1981, 67).

21. As of 1954, some 96.6 percent of Koreans in Japan were from South Korea, and only 2.4 percent were from North Korea (Lee 1981c, 104).

22. For more on the relationship of Supreme Commander of the Allied Powers (SCAP) to Koreans in Japan, see Lee (1981a).

23. At that time, North Korea–affiliated Koreans exceeded those affiliated with South Korea by almost 2.5 times (B AG 232 105-002 "Problème du rapatriement des Coréens du Japon, dossier I: Généralités," 27/02/1953–11/10/1957. "Fundamental Conditions of Livelihood of Certain Koreans Residing in Japan." Written by Masutarô Inoue, JRC, November 1956).

24. B AG 232 105-002 "Probléme du rapatriement des Coréens du Japon, dossier I: Généralités," 27/02/1953–11/10/1957. "Fundamental Conditions of Livelihood of Certain Koreans Residing in Japan." Written by Masutarô Inoue, JRC, November 1956.
25. According to a report for the ICRC, 75 percent of Zainichi Koreans loyal to South Korea did not support the Rhee government. Having said this, such exact figures on these matters are highly contentious (B AG 232 105-025 "An Analysis and Appraisal of the Problems of Koreans in Japan and the Role of the International Committee of the Red Cross and Other Agencies in their Solution." Hallam C. Shorrock Jr. 15 July 1959, Seoul, Korea 15/07/59-15/07/59, p. 34).
26. Lee claims that the ultimate blame for South Korea's neglect of Zainichi Koreans should not be placed solely on the Rhee administration, since Mindan never gained the confidence of the majority of Koreans in Japan (Lee 1981c, 97).
27. This latter relationship was at times a tenuous one. For example, an ICRC report of the time stated, "Recently the President of Mindan, Mr. Kim Jae Hwa announced that he would no longer support the [ROK] Korean Mission to Japan, and spoke bitterly about the Rhee Government: 'Mindan has been asking for help for ten years, but in vain. Four or five years ago Mindan requested $2,000,000 to help Koreans [in Japan] achieve a better standard of living and establish anti-Communist schools. But we have received nothing.'" (B AG 232 105-025 "An Analysis and Appraisal of the Problems of Koreans in Japan and the Role of the International Committee of the Red Cross and Other Agencies in their Solution." Hallam C. Shorrock Jr. 15 July 1959, Seoul, Korea 15/07/59-15/07/59 p. 32).
28. B AG 232 105-025 "An Analysis and Appraisal of the Problems of Koreans in Japan and the Role of the International Committee of the Red Cross and Other Agencies in their Solution." Hallam C. Shorrock Jr. 15 July 1959, Seoul, Korea 15/07/59-15/07/59 pp. 32–33.
29. In a report collated by the Ministry of Justice of Japan on 26 April 1956, Roger Gallopin, executive director of the ICRC, explained that the South Korean government was concerned about the growing contact between North Korea and Japan. In an effort to block the repatriation project, the Rhee government made it a precondition for the normalization of Japan–South Korea diplomatic relations that Japan should have no relations with North Korea (B AG 232 105-019.01 18/03/1960–31/12/1960. "A Short Account on the Korean Question").
30. B AG 232 105-025 "An Analysis and Appraisal of the Problems of Koreans in Japan and the Role of the International Committee of the Red Cross and Other Agencies in their Solution." Hallam C. Shorrock Jr. 15 July 1959, Seoul, Korea 15/07/59-15/07/59.
31. B AG 232 105-008.02 "Résolution de la Croix-Rouge Japonaise du 20 Janvier 1959 et dépliant intitulé: 'Korean repatriation question,' publié par la Croix-Rouge Japonaise," 20/01/1959–03/03/1959, 14 February 1959.
32. B AG 232 105-008.02. "Résolution de la Croix-Rouge Japonaise du 20 Janvier 1959 et dépliant intitulé: 'Korean repatriation question,' publié par la Croix-Rouge Japonaise" 20/01/1959–03/03/1959, Republic of Korea Ministry of Foreign Affairs, 1 March 1959.
33. According to a 15 February 1959 *New York Times* article, a spokesperson for the Rhee government asserted that the Japanese government was "collaborating

with a Communist slave labor scheme," and questioned if Japan was truly pursuing humanitarian motives.

34. B AG 232 105-007.02 "Demandes écrites de particuliers ou d'associations de Coréens, réactions aux pourparlers entre le Japon et la République démocratique populaire de Corée concernant le rapatriament des Coréens vers la Corée-du-Nord," 29/01/1959-25/06/1959.

35. In September 1955, Kim Il-sung announced, "The DPRK will try to arrange repatriation if the Koreans in Japan wish to return." But Kim's statement was tempered by his suggestion that Zainichi Koreans should work to establish themselves in Japan and contribute to the unification of Korea by fostering a closer relationship between Japan and the DPRK (Lee 1981c, 98–99).

36. B AG 232 105-006.03 "Copies pour information transmises par la Croix-Rouge Japonaise 07/01/1958-01/11/1958." "Request on Collective Repatriation of Koreans from Japan," 8 October 1958.

37. B AG 232 105-006.03 "Copies pour information transmises par la Croix-Rouge Japonaise" 07/01/1958-01/11/1958, "Livelihood and Education after Repatriation Guaranteed, Only the Attitude of Japanese Government Left unsettled," The General League of Koreans, 1 November 1958, p. 2.

38. "Answers of Vice-Premier Kim Il to the questions put by the correspondent of the Korean Central News Agency in connection with earliest realization of the urgent desire of the Korean nationals to return home from Japan" (DPRK 1959, 13–16).

39. Nam Keun Woo (2012) argues that North Korea pursued economic motives and that the political gains to be made by the repatriation project were peripheral. Nam suggests that North Korea viewed an influx of labor power as desirous for the country's seven-year economic plan (1961–70). While the potential benefits of returnees as a labor force were surely considered by the North Korean government, to reduce the motivations of North Korea to economics is to overlook North Korean efforts to play a leading role in the region and devalues the significance of the repatriation project as a broader propaganda win for the communist bloc. Furthermore, there was no way that Ch'ongryŏn could guarantee it would obtain the required number of able-bodied workers. The ICRC warned Ch'ongryŏn against rejecting applicants on the basis of age and health (with the exception of contagious disease, in which case applicants had to wait until they were medically cleared to travel). Consequently, North Korea was compelled to accept children, the elderly, and others who may have been more likely to be a drain on state resources, rather than a benefit.

40. B AG 232 105-025 "An Analysis and Appraisal of the Problems of Koreans in Japan and the Role of the International Committee of the Red Cross and Other Agencies in their Solution." Hallam C. Shorrock Jr. 15 July 1959, Seoul, Korea 15/07/59-15/07/59. I have paraphrased the original language.

41. An article in the 24 October 1958 edition of the *Asahi Evening News* explained, "A vigorous nationwide movement to expedite repatriation of Korean residents wishing to return to North Korea was launched this week. The League of Korean Residents in Japan, an organization representing those wanting to return to North Korea, announced that nationwide rallies will be held on Thursday next week."

42. According to returnees who recalled the events leading up to the repatriation.
43. One interviewee told me that, as a result of the repatriation of Korean criminals, Japanese Yakuza gangs established a foothold in North Korea. Yakuza members could be identified by their elaborate tattoos that differed from North Korean ideological designs.
44. Interview with François Bugnion, the ICRC Director for International Law and Co-operation (interviewed by author. Geneva, 5 August 2014).
45. In 1971 North Korea's Man'gyŏngbong ferry established a regular link between the two countries. The Man'gyŏngbong operated until 1992, when the Ch'ongryŏn funded Man'gyŏngbong 92, built for Kim Il-sung's eightieth birthday, replaced it.
46. Interview with François Bugnion (interviewed by author. Geneva, 5 August 2014).
47. The same sort of screening or confirmation of free will process was conducted in UN prisoner-of-war camps during the Korean War, provoking massive opposition from North Korea, China, and the Soviet Union. This was the major factor in delaying the end of the war and is likely to have been in the minds of the ICRC staff who devised the repatriation screening.
48. B AG 232 105-028.02 "Rapports sur les convois" 17/01/1961–28/12/1964, 20 July 1961.
49. Prior to moving to the JRC Center in Niigata, all prospective repatriates were required to register their interest at an ICRC registration window. Such windows were set up throughout Japan.
50. The maximum a person could take with them was ¥45,000. Any amount exceeding this had to be left in Japan, in a Japanese bank account in the owner's name. Furthermore, repatriates were not permitted to take with them government bonds, share-certificates, deposit notes, or insurance certificates (JRC 1959, 4).
51. Morris-Suzuki writes that the booklet provoked months of heated debate between Ch'ongryŏn and the North Korean delegation, the Japanese government, and the ICRC. North Korea was strongly opposed to the screening of prospective repatriates and pressured the ICRC to abandon the guidebook. The JRC responded to Ch'ongryŏn pressure by altering the doors of the Special Rooms (in some cases removing them entirely) and changing the guidebook with a number of supplementary explanations (Morris-Suzuki 2007, 211–13).
52. B AG 232 105-028.02 "Rapports sur les convois" 17/01/1961–28/12/1964. "Report regarding the 67th ships," 19 July 1961.
53. B AG 232 105-028.02 "Rapports sur les convois" 17/01/1961–28/12/1964. Ship No 52, Op. No.17, Room 2," 14 January 1962.
54. B AG 232 105-015.01 "Extraits des procès-verbaux des séances du Comité, plénières, de la Présidence," 03/09/1959–28/12/1959, Annex 3.
55. The doors of the Special Rooms had been removed from their hinges and replaced with fabric that allowed for those outside to hear what was being said inside (Morris-Suzuki 2007, 211–13).
56. The Calcutta Accord formally agreed to the repatriation of Koreans from Japan to the DPRK. Representatives from the DPRK's Red Cross Society and the JRC signed the accord on 13 August 1959.

57. One such occasion is particularly representative of the atmosphere at the docks in the early years of the repatriations: On 7 April 1962, 227 people left Niigata on board the Soviet liner, *Norilsk*. The passengers, many of them teenagers, were cheered off by a crowd continuously shouting *"Bansai"* and *"Mansei,"* followed by a triple salvo of handclapping (B AG 232 105-028.02. "Rapports sur les convois" 17/01/1961–28/12/1964. "Report on Repatriation Ship No. 91. Norilsk," 9 April 1962).

58. B AG 232 105-019.01 "Monthly reports on the repatriation to North Korea by the Immigration Bureau," Ministry of Justice of Japan.

59. B AG 232 105-019.01 "Monthly reports on the repatriation to North Korea by the Immigration Bureau," Ministry of Justice of Japan.

60. B AG 232 105-019.01 "Monthly reports on the repatriation to North Korea by the Immigration Bureau," Ministry of Justice of Japan.

61. B AG 232 105-033 "Probléme du rapatriement des Coréens du Japon," dossier XXI 14/11/1962-31/12/1967, "The Unification of Fatherland," 14 November 1962.

62. B AG 232 105-033 "Probléme du rapatriement des Coréens du Japon," dossier XXI 14/11/1962-31/12/1967, "Happy Life of Repatriates seen in figures," 19 May 1964.

63. B AG 232 105-033 "Probléme du rapatriement des Coréens du Japon," dossier XXI 14/11/1962-31/12/1967, "Monthly report on repatriation," 31 December 1967 p.5.

64. A report by the Immigration Control Bureau of the Ministry of Justice of Japan posits that numbers decreased due to the reluctance of prospective repatriates to go to North Korea during winter (B AG 232 105-019.01). It is also significant that, according to my interviewees, reports were coming out of North Korea that conditions were much harder than expected, including difficulties finding resources for heating homes and difficulties locating food and other basic resources. Furthermore, at this time the Japanese economy was noticeably improving. These factors likely deterred some individuals from emigrating to North Korea.

65. B AG 232 105-032.02 "Rapports sur les convois" 23/01/1965-23/12/1967, "Statistique des Coréens du Japon rapatriés," p. 1.

66. B AG 232 105-028.04 "Probléme du libre passage entre la Corée-du-Nord et le Japon" 05/06/1963-28/12/1964. "The People's Korea, 'Free-Travel Movement' Winning Support from Abroad," 21 August 1963.

67. B AG 232 105-028.04 "Probléme du libre passage entre la Corée-du-Nord et le Japon" 05/06/1963-28/12/1964. "Central Standing Committee of General Association of Korean Residents in Japan," 20 June 1963.

68. B AG 232 105-028.04 "Probléme du libre passage entre la Corée-du-Nord et le Japon" 05/06/1963-28/12/1964 (file no. 2798).

69. B AG 232 105-028.04 "Probléme du libre passage entre la Corée-du-Nord et le Japon" 05/06/1963-28/12/1964 (file no. 2535).

70. B AG 232 105-028.04 "Probléme du libre passage entre la Corée-du-Nord et le Japon" 05/06/1963-28/12/1964, *Yomiuri Shimbun*, Kaji Onose, "Free Travel Between Japan, North Korea is Political Aim," 14 June 1964.

71. B AG 232 105-028.04 "Probléme du libre passage entre la Corée-du-Nord et le Japon" 05/06/1963-28/12/1964, The Mainichi, "Special Consideration to be

Studied on Visit to and from North Korea," Ministry of Justice, 17 December 1964.

72. For more on the status of Zainichi Koreans in Japan, see Tai (2004) and Chapman (2008).

73. B AG 232 105-033 "Probléme du rapatriement des Coréens du Japon," dossier XXI 14/11/1962-31/12/1967. The Mainichi Daily News, "N. Korean Repatriation Accord to be Suspended," 21 April 1967.

74. B AG 232 105-033 "Probléme du rapatriement des Coréens du Japon," dossier XXI 14/11/1962-31/12/1967. The Japan Times, "N. Korea Demands Japan Retain Repatriation Pact," 24 April 1967.

75. An agreement made between the Japan Red Cross and the DPRK Red Cross during the Colombo Talks (27 November 1967–24 January 1968) stated that Koreans who had registered for repatriation but who had missed the November deadline would be permitted to return on board vessels provided by North Korea and using Exit Certificates provided by the Japanese government. Anyone leaving Japan for North Korea after 1 August 1968 would leave "as any other foreigner leaves Japan" (B AG 232 105-036 "Prolongation du rapatriement des Coréens du Japon en Corée du Nord. Proposition d'une nouvelle solution pour le rapatriement" 05/01/1968-19/03/1970).

2

Marriage and Mobility

It was a shotgun wedding, and everyone was invited.

For months, the bride and groom had kept their liaisons a secret, meeting outside of Tsuruhashi and the Koreatown bubble, away from prying eyes and gossiping grandmothers. But with an unexpected pregnancy, there was no hiding it. Despite such inauspicious circumstances, the timing, agreed the wedding guests, could have been worse. Both bride and groom had been in Japan for several years, both had family around them, and both were well known throughout the nascent returnee networks. As such, the celebrations were a who's who of people involved with the resettlement of returnees from North Korea. Representatives from civic groups, a teacher from the Japanese language school frequented by returnees to Osaka, journalists, and an assortment of familiar faces from the returnee community huddled together for the group photo. The guests, some of whom had contributed to the relocation of the bride and the groom to Japan, reinterpreted a potential scandal as an event symbolizing the success of their work assisting escapees from North Korea.

This chapter explores how people on the margins of society—in this case, returnee families from North Korea—strategically use marriage as a means for building alliances. The marriage of Ko Hyewŏn and Yi Minch'ŏl was a climactic point in the migratory histories of two families that span almost a hundred years. Each generation of both families was born in a different political state: colonial Korea (Chosŏn), Japan, and North Korea. In each place, the Ko and the Yi families had married endogenously—within the loosely organized boundaries of their migrant group, like so many others in their community. They practiced intramarriage as both a protective response to fluctuating and sometimes life-threatening sociopolitical conditions, and as a positive response to perceived similarities in their families' histories. Unbeknownst to the families who migrated between Japan and the two Koreas, intramarriage as a survival strategy also inadvertently increased the social distance between themselves and their host society, both in North Korea and in Japan. It helped to ensure that, for each generation, migration has been the defining feature of their family identity, narrative, and culture.

In North Korea the low sociopolitical status assigned to repatriates from Japan directly influenced the marriage strategies of repatriate families. Associations with both the former colonizer and South Korea politically tainted repatriated Koreans in the eyes of North Koreans. Consequently, North Koreans avoided marrying repatriates for fear of damaging their own sociopolitical status. One interviewee explained, "Native North Koreans never wanted to marry repatriates or their children. They knew it would be detrimental to their prospects for joining the Party and earning a decent living."

There were, of course, rule breakers, those who chose to marry for love or who used marriage as a way of trying to move up the social ladder. In a situation where a repatriate family had economic means but low sociopolitical status, creating an alliance with a North Korean family of comparatively high sociopolitical standing was a means for improving their life chances. Even if the North Korean family was economically struggling, it was hoped that a marriage alliance would improve the sociopolitical standing of the repatriate family's progeny. For North Koreans, marrying with an economically affluent family from Japan was a risk requiring careful consideration. If the repatriate family had a reliable access to goods and capital from Japan, the material benefits of such an alliance might be useful in weathering food shortages and paying off aggressive cadres. But such marital strategies also had a downside. One interviewee, for instance, told me that his brother had married a local North Korean woman. When his family decided to leave for China, his wife's family, well established in North Korea, would not permit her to leave. Consequently, his brother remains in North Korea with his wife and children. Although North Korea's sociopolitical system constrained repatriates' aspirations, families with some economic capital could negotiate their marginalized status with various measures of success.

What can we learn from family narratives shaped by displacement? What can intimate stories of marriage and movement reveal about migration as a general process? Anthropologist Kirin Narayan's ethnography of her life growing up in India likens family narratives to a collection of beads, in that they are both portable and replete with histories, places, and people (Narayan 2007, 4). The metaphorical story beads are polished as the teller crafts the narrative more finely each time. Similarly, George Gmelch noticed that, through the repeated telling of their stories, the Barbadian migrants with whom he worked had crystallized memories of their migrations as a life event with a clear beginning, middle, and end (Gmelch 1992, 283). Returnees who had written about their experiences escaping North Korea or who had given public talks of their struggles resettling in Japan presented personal histories carefully organized in such a linear fashion. In these cases, clearly defined themes of political persecution, hunger, loss of family, border crossing, and salvation emerged from within well-crafted narratives. In contrast, men and women recently arrived in Japan, or those who had not previously discussed their migrations, carried with them roughly cut fragments of memory that oscillated unpredictably between points in time. "Every memory falters, skips, adorns," writes Dina Nayeri of her own experiences working with refugees. "Every story takes on mythic or hagiographic qualities because the mind is thirsty for meaning" (Nayeri 2019, 183). Whether rounded and smooth, or jagged around the edges, my conversations with returnees were not a search for precision, nor for truth. Rather, interviews and informal conversations were opportunities for moments of reflection, during which we each contributed to creating a version of the past from which the returnee might draw meaning.

The process of constructing self-narratives is a communal project. People require the help of others to gather together memories and create a sensation of belonging in space and time. But in the turmoil of forced migration, the people required for such self-referencing and community building—family and friends—are often scattered far and wide. Evidence of generations of crisis-propelled movement emerges, especially from the narratives of refugees from North Korea. For people unable to return to their country, the creative process of remembering the past is central to reassembling a long-distance, transnational community, and to rethreading the beads of self-narrative. Revising Narayan's metaphor, memories form beads on a string that comprise a person's identity. Each new bead represents a new experience and memory. When a person migrates, leaving behind family, friends, and a childhood home, the string of beads is vigorously shaken and threatens to come undone, spilling the beads. In this vein, forced migration and displacement scatters the beads and fragments a person's sense of self.

The biographies of the Ko and the Yi families are representative of a growing body of anthropological research that uses oral histories and everyday narratives of mobility that may otherwise be obscured in macro analyses (Brettell 2003, 23–46; Freeman 2001; Gmelch 1992; Guarnizo 1997). Gmelch, for instance, uses the oral histories of Barbadians who migrated to the United Kingdom to explore issues of racial identity, social mobility, and economic change in postwar Britain and Barbados. Such oral testimonies offer subjective examples in which the migrants are agents of cultural and economic change in both the sending and receiving countries (Gmelch 1992, 3–8).

Reflecting the complexities of mobility, migrants' intimate narratives change according to class, gender, and generational differences. Individual recollections, whether smooth and linear in form or unpolished and serpentine, provide insights into, for example, complex religious and political dynamics emerging between family who emigrate and those who stay (Glick

Schiller and Fouron 2001; Levitt 2001), into the strategies that migrants use to contest restrictive immigration and labor policies (Freeman 2011), the ethnic and class-based tensions that emerge between new arrivals and the host society (Tsuda 2003), the economic pressures contributing to the decision to emigrate, and the hazards of irregular migration (Lucht 2012), and the role of return migration for facilitating upward mobility back home (Brettell 2003, chap. 3).

Family narratives are rarely regarded as carrying the same import as official histories, but they provide insights on economic, political, and geopolitical changes far beyond the intimate sphere of kin groups. A story of family migration, for example, is embedded within broader dynamics compelling people to move in particular directions at particular times. Where the previous chapter drew on official records documenting the repatriation project, this chapter shifts focus, bringing to the fore returnees' memories of displacement, transnational movement, and alliance building.

The narratives that follow are selected from two families now resident in Osaka, Japan. Both families have completed multiple migrations between the Korean Peninsula and Japan over a century. With multiple generations resorting to emigration and intramarriage as a means to negotiate periods of economic and political insecurity, a particular culture of mobility, an "ethos of migration" (Chamberlain [1997] 2017, 51) has emerged within the families in this chapter. Historian Mary Chamberlain, a pioneer of using oral histories to understand migration, suggests that such a dynamic gives a family meaning and determines communal behavior that in turn lays the groundwork for further migration. Returnees' strategies of alliance building and their memories of moving between Japan and the two Koreas have become embedded in family narratives that are transferred and transformed intergenerationally. The oral histories of multigenerational migrations are a window to understanding the factors perpetuating movement, why so many people were channeled in particular directions at particular times, and how marriage becomes a strategy for survival.

The Mobile Family

Movement-centric family narratives highlight the role of migration as a normal and legitimate response to crisis.[1] The Yi family's migration narrative develops through the story of Yi Minch'ŏl, a returnee from North Korea in his late twenties. Funai Kaori is at the center of the Ko family's story. Kaori is ethnically Japanese; she married a Zainichi Korean man in the early 1960s and together they migrated to North Korea.

I met Minch'ŏl and his wife, Hyewŏn, four years after their sudden wedding. The young couple that had hurried down the aisle were by then parents to a four-year-old boy. At a little over five foot three inches, Minch'ŏl's modest stature belied his infectious energy, and the positivity that had paid off since his arrival in Japan in 2003. Not long after touching down in Osaka, Minch'ŏl found work moving stock on the shop floor of a Tsuruhashi kimchi factory, a position that had been occupied by a succession of returnees over the years. Later, with the help of Japanese language teacher Akiyama Ayako, he was hired in an Osaka-based trading company. Minch'ŏl had worked hard on his language skills. He was multilingual, speaking Mandarin (he had learned it during his time working undocumented in Northeast China), Korean, Japanese, and some English. Although hired to record basic stock movements—in and out of the company warehouse—his hard work and gregarious manner caught the eye of his boss, a Zainichi Korean. He soon found himself being dispatched to meetings in South Korea and China as the company expanded.

Over several meetings with Minch'ŏl and his extended family, an in-depth family history emerged with displacement and mobility as defining characteristics. The migration genealogies of the Yi and Ko families intertwine with significant geopolitical and ideological transitions occurring across East Asia over the past hundred years. In each time period political instability compelled the Yi and the Ko families, like thousands of others, to respond to structural pressures by emigrating. Their stories contrast with those who decided it was better to stay put, or those who often had a vested economic and social interest in not moving. Those compelled to migrate did so in response to a combination of negative push factors and positive pull factors—including, for instance, the likelihood of continued unemployment in Japan on the one hand and the promise of employment in North Korea on the other. In some cases, families chose to divide their members: perhaps an eldest son stayed at home to manage the family business while the younger siblings took their chances through emigration. The mobility of the two families in this chapter offers a glimpse into the broader mass movements taking place between the Korean Peninsula and Japan in the twentieth century.

The Yi Family

Minch'ŏl's family had never struggled with money in North Korea. His father, Pak Byŏngho, had worked as a doctor, and his mother, Yi Soyi, had been an instructor in a teaching college. Although their salaries were modest by Western standards, his family enjoyed the benefit of informal cash payments from patients and students. He even had an uncle in the Korean Workers' Party. These achievements were even more impressive when considering the unfavorable beginnings of his family's migrations some seventy years earlier. In early March 1948, Yi Mansik, Minch'ŏl's maternal great-grandfather; Sukcha, Minch'ŏl's great-grandmother; and their sons, Mansŏk and Mansu, slammed shut the door on a Cheju Island home they would never see again. The four of them bundled the family's belongings into a rickety wooden cart and hurried down the dirt road to a pier, where they negotiated a price they could afford and boarded a small fishing boat bound for Japan. Even as their island home disappeared over the horizon, Mansik, a proud man, vowed that his children would remember their Cheju heritage. Among the few possessions they carried that day was their *ch'ŏkbo* (ancestral book), a tome Mansik's father had made him memorize as a child. Over too many evenings to count, the family patriarch had reached for the ancestral book, thumbing through the worn pages for a family favorite and bringing to life the exploits of their more illustrious forebears.

The timing of their abrupt departure was fortunate. Mansik and his family were part of a mass migration of some forty thousand refugees escaping the escalating violence on Cheju Island (Cumings 2010, 121). Demonstrations against the formation of a South Korean interim government on the March anniversary of the Korean independence movement had turned into armed clashes between locals and the American-supported Korean constabulary. A week later the demonstrators confronted police, demanding the release of prisoners. During the fighting that ensued, police panicked and fired on the crowd, killing five protestors (Merrill 1980, 154). Alarmed at events on Cheju and fearful of a communist takeover, the mainland government fortified security forces with an additional four hundred police and extreme right-wing Northwest Youth Group members. With the arrival of the paramilitary force the violence further intensified. On 3 April 1948 attacks on police stations signaled the beginning of the Cheju Uprising along the island's north coast. In the months that followed, the violence spread across the island, with battles between locals opposed to dividing Korea into two and the mainland constabulary escalating. In an effort to contain guerrilla activities, the US Navy blockaded Cheju and the South Korean government declared the entire interior of the island an enemy zone. In the fighting that followed, "more than half of all villages were burned and destroyed, and civilians thought to be aiding the insurgents were massacred" (Cumings 2010, 128).[2]

Unaware of how fortunate they had been, wrapped up against the cold of the night sky, Mansik and Sukcha followed a stream of flimsy-looking vessels bobbing up and down on the Sea of Japan/East Sea. The journey east, toward Japan, took several days. Upon arrival, Mansik and Sukcha found a place to sleep for the night on the shoreline, along with throngs of other refugees fleeing Cheju.

Life in Japan for the Yi family was never going to be easy. Japan was still recovering from the damage inflicted by American bombing, and a fully functioning economy had yet to emerge. The Yi family found themselves a house sardined into the already overcrowded areas of Tsuruhashi, Osaka. Mansik found work alongside other Cheju Koreans, distilling and selling bootleg alcohol on the black market. But the political tensions of the homeland followed the Yi family to Osaka. Mansik admired the DPRK's new leader, Kim Il-sung, but after hearing what had happened to supporters of North Korea on Cheju, he was cautious about getting involved in politics. The reality was that he was too busy eking out a living to join other Koreans protesting the escalating conflict in the homeland. Although Mansik had decided to steer clear of the political spillover from a newly independent Korea, his wife, Sukcha, had made it her reason to exist.

At Sukcha's behest their sons, Mansŏk and Mansu, joined Ch'ongryŏn, the North Korea–affiliated organization that had been so active in building schools for Korean children. In collaboration with the sons of several other Cheju Island families, the two young men made a living running gambling (pachinko) parlors.³ Mansik and Sukcha used a matchmaker to introduce their eldest son, Mansŏk, to Sŏngcha, a woman whose family was also from Cheju. Mansŏk and Sŏngcha married and the new bride moved into the family's one-bedroom home.

One day in late 1959 Sukcha returned home from a Ch'ongryŏn meeting and excitedly announced that they were to be among the first patriots returning to the homeland. Mansik struggled to hide his disapproval. He had watched the Ch'ongryŏn cars crawling through his neighborhood, banners flying in support of Kim Il-sung and loudspeakers promising all manner of things in North Korea. But he had his doubts that the country could have recovered so quickly since the Korean War. If Mansik did have concerns, they were quickly dismissed. Sukcha had long been the driving force of the family, expanding the Yi's social networks throughout the Osaka Korean community. Mansik could do little but reluctantly acquiesce to her relocation plans. That evening he announced the family's impending move to his children. The couple's eldest son, Mansŏk, would join his parents. Mansŏk knew how to explain the move to his wife, telling her, "In North Korea, our children can have a real education. You can have a home to be proud of, and I can have a decent job." Mansŏk's wife, Sŏngcha, realized she had little say in the matter and agreed that they would go with the family. If things were not as promised, they could always return, she reasoned. Mansik's youngest son, Mansu, balked at the idea of emigrating to North Korea. Business was starting to pick up at the pachinko parlor. More important, he told himself, he was in love. He kept his romance a secret, though, as he knew his mother would never approve of his Japanese girlfriend. After much negotiation with his father and older brother he promised to join his family within two years. In the meantime, he would take care of the business and settle the Yi family accounts.

Mansik, Sukcha, their son Mansŏk, daughter-in-law Sŏngcha, and grand-daughter Soyi boarded a seven-carriage train on a blustery spring evening in 1960. Throughout the night, as the train sped toward Niigata, children curled up at the feet of mothers and fathers. Others, too excited to sleep, sipped tea and kept watch for the morning light. At each station along the way, Ch'ongryŏn-organized crowds waved DPRK flags and regaled waiting passengers with political songs. Teenaged Korean girls poured fresh pots of tea at carriage windows and Japanese police–some in uniform, others in plain clothes–stood guard against Mindan protests.[4] A low hum of excitement permeated the carriages each time the train edged out of a station and ever closer to the docks from where the Yi family would leave Japan.

Upon arriving at the Niigata Red Cross Center, the Yis rested in their temporary room, shared with several other families, and waited for their turn with the Red Cross interviewers. "Are you all traveling to North Korea out of your own volition? Is there any reason why you shouldn't be going to North Korea? Have any of you committed any crimes while in Japan?" The Japanese interpreter lobbed question after question to the Yis. On behalf of the family, Mansik confirmed their independent desire to leave for the DPRK. After a cold night in the waiting room, the Yi family boarded the Soviet transport ship, and cast off for North Korea.

In meetings across Japan, Ch'ongryŏn had described North Korea as heaven on earth to wide-eyed Zainichi Koreans, so it was difficult for Mansik and his family to hide their shock when the ship docked in Ch'ŏngjin and they were greeted by what Sukcha later described as "dirty, skinny-looking creatures." They were further taken aback with the apartment that party cadres ushered them into several days later. "It appeared complete from the outside, but inside there was no plumbing. Every day we had to go to the nearby stream to fetch water. When the stream froze, we carried home chunks of ice and waited for them to melt. And heating? Oh no. There was no heating. It was like going back to the Stone Age. You got heating if you could make a fire. And you only got fire if you had something to burn," Mansŏk remembered. This was the beginning of a dark time for the Yi family. Only six months after arriving in North Korea, Yi Mansik, the patriarch of the family, died in his sleep. "It was the old who suffered the most," Mansik's granddaughter, Soyi, would recall half a century later. "It was too cold for the elderly and they had no reason to live and nothing to do." Shortly after her husband's death, on a freezing winter's morning, Sukcha also passed away.

The passing of Mansik and Sukcha happened in quick succession and had a profound effect on the family. Without realizing it, however, Mansik and Sukcha's remaining family members were in an advantageous situation, compared to other repatriates. While they had lived in Japan, their generous financial contributions to Ch'ongryŏn and Sukcha's tireless campaigning on

Figure 2.1. Niigata, Japan. Family and friends wave goodbye to repatriates as they set sail for North Korea. Many would never see their loved ones again. © Photothèque CICR (DR)/ (Photographer: S.N., confidentiality level: public). Taken some time between 1959 and 1963.

behalf of the organization had not gone unnoticed by the upper echelon of Ch'ongryŏn's leadership. Their growing wealth further helped catch the eye of North Korea's elites. Mansu, the son they had left behind in Japan, continued to grow the family pachinko business. From his accumulating wealth, Mansu sent a steady stream of packages filled with clothes, food, medicine, and other goods to his brother in North Korea. Mansŏk and Sŏngcha used these items to bribe low-level cadres and to encourage favorable treatment from their daughter's schoolteachers. The couple's conscientious nurturing of political networks prompted local officials to select their family for special treatment. Following the death of his parents, the state allocated Mansŏk and Sŏngcha a new apartment in the center of Sinŭiju, a trading town on the Sino-Korean border. The apartment had running water and sporadic electricity. More importantly for the Yi family, living near the border presented opportunities for illicit trade with Koreans in China. Using Mansu's remittances and items imported from Japan, Mansŏk and Sŏngcha could trade for things that were beyond the reach of ordinary North Koreans. All the while, the Yis were careful to maintain salubrious relations with party members, distributing generous gifts to border guards and provincial government officials, and hosting lavish parties fueled by imported Japanese alcohol.

Throughout the 1980s Mansŏk managed a machine factory and Sŏngcha raised three sons in addition to her daughter, Soyi. Soyi finished high school at seventeen, and subsequently started college. Encouraged by her mother, she trained as a teacher. Shortly after Soyi's graduation, Sŏngcha decided it was time for her to marry. Sŏngcha's friend, also a repatriate from Japan, put her in contact with a matchmaker specializing in matching repatriates who could trace their origins to Cheju Island. After only two meetings–one with parents and one without–the match was made between the Yis and the Paks. At twenty years old, Soyi married Pak Byŏngho. Byŏngho, born in Nagasaki, had also moved to North Korea with his family as a young child. Unlike most other families they knew, the Yis did not have to borrow money for the wedding, since Mansu sent enough Japanese yen to pay for the entire ceremony. The wedding celebrations continued for two days. Sŏngcha and Mansŏk invited all the local cadres and fed them well. The mountain of shoes piled high at the front door of their apartment was a talking point of the town for months afterwards.

Byŏngho's family had also stridently supported Ch'ongryŏn while in Japan and the marriage was a union of two families with comparatively similar levels of political capital and material wealth. Byŏngho proudly told whoever was willing to listen that he traced his lineage to Cheju communists. Consequently, the state also gave his family favorable treatment in terms of employment and education opportunities that were unavailable to most repatriates. At twenty-three years old, Byŏngho had graduated from university and was working as a doctor in the Sinŭiju People's Hospital. The couple supplemented their income with black market trading, fostering good relations with both border guards and the merchants who plied their trade between Dandong and Sinŭiju. For the Yi family, it seemed that Ch'ongryŏn's promises had borne fruit.

Soyi's career continued to flourish. She found work teaching in a local college. As a government official she had a stable, albeit modest, salary and she regularly received monetary gifts from students' parents. Local officials also permitted Soyi to visit her brothers in Pyongyang. She explained, "I had family in the Korean Workers' Party. Only about 1,000 people who'd come from Japan were able to live well and rise within the ranks of the Party. This was because, like our family, they'd shown unwavering support for the Party while they were in Japan." But all was not well behind the family's glowing façade. Soyi and Byŏngho's marriage had started to unravel. "My parent's relationship was actually really bad at that time," Soyi's daughter recalled during an interview in Osaka. "They were always fighting, but the government wouldn't let them divorce so they just continued on."

The Yis' fortunes were about to take a further turn for the worse. In early 1994, just months before the July death of North Korean leader Kim Il-sung, Sŏngcha died. In the years that followed the loss of the matriarch of the family, the Yi family's trade connections in China rendered them better off than most. But their insulation also attracted attention from native North Koreans, including state cadres who were themselves struggling to make ends meet in increasingly difficult conditions. The Yi family's privileged status came to an abrupt end in 1999, when security officers arrested Soyi's father, Mansŏk, for illegal trading. Soon after, Soyi's husband Byŏngho died. Soyi had noticed Byŏngho's weight loss but had not realized the seriousness of his condition until he collapsed one evening. Perhaps it was his drinking. Perhaps his feelings of powerlessness, treating patients using ancient equipment and next to no medicine, exhausted him to a point of no return. Whatever the reason, the double blow of Mansŏk's detention and Byŏngho's death sent shockwaves through the Yi family. Soyi remembered,

> My father was arrested. State security interrogated him, and we knew that our own punishment would be forthcoming. Then I suddenly lost my job. Sure enough, not long after, local officials ordered me to join a special work party. We had a terrible task—disposing of the corpses of people who'd died during the famine. My husband was dead, I had no job and no way to support my family, my father was missing, and my children would never be able to wash off the dirt from his arrest. My father never returned home from the interrogation center. They took everything from me.

The anxiety she felt while living as an enemy of the state compelled Soyi to leave North Korea with her son, Minch'ŏl, in 2002. Soyi's daughter followed later. Her experiences while in state custody and her years hiding in China meant Soyi's body and mind were, in her own words, "broken by North Korea." In Japan, with the help of activist groups, she found part-time work as a caregiver in a retirement home. She worked in the home for several years until her aches and pains forced her to resign. She now lives from week to week on state welfare.

Sitting across from Soyi's son, Minch'ŏl, in a Korean restaurant, as he meticulously spread leaves of kimchi across the hot grill, it became clear that he was being modest in deflecting suggestions of his success. His family owned two cars, they rented an apartment outside of Tsuruhashi, and he had recently supported his wife in opening a retail store. "Hyewŏn imports clothes from South Korea and sells them to Japanese housewives. They're crazy about Korean-style things here. You've been to her store, right?" he asked. I nodded, recalling the cramped store hidden deep within the maze of Tsuruhashi market. Women's clothes hung from floor to ceiling, from wall to wall. "She flies back and forth between Korea and Japan three times a month, sourcing new clothes. She gets to Seoul in the afternoon and shops all night in Tongdaemun market, returning to Osaka in the morning. She's got a good sense for what Japanese women like. The rent's expensive, but she's happy, so I'm also happy." Hyewŏn had deliberately sought out retail space in the Tsuruhashi area to capitalize on the growing popularity of Korean fashion. In recent years Tsuruhashi had become a domestic tourist attraction, particularly for Japanese women interested in Korean music, fashion, and dramas. With the number of Korean immigrants in the area also increasing, Hyewŏn hoped her store would serve both Japanese visitors and new arrivals from South Korea.

Migration as a response to crisis and critical junctures at the macro level, and the strategy of dividing and remaking family, are common to many Korean families' movements between the Korean Peninsula and Japan. The Yi family's narrative demonstrates the extent to which successive generations migrated as a response to deteriorating living conditions in one place and the promise of something better elsewhere. Similar to tens of thousands of others at the time, the Yis fled Cheju Island because of ideologically motivated violence. They smuggled themselves to Osaka, and in doing so they followed thousands of other Korean families who had made the sea journey from rural Cheju to industrial Osaka. In Japan the Yi family built social networks within the Zainichi Korean community—working, living, socializing, and becoming politicized with others from Cheju. Their membership in Ch'ongryŏn was as much an expression of political solidarity with North Korea as it was a vote of no confidence in the Rhee regime. For new arrivals, membership in the Ch'ongryŏn organization also assisted with expanding a customer base required for doing business. The family's involvement in Ch'ongryŏn offered Sukcha renewed purpose as she led the way in campaigning for the repatriation project. When the opportunity arose to return to North Korea, Sukcha was the driving force behind the family's relocation.

Like so many others who made the journey, the Yis divided their family with the expectation that they would be permitted to visit each other. The youngest son stayed in Japan where he would later play a crucial role in supporting his parents and siblings. The Yis' resettlement in North Korea was initially less troubled than it was for most repatriates. Their comparative wealth and Sukcha's ideological zeal accorded them favored status. In the years following their arrival, it appeared as though migration to North Korea had been a wise move, but the fate of the whole family was doomed by the actions of one member and the state that condemned them all through him. As is the case with many North Koreans who live in the northern border regions, Mansŏk, Minch'ŏl's grandfather, brought in extra income by trading privately with Korean-Chinese. Unbeknownst to them at the time, the Yi family's comparative comfort attracted the ire of local cadres. It was perhaps only a matter of time before Mansŏk would be arrested. Soyi concluded that they had two choices left: leave North Korea forever, or be condemned to die in the mountains.

The Ko Family

On my way to and from the Tsuruhashi train station I often passed Hyewŏn in her clothing store. It became a ritual of sorts; I would ride by her store on my folding bike and wave one handed. If not busy, Hyewŏn, hair pulled back into a ponytail, pencil behind her ear, waved back, often clutching her mobile phone in one hand and some women's clothes in the other. Hyewŏn also came from several generations of reluctant nomads moving back and forth across the Sea of Japan/East Sea. Her family's migration narrative, while exhibiting similarities to Minch'ŏl's, differs in a few notable details. First, her great-grandparents and grandparents were not wealthy, nor did they have the same political capital as Minch'ŏl's forebears. Furthermore, Hyewŏn's grandmother, the matriarch of the family who had played such a pivotal role in Hyewŏn's escape from North Korea, is Japanese. These differences meant that, although the Ko family also migrated to North Korea in the early days of the repatriation project, their lives were significantly more challenging than the Yi family's.

Ko Hyewŏn was born in Ryanggang Province, North Korea, in 1985. She grew up in a close-knit family, consisting of her brother, her mother and father, and her grandmother. In contrast to Minch'ŏl's family, the Kos struggled to make ends meet. Hyewŏn's father died when she was eight years old and, at the height of the famine, Hyewŏn's mother pulled her out of school to earn money in the local markets. From ten years old, Hyewŏn worked and slept in the markets where she witnessed people dying from starvation.

She had always had a close relationship with her grandmother, Kaori. In the times when she was not selling goods imported from China and locally brewed rice wine, Hyewŏn helped her grandmother foraging for mushrooms and tree bark on the outskirts of Hyesan. Her mother used whatever they brought home as filler for soups. On the occasions when Hyewŏn and Kaori were able to catch frogs, they made a little extra money by trading them across the border with Chinese.[5] During their frequent scavenging trips, Kaori sang Japanese songs and told Hyewŏn stories about life before she came to North Korea.

Kaori liked to remind Hyewŏn that their family was different from others. "I didn't have to come to North Korea," she impressed on her granddaughter. "I did it for your grandfather." Kaori was one of some 6,750 Japanese who migrated to the DPRK. Most Japanese were either women married to Korean men, or the children of relationships between Korean men and Japanese women.[6] Kaori was born in 1941, in the Hokuriku region, in the northwest part of Honshu Island. She completed middle school in 1957 and graduated high school in 1958. She found employment as a seamstress and worked in the same factory for two years, sewing trousers for businessmen and finishing the collars on pearl-white business shirts.

In early 1960, on a rare night out, she met a handsome man at a social event. "I'd never been to a dancehall before. I didn't even know what I was supposed to do," she told me. "So, I just sat there until I was asked to dance. My friends and I went outside for some air, and one by one they drifted off until I was left with the man who would become my husband. We were married on 2 December 1960," she smiled. From that evening, Kaori and Katashi, at that time using a Japanese name, started seeing each other. It did not matter to Kaori that her new beau was Korean. Until that point, she had never even heard of a Zainichi Korean, and Katashi seemed so Japanese that it hardly seemed to matter.

Like so many Koreans who moved to Japan during the colonial period only to later leave for North Korea, the Yi and the Ko families had much in common. Japanese land reforms and skyrocketing rent forced many Korean families like the Kos and the Yis off the lands they had worked for generations. Moved by the same need for better living conditions and a dependable income, Katashi's parents migrated separately to Japan from the southeast of the Korean Peninsula during the colonial years. His father was from South Kyŏngsang Province, and his mother's family came from South Chŏlla Province, in the southwest of the peninsula. At the time, a union between families from these regions would have been a difficult proposition, but living outside of the homeland and as a minority in Japan, regional rivalries could, on occasion, be put aside. In the expanding urban sprawl of Osaka, Katashi's father found work in a steel factory, making armaments for the Japanese advance across Asia. Through a mixture of luck and hustle in the black markets, the Ko family survived both American bombing and the chronic food shortages of the immediate postwar period. But, as for so many Koreans, life in Japan continued to be a struggle. When rumors started circulating that Kim Il-sung had invited Korean comrades to return to the homeland, it seemed like a sign they could not ignore.

Amid much fanfare, on 18 September 1961 Kaori, Katashi, his three brothers, one sister-in-law, and his parents boarded a ship at Niigata and cast off for their new home. Kaori's parents, reluctant to let her go, took comfort in the knowledge imparted by Ch'ongryŏn officials that, if she was not happy, they would let her return home after three years.[7] Katashi's family had never had money, nor had they been especially active in Ch'ongryŏn. The hope that life in North Korea might offer a path out of poverty, and the promise of free education—in Korean—were enough reasons to sign up for repatriation. Kaori recalled the days following their arrival:

> We went on board the 63rd ship. It carried about 1,300 people, the largest number to go to North Korea during the repatriations. After we arrived, we took a train to Sinŭiju, in the northwest. Once we arrived in Sinŭiju we had to wait again, until we were directed to board another train, this time to Ryanggang, a province in the northeast. The train was full, but everyone was so quiet that I could hear them wriggling around in discomfort. It was the lice! The lice in the seats were devouring them. And so, we spent six hours wriggling around until we arrived in Ryanggang where again we waited. This time we stayed in a government center for a month while they organized an apartment. Finally, we moved into a place on the fourth floor of a building on the outskirts of Hyesan city. My husband and I were so impressed because it had under floor heating. Things were going to be alright after all, we thought. But, when we looked closer, we discovered that the light switches didn't work, and nothing happened when we tried to start the heating. It dawned on us that there wasn't any electricity, nor was there any running water for the toilet or for bathing. There wasn't any sewage system. From that time on I had to find wood or rubbish to burn and heat the floor.

Katashi and Kaori were resettled in Hyesan on the North Korean frontier, close to Paektu Mountain. The area is known for two things: its copper mine that opened the year before Katashi and Kaori arrived, and the freezing winters. For repatriates dispatched to this area of North Korea, life was a struggle against the elements. Resettling into their new home brought a host of unexpected challenges. Fellow repatriates told Katashi, "You need to put Japan behind you," and advised him to revert to his Korean name, Dohyŏn. With a new name and a new focus, Dohyŏn set the rules for his family: inside the home Japanese language and Japanese cooking was acceptable, but outside there was to be no talk of Japan, no speaking Japanese, and certainly no criticism of their new home. Dohyŏn finished the training he had started in Japan and the state assigned him work as an optometrist. Kaori was afforded no such benefits. She did not speak Korean and her daily routine involved little else besides collecting water and refuse to heat their apartment, and cooking for her family.

> The town where we lived was so strange, there were no shops! Nothing was sold anywhere. I was shocked. One thing that I had in my favor was that my sisters in Japan sent me parcels with food and other supplies. I learned

early on that the native North Koreans wanted Japanese clothes and food, so I traded many of the things she sent me with them. My daughters and I grew some potatoes in a little plot behind our apartment, but we'd also trade most of these for rice. By trading and growing our own food, I was able to make my husband the kind of dishes he liked.

Each day, Dohyŏn left for work with a lunchbox of rice and kimchi under his arm, the fruits of Kaori's careful trading and cultivation. Once he had left Kaori began the day's chores: collecting what was needed for the house, sourcing food, and preparing the evening meal. She told me that she felt a desperate frustration while living in North Korea. Her husband and parents-in-law were the reason she had left Japan, but she was unable to complain because they were all suffering together. In her own words, she lived a quiet life, raising her children in a town in which there were a number of other Japanese wives. Although she would see the other wives around the town, she confessed to me that she was exceedingly lonely: "The Japanese wives got together once a month to catch up on the latest news from home. If we saw each other in the street, we'd greet each other. But you'd never make a show of your Japanese side. You'd never speak openly in Japanese or say anything that showed your difference. You had to keep quiet, because you never knew who was listening. I was so worried about exposing my Japanese side that I had trouble making friends." Kaori struggled the most in her family, unable or perhaps unwilling to learn Korean as fast as Dohyŏn would have liked. Kaori's trading and Dohyŏn's meager salary was enough to keep the family in relative comfort, but as immigrants from Japan their chances for upward mobility were limited. Dohyŏn's fondness for homemade *soju* was also becoming a problem, causing further concern for Kaori.

In the early 1990s the Ko family experienced a series of tragedies. First, after several months of illness, Dohyŏn succumbed to liver disease and passed away. Kaori reflected on his death, telling me that she had never felt close to her husband. Furthermore, although her two sisters sent packages full of food, clothes, and medicine, life in the northern provinces took a devastating toll on her family during the famine years. "I had six children, but four of them died in North Korea," she explained, taking the pencil out of my hand to add a stroke, signifying death, across each of the symbols representing a son or a daughter on her genealogy chart. Kaori paused, pencil in hand, "This was when I decided I had to leave."

I heard from the other Japanese wives that there was a way to contact your family without the government knowing. I just needed to bribe the border guards and cross into China to call my mother. In 2000 I sneaked into China. While I was in China, I met with a people smuggler and asked if he would take me to Japan, but it was too expensive. I had nothing, no money or anything I could trade with him, so I returned to North Korea. Later, I returned to China and again spoke to a broker who encouraged me to leave for Japan saying, "Let's go. I can take you there and you can pay me later." This was what I needed to hear. I left with the broker and decided never to return to North Korea. Instead, I stayed for six months with the broker in his home in Yanji, China. When I felt safe, I went to the Japanese consulate and asked them for help with returning to Japan. After some time, an embassy worker escorted me from Beijing to Haneda Airport, Tokyo.

Kaori's journey, simplified above, brought her full circle back to Japan. Following her return, Kaori worked in an Osaka market and gave talks on her life in North Korea to curious Japanese. She repaid her debt to the broker, while covering her daily expenses and putting away a little savings each week until she could afford the fee needed to smuggle her eldest daughter, Yunsŏk, out of North Korea.[8]

Once she arrived in Japan, Yunsŏk found factory work through a newspaper advertisement. The two of them saved their wages until they had enough money to pay a broker to smuggle Yunsŏk's niece and nephew, Hyewŏn and Hosŏng, out of North Korea, to the Japanese consulate-general in Shenyang. Kaori still has one daughter, Yunhŭi, remaining in North Korea. Meanwhile, Yunsŏk works in a Tokyo factory alongside her nephew, Hosŏng. Again, Kaori and Yunsŏk are pooling their savings with the intention of paying for Yunhŭi to escape North Korea for Japan. But Yunhŭi had not been heard from in months and Kaori was worried that she had been arrested.

More than fifteen years have passed since Kaori returned to Japan. Now in her mid-seventies, she is no longer able to work. Instead, she spends her days giving talks to Japanese about her experiences. On special occasions, such as the New Year, family birthdays, and *ch'usŏk* (harvest festival) she meets with her daughter and grandchildren. Together they commemorate the death day of her husband. Kaori still has two sisters living in Japan, the same sisters who helped her family survive in North Korea. But her bond with her Japanese family has eroded. She blames the constant burden her sisters carried in sustaining her in North Korea for their strained relationship.

The marriage of Kaori's granddaughter, Hyewŏn to Minch'ŏl continued a pattern of endogamous marriage between families whose narrative is distinguished by a series of forced migrations between Japan and the two Koreas. It is likely that the Yi and the Ko families' migration experiences have not yet reached a conclusion. The emergence of affordable air travel now enables Hyewŏn and Minch'ŏl to move freely between Japan, South Korea, and China for business. They hope that their son, Minjae, will be proud of his North Korea–born parents and his Korean heritage. Minch'ŏl told me that he is considering sending Minjae to South Korea when he is older, so that he can learn to speak Korean. "He has to know where he's from," Minch'ŏl impressed on me. "Where is he from?" I probed. "He's Korean," Minch'ŏl replied. Hesitating, he added, "Not South Korean, but also not North Korean. He's certainly not Japanese. He's just Korean. But . . . I see what you're doing, Markus." We both smiled, clinking our beers together.

Frustrated social mobility characterizes the Ko family's migratory biography. In North Korea Katashi/Dohyŏn was a skilled worker, but his family background and his Japanese wife made it unlikely that he or his descendants would improve their social standing. The Ko family's political status was so significantly low that they were considered enemies of the state. Lacking in political influence and without the Yi's financial capacity to negotiate their inferior status, the Kos would never improve their lives as long as they stayed in North Korea.

When Hyewŏn's mother withdrew her from school to work in the black market, it was as an act of desperation to prevent the family from starving. When Kaori escaped North Korea, promising the people smuggler that she would pay him when she got to Japan, it was because she felt she had already lost so much. And, when she worked every day in the Osaka supermarket until she could pay the broker to bring her family to Japan, it was because she knew she could not go on without knowing the fate of her family she had left behind.

Reflections on Genealogies of Family Migration

From Cheju Island to Osaka, Kobe, or Tokyo; from Japan to Pyongyang, Hyesan, or Sinŭiju; and back to Osaka some fifty years later, mobility, displacement, and resettlement have shaped the lives of Zainichi Korean families in Japan and in North Korea. As fugitives who moved to survive, as workers who toiled in factories, mines, and forests throughout Japan, the Kos, the Yis, and others went to North Korea and were resettled according to their political biographies, their financial capacity, and their demonstrable skills. Consequently, in Japan and in North Korea, particular cities, towns, and villages became home to communities of Zainichi Korean migrants.

The genealogies of the Yis and the Kos offer nuance to the abstractions of migration theory. Across four or five generations, continuous movement and precarity shaped the lives of the families now returning from North Korea. Families like the Yis felt compelled to leave Cheju Island due to the Japanese colonial government's land reforms. Others were forced to flee increasing violence in the postcolonial years as the Rhee government clamped down on opposition. Japan, however, did not always offer Koreans a better life. The host society regarded Koreans as subordinates and, when the opportunity arose, the state withdrew what limited rights they had been afforded as citizens of empire. Similarly, repatriates' experiences in North Korea impressed on the new arrivals their outsider status and underlined the mismatch between North Korean propaganda and everyday life.

For both the Yis and the Kos, transnational relationships between divided families have been critical for their survival. In the case of the Yis, dividing family between Japan and North Korea enabled them to prosper in North Korea. For the Kos, Kaori's relationship with her sisters in Japan contributed to sustaining the family and later facilitated her return. Relationships that connected these families beyond their immediate time and place offered a means to manage strained socioeconomic conditions and even, in a few cases, to enter into the North Korean political elite. However, both families endured economic hardship, untimely and unnecessary death, and political persecution.

The lives of these two families reveal some of the hidden social rules for people on the move. First, each generation of the Yis and the Kos was born in a different political and geographic space to their parents: the first generation was born in colonial Korea, as it was then part of the Empire of Japan (Kaori was born in Japan proper). As a consequence of their parents' migration from colonial Korea, the next generation of each family was born in occupied Japan, which was administered by the United States until 1952. Since both families were part of the repatriation project, the generation that followed was born in North Korea. The newest generation is being born after a return to Japan. The significance of a transnational birthing pattern highlights the transient characteristics of the families and their familial, emotional, and material connections to multiple places. The movement back and forth between Japan and the two Koreas also explains the difficulty that some interlocutors experience in articulating where home is to them. For Kaori, the answer appeared straightforward: she is Japanese, and home is Japan. But for ethnic Koreans who repatriated to North Korea, the question was often more complicated. Returnees' multiple migrations have resulted in their feeling a sense of belonging to everywhere and nowhere at the same time. In a few cases, feelings of displacement are resolved by identifying not with a Japanese or Korean identity, but with a third way—a hybrid identity located outside of both Zainichi Korean communities and the majority Japanese society (see Chapman 2004).

For some returnees, multiple migrations have had an alienating effect, fostering a sense of permanent displacement. During a tea break in between teaching classes, Sŏn Donghyŏn considered the question of belonging, "I married another Zainichi Korean in North Korea, so it made sense for us to try and get back to Japan. But when we returned to Japan, we returned to the Zainichi community. So, we are Zainichi Korean." Donghyŏn located his family within a diasporic community, but he did so with the experience of returning to the ethnic homeland only to discover it was no longer home.

In response to extreme social pressure, both families in this chapter transformed items sent from Japan into social and political capital, by trading with locals and bribing the authorities. Another way of negotiating their outsider status was to relinquish particular symbols of their identity that state and society regarded as ideologically subversive. Repatriates to North Korea learned to use only their Korean name, to speak only Korean, and to discard family records so as to obscure kinship connections to Japan and South Korea.

With opportunities for upward mobility limited in both Japan and in North Korea, Zainichi Koreans have been inclined to make alliances endogamously and homogenously, demonstrating a marriage preference for families with a similar migratory biography. The Ko and the Yi families used Zainichi Korean matchmakers to introduce their children to partners with a background as close to their own migratory experiences as possible. In postwar Japan migrants from Cheju Island married other Cheju islanders. In North Korea repatriates formed alliances with other repatriates. And in contemporary Japan, returnees may be inclined to marry other returnees, as in the case of Ko Hyewŏn and Yi Minch'ŏl.

The oral histories of the two families discussed in this chapter show how intramarriage—the joining of families with similar ethnic and migratory histories—is used as a strategy for fostering resilience against pressures from the host society. The joining of families for whom forced migration is a shared experience has subsequently encouraged an ethos of migration to emerge. With displacement and migration at the heart of these families' personal narratives, it becomes more likely that they will again in the future resort to migration as a response to critical junctures and macro pressures.

In the next chapter we move on from the early days of the mass exodus from Japan to better understand what life was like for the men, women, and children who arrived in Kim Il-sung's revolutionary homeland. Some repatriates were offered opportunities that had eluded them in Japan. But for many, life in North Korea required a careful management of ethnic and political identities. Over time, the feelings of belonging that had initially drawn so many Zainichi Korean families to North Korea shifted, and repatriates again dreamed of a return home. This time a longing for home was directed to neither of the Koreas, but rather back to friends, family, and Korean communities they had left behind in Japan.

Notes

1. The majority of my interviewees had never written down their experiences, been interviewed, or spoken with a researcher. Consequently, we worked together to establish a timeline that would scaffold their memories. The timeline ran the bottom of a landscape A4 piece of paper, starting in 1900 and reaching to the

present. On the timeline we charted moments of significance to the interviewee's family and mapped these onto changes happening at the macro level. For example, Korean independence (15 August 1945), the Cheju Uprising (3 April 1948–May 1949), The Korean War (25 June 1950–27 July 1953), the beginning of the repatriation project (December 1959), the Treaty on Basic Relations between Japan and the Republic of Korea (1965), the beginning of family visitations from Japan (from the late 1970s), the abduction revelations (2002), and the implementation of Japanese sanctions on travel and trade with the DPRK (October 2006).

2. For more on the Cheju Uprising, see Cumings (2010, 121–31), and Miyoshi Jager (2013, 47–54).

3. Pachinko is a Japanese gambling game similar to Western slot machines. For an interesting read on Koreans' involvement in the pachinko trade, see the fictional account *Pachinko* (Lee 2017).

4. Mindan and Ch'ongryŏn affiliates clashed on a number of occasions. On 16 November 1959, for example, five hundred Koreans affiliated with Mindan and the Great Japan Patriotic Party converged on a Ch'ongryŏn rally in Kokaido, Tokyo. According to the incident report, several hundred persons subsequently participated in a violent battle (B AG 232 105-015.05 "Copies de déclarations officielles, de notes, de télégrammes, pour information transmises par la Criox-Rouge Japonaise." 04/09/1959–26/12/1959).

5. Kaori told me that the Chinese merchants with whom she traded ate the frogs' legs and used what was left to make oil.

6. Under Japanese law at that time, children of a Korean man and a Japanese woman were considered Korean if the couple was officially married and Japanese if they were not (Morris-Suzuki 2009, 6).

7. Japanese migrants to North Korea believed that they would be permitted to return to Japan after three years. This proved to be a fabrication and they were not permitted to return.

8. The people smuggler quoted the cost as 400,000 yen (approximately US$3,500). The cost of paying a smuggler to bring family safely out of North Korea and through China has fluctuated over time but is now considerably higher than it was in the early 2000s.

3

Becoming a Foreigner
in North Korea

Prospective repatriates arrived in Niigata from across Japan. Families like the Kos and the Yis disembarked from trains and climbed on board buses headed for the Red Cross Center. Men, women, and children dragging suitcases stuffed full of clothes and family keepsakes were fed and given sleeping quarters for the duration of their stay in Niigata.[1] Those awaiting an interview with ICRC staff bathed in the communal baths, styled their hair in the Center's barber, and bought extra supplies in the store (figure 3.1).

Repatriates stored their luggage and other large items destined for North Korea in nearby warehouses, and from there cranes loaded them onto the waiting passenger liner.[2] In the wintertime, snow piled up high around the walls of the Center and the families inside shivered. During especially heavy snowfalls, departures from Niigata were suspended. In the summertime, families spread out blankets in the Center's gardens, practicing their Korean over picnics and imagining what awaited them across the sea.

It usually took no more than a few days to complete the formalities of confirming free will. Prior to each trip, JRC officials compiled a list of repatriates before handing it to DPRK Red Cross staff. Nervous men, women, and children then took a bus for the dock, where a Japanese immigration official moved smartly up and down the line with pen and clipboard for a final identification check. "Kim family? How many people? How many pieces of luggage?" A few simple questions concluded the Japanese state's duty of care. The journey to North Korea took three days and two nights. "It was terrible," Hiroko recalled. "We were in the bottom of the ship and I remember the awful smell of all those people in that tiny space. It was summer and everything stank. The trip was so boring and made worse because I couldn't sleep. So, I climbed up to the deck to get some air. Imagine my shock upon reaching the deck and finding groups of armed soldiers staring at me. I was terrified."

Figure 3.1. Niigata, Japan. A young repatriate examines the bicycles for sale in the Niigata Red Cross Center store. © Photothèque CICR (DR)/ (Photograph by Elsa Casal, confidentiality level: public). Date: sometime between 1959 and 1963.

Hiroko's memories of the journey from Niigata are marked by discomfort, boredom, and apprehension of what awaited her in North Korea. The soldiers she stumbled on were Soviet troops assigned to protect the vessels from a possible South Korean attack. But it was not always so unnerving. Romancing couples danced across the promenade. Single men chain-smoked while hunched over card games, and children chased each other through the ship's labyrinth of passages and sleeping berths.

In the early light of the morning, North Korea appeared as a faint smudge between the ocean and the sky. Bit by bit, the smudge grew into a shimmering green of mountains. Excited passengers emerged from below the deck, squinting for a first glimpse of their new home. As the ship docked at Ch'ŏngjin, the call to disembark crackled through the loudspeakers. Passengers crowded the deck and cries of *Manse!* (hurrah) rippled through the new arrivals as men, women and children threw up their hands in celebration. But not everyone was so animated. Steadying themselves against the ship's railings, some stared in a mixture of wonder and horror at the state-organized greeting party. Kim Hyŏnjae recalled his parents' first impressions: "My mother told me how distressed she was by their appearance. Their skin was black and worn, their clothes were drab and unkempt. They looked like they'd had very hard lives." Hyŏnjae's mother's reaction at seeing the locals for the first time accords with other interviewees who recounted their arrival stories to me. In the eyes of the new arrivals, the people gathered together at the end of the gangway, lackadaisically waving DPRK flags and clutching flowers, appeared vastly different from the passionate, healthy young patriots they had seen in North Korean propaganda leaflets.

Some of the new arrivals had studied in Ch'ongryŏn schools in Japan, learning North Korean revolutionary history and Korean language. Others felt more comfortable speaking in Japanese, having spent their entire lives in Japan. Either way, once they disembarked, cadres marked by armbands directed the new arrivals into a warehouse-sized building with instructions to wait. "They handed out some rice for the children and ordered us to prepare for travel to our new homes. While we waited, government workers gave us lessons about the country and Kim Il-sung–ideological lessons," Hiroko recalled. Officious men in rough textured suits went from family to family, stopping to record their place of origin in Japan, occupation, age, special skills, and family composition.[3] The wait in the processing center could take up to four days, depending on how prepared officials were for each new batch of repatriates. On the day of their onward journey, state officials ushered them out of the warehouse and onto trains. Those who had political connections through Ch'ongryŏn or money to bribe officials might find themselves later disembarking in the capital, Pyongyang, a favorable location in terms of infrastructure, employment, and proximity to power. The majority of new arrivals, however, were bound for cities, towns, and villages scattered throughout the country.

By 1965, five years after the repatriation project began, some eighty-three thousand Koreans and more than six thousand Japanese had emigrated to North Korea. In a dispatch from the Central Committee of the DPRK's Red Cross Society to the ICRC, North Korean officials lauded the successes of those who had already made the journey. "Returnees have been leading a happy life in the warm bosom of their motherland, devoting themselves to socialist construction of the country," the letter boasted. "Thus, some 2,000 of them have been awarded the state commendation of all classes, the title of Labor Hero included. Moreover, 990 returnees have been elected to deputies of the People's Assembly of all levels including the Supreme People's Assembly, thereby taking part directly in the administration of the Government."[4]

Arriving at the ICRC's headquarters in Geneva, the report came tucked inside a glossy booklet produced by the Pyongyang Foreign Languages Publishing House. Replete with full-page photos of a smiling Kim Il-sung locked arm in arm with gleeful repatriated children, the booklet claimed that return to "their glorious fatherland" afforded repatriates educational and medical services denied them in Japan. In some cases, these declarations were true. However, by the mid-1960s it was clear that life in "the glorious fatherland" had not resolved the everyday struggles of many Zainichi Koreans who had made the journey.

While the outward migration of North Koreans into China and on to South Korea is not a new phenomenon (Bell 2013a, 2013b, 2014; Jung 2013; Kim 2013; Koo 2016; Lankov 2006; Song 2013), very little has been said about emigration *to* North Korea, the motivations for migrating to one of the most closed societies in the world, and what happens to the people who move there. At the height of the Cold War, families on the front lines of the ideological standoff between the two power blocs internalized these ruptures in complex, contradictory ways that reshaped their understanding of themselves and their communities. The division of the Korean Peninsula and the movement of Zainichi Koreans to the DPRK, for instance, impacted already complicated ideological and kinship alliances, shattering communities and shaping new identities for those who moved and the people they left behind.

This chapter shows how immigrants to North Korea managed their identities as a strategy to emotionally survive state persecution and social alienation. Two prominent tropes emerged in conversations with returnees from North Korea: hope that life in North Korea would offer repatriates a chance for upward social and economic mobility denied them in Japan, and disappointment when it became clear that it would present neither improved opportunities nor a homeland in which to belong. Instead, the reality of living in North Korea as politically low-status immigrants forced a rethinking of repatriates' sense of self, and their relationships to both the communities from which they departed and those in which they were received. Because the DPRK state and society treated immigrants from Japan as outsiders, feelings of rejection and alienation moved repatriates to reexamine their understanding of home, and to reimagine their experiences in Japan in a more positive light. Repatriates' responses to social exclusion provided opportunities for new understandings of belonging to emerge, as individuals who considered themselves Korean patriots developed strong emotional "translocal identifications" (Conradson and McKay 2007, 168) that connected them not to the nation of Japan, but to ethnic Korean communities within Japan. These factors contributed to the emergence of what Edward Said describes as a "plurality of vision" (Said 2000, 186), in which immigrants simultaneously identify with aspects of both the old and the new, the sending country and the host country.

Interviewees recalled a pre-repatriation fervor. They talked of a desire to be part of an independent country built by and for Koreans—ethnonationalist, revolutionary and anti-imperial in character. But emotions of longing and belonging shifted following their arrival in North Korea as frictions between locals and newcomers became more pronounced. Conflicting emotions pulled on repatriate families—feelings of ethnic pride and political loyalty to North Korea from one side, and the lived experience of being treated like a foreigner in the homeland from the other.

Migration and Emotions

There was a noticeable difference between repatriates who emigrated to North Korea in the early 1960s and those who emigrated starting in the late 1960s. Those who left earlier were often motivated by both a desire to escape a hardscrabble life of persecution and poverty in Japan, and out of support for the fledgling homeland. Earlier repatriates put their trust in Kim Il-sung's promises for a better life, hoping for a stake in rebuilding the DPRK. Later arrivals, however, often included recent high school graduates, the second or third sons in a family with Ch'ongryŏn membership, and people with nothing left to lose. One former Ch'ongryŏn member told me that, on politically auspicious occasions, Ch'ongryŏn would send groups of young members to North Korea as tribute to the leadership.[5] Those who emigrated in the 1970s and after would also have had a better understanding of what awaited them in North Korea since by this time the gap between propaganda and reality had been exposed in repatriates' carefully worded letters home.

For early repatriates in particular, their experiences in the DPRK were starkly different from what most of them had expected. Hope for a prosperous life in the ethnic homeland gradually turned to disappointment. Although many were unaware of it at the time of arrival, their association with the former colonizer, Japan, marked them as symbolically polluted individuals: embodied representations of Korea's subjugation under foreign rule. With the exception of a select few, repatriates' relationship to the North Korean state and the indigenous population provoked a distinct shift in how many identified themselves, from patriotic revolutionaries to Zainichi Koreans.

Migration shapes emotional processes and understandings of the self for the person who moves, those who remain behind, and the receiving community.[6] In this chapter, the relationship of migration to emotions (see Baldassar 2008; Skrbiš 2008; Svašek 2010), of migration to identity (see Brubaker and Cooper 2000), and of migration to the self (see Walkerdine 2006; Whittaker 1992) underline the importance of inner life processes for reflecting moments of both crisis and the everyday. The words "self" and "identity" are often used synonymously to describe an innate character that exists out of sight but is nevertheless foundational to a person's being. But in fact the self is not the same as identity. Where the self is similar to concepts like the mind, ego, soul, spirit, and psyche (Whittaker 1992, 200), identity is something multiple, in that people may have an infinite number of identities that they deploy to their advantage in situations of both stress and opportunity.

A person's self is not an atemporal, bounded repository into which experiences are passively accumulated. Rather, the self is in an ongoing relationship with the world, and is continuously shaped through interactions with others, with the material environment, with memories of the past, and with imagined futures (Svašek 2010, 868). A person does not even have to exist in one place or time for an experience to have a profound impact on his or her self. My interviewees, for instance, recalled family who had perished during the North Korean famine and how, even now, memories of their lost family shape their thoughts and behaviors. For all of us, deceased family exercise a strong pull on their living kin. For North Koreans in exile, such recollections are further tied up with a nostalgia for a simple life in North Korea, guilt for leaving family behind, fond memories of family gatherings and making do with whatever resources were available, and betrayal by a state that failed to protect them.

Managing Identities

The narratives of migrants moving between Japan and North Korea span several generations and create overlapping identifications between localities in both the sending and receiving countries. These migrations disrupt and complicate, destabilizing the idea of home for people who move and for family members who are impacted by the social and economic consequences of human mobility. The experience of leaving home threatens to generate a perpetual feeling of being out of place and outside of time. How people present themselves, how they interact in particular situations and deploy particular identities into specific social worlds is something sociologist Erving Goffman refers to as "acting out a line"–producing a pattern of verbal and nonverbal acts by which a person expresses his or her view and relationship to others around them (Goffman 1967, 5). Producing and reproducing multiple identities is a strategy for managing social interactions.

For immigrants in particular, cross-cultural identity management (Cupach and Tadasu 1993)–organizing one's performance to suit audiences within and outside of one's cultural group–is a strategy for passing through social worlds with as little friction as possible.

Many repatriates had spent their entire lives in Japan. They left behind a familiar community and social system and arrived in a society that was war-ready and hostile to outsiders. I met Kim Yujin through a church group in Seoul, South Korea. Yujin escaped to South Korea in 2005. Born in North Korea in 1987, he recalled growing up with children whose parents and grandparents had emigrated from Japan. In a Seoul coffee shop, he explained the relationship of native-born North Koreans to the newcomers:

> The Chaepo[7] had skills that most people didn't have. They could make origami flowers for weddings, fix electronics, and they worked really hard, despite all the prejudice they experienced. They also married within their own group, with people who had a similar level of *sŏngbun,*[8] and with others from Japan. When I was fifteen, I knew a man from Japan. He was fifty-eight years old, handsome, and softly spoken. He'd gone to college and got training in chemistry and welding. He was good at math and visited families in our neighborhood to help them with their household budget. It was all useless though. People saw him as a threat because he was from outside North Korea. So, he didn't have any friends. The fact is that in North Korea, you can't simply be nice to other people, because they'll use you to their own ends and they won't let you in. It was clear that he hadn't adapted to the North Korean way of life, despite having lived there for almost thirty years.

Drawing comparisons to his life in South Korea, Yujin explained that in North Korea, the feeling code–an unspoken but tacitly understood means of communication–is different from the code in South Korea or Japan.[9] North Korean people have become adept at shielding their emotions as a way to protect themselves from political recriminations. "In my experience," Yujin reflected, "we treated them [repatriates] like strangers. We treated them as if they were Japanese and there was no chance for them to become like us." Yujin's recollections echoed another North Korean interviewee who remembered his repatriate friend telling him, "We [repatriates] get married, but only to each other. We talk, but only to each other. We live together, but not with others."

Repatriates were well aware of the differences between them and local Koreans. New arrivals to the DPRK also understood that they often had more in common with others from Japan than with the locals. Interviewees explained that, upon meeting for the first time, repatriates mutually acknowledged their shared origins by introducing themselves using their name, place of origin in Japan, and the number of the ship they had arrived on. This was also a means through which seniority was established between repatriates. Those who had been in North Korea longer were regarded as having accumulated more knowledge of the host society and as having an obligation to look out for new arrivals by sharing information and, when necessary, warning others on what not to do.

Life in North Korea

The majority of repatriates arrived in North Korea between 1959 and 1964.[10] The North Korean state initially received immigrants from Japan with enthusiasm. But the propaganda value of new arrivals and their usefulness as an economic conduit connecting the two countries failed to offset suspicions that returning comrades were little different from the former Japanese colonizers.

New arrivals' resettlement was shaped by their low sociopolitical status and the political and economic changes taking place at the regional and global levels. Several events in particular impacted the experiences of repatriates from Japan: the establishment of a regular ferry service running between North Korea and Japan in 1971, the loosening of restrictions on family visitations in 1979, the 1991 breakup of the Soviet Union, the subsequent North Korean famine, and the political fallout from the 2002 Japan–North Korea summit.

Hostile Forces

The DPRK state classifies the population into three broad sociopolitical groups: hostile forces, neutral forces (also known as the wavering class), and friendly forces. These categories are hereditary and prevent the upward mobility of all but a few individuals.[11] New arrivals from Japan were organized according to the government's assessment of their family background, political contributions, and perceived value to the state. But even before arriving, their association with the former colonizer and the southern (ROK) origins of new arrivals limited the opportunities available to most repatriates and circumscribed their relationships to the state and the broader population. As it continues to do for native North Koreans, repatriates' *sŏngbun* (sociopolitical status) limited both marriage and career prospects. Kim Mi, who escaped North Korea for Japan in 2011, explained, "In our town, in South P'yŏng'an province, there were lots of people from Japan. They worked skilled jobs as researchers, doctors, and engineers–not as laborers. They were allocated these jobs because they had received a high level of education in Japan. But, because of their bad *sŏngbun*, they could never get into the party, so their lives had no hope." Doctors, educators, and other such skilled workers in North Korea are afforded a level of social respect according to their status. But without party membership, their children are limited in employment opportunities, in their marriage choices, and in their chances of moving up the socioeconomic ladder. Kim Yujin remembered the repatriated families differently. He told me, "There were two things that everyone knew about repatriates: first, their political status was bad. Second, lots of them were sent to the coalmines. The problem was that they were outsiders. They spoke, acted, and thought differently to us [natives]. And they had family in Japan, so they could leave [the DPRK] at any time. Of course, they couldn't actually leave, but that was what people thought."

A person's relationship to the state was dependent on the political and economic capital each family brought with them, and the period in which they arrived in North Korea. But suspected divided loyalties made it difficult for repatriates to build trust with the host society. Military service, for example, was and continues to be an important means for the state to enculturate its citizens, transmitting political and social ideas through the militarization of young men and women. Early repatriates were not permitted to carry out compulsory military service. The state was concerned that young repatriates would spread corrupt ideology within the military. On a practical level, new arrivals from Japan struggled to communicate in Korean, and many could not speak well enough to work alongside North Koreans. On the rare occasions when young repatriates were permitted to serve, they were more likely to be conscripted into office administration roles. Denied the opportunity to serve the country, to pass through what ethnologist Arnold van Gennep refers to as a rite of passage ([1909] 1960), repatriates as a group were unable to move from the outer to the inner circles of North Korean social and political life.

There were exceptions. Kim Hyŏnjae, now working for a removal company in Osaka, told me that in the late 1960s, Pyongyang created a special forces unit comprised entirely of young men from Japan. The Returnees Unit, he explained, remembering the experiences of a friend who had served in the unit, was based in the mountains of North P'yŏng'an Province, in a town called Kusŏng. Chief of Staff Kim Ch'angbong (a man Kim Il-sung later purged), took charge of training new recruits. The unit recruited young repatriates who spoke both Japanese and Korean and was tasked with long-range, covert operations. Specifically, the Returnees Unit was formed with the mission of making Japan an outpost for the unification of the two Koreas. "They were trained to go undetected through South Korea and enter Japan by boat. Once they had infiltrated Japan, they would work as spies to strengthen the Ch'ongryŏn organization," Hyŏnjae told me. In the early 1980s, after the unit was disbanded, members struggled to adapt to civilian society. Former returnee special forces such as Hyŏnjae's friend, young men who had spent their service isolated from the regular military and who now found themselves unemployed and listless, reportedly formed gangs and lived off the land, terrorizing the residents of P'yŏng'an.

Most first-generation repatriates, however, did not serve in the DPRK military. Consequently, the state looked for alternative ways to nurture their loyalties. Throughout the country, cadres of the Korean Workers' Party tried to control new arrivals by means of political meetings[12] and self-criticism sessions, state-directed surveillance through a vast network of informants[13] and the threat of exile to the mountains for those who resisted. State discipline started at the top of the political food chain. In the 1960s Kim Il-sung launched a series of purges of opponents as part of a broader effort to secure a monolithic ideological system and strengthen his leadership (Buzo 1999, 59). Although party purges would become less frequent, the disappearance of politically suspect individuals continued throughout Kim's time in power. During the 1970s, for example, the state confiscated the wealth of an unknown number of repatriate families before disappearing them into labor camps.[14] The DPRK's persecution of repatriate families was made worse by a tightening of sanctions as Tokyo moved to block all Japan-DPRK trade. Although it would still be possible to send money and goods to family in North Korea, the days of bulk-exporting automobiles, bicycles, refrigerators, washing machines, stereos, and pianos were coming to an end.[15] Yujin described how the sanctions impacted his community: "There were still things like video recorders and DVDs in the markets, but they were imported from China, not Japan. Also, things weren't as cheap anymore, and Chaepo families had nothing to sell."

Divided Loyalties, Dividing Identities

Prior to arrival in North Korea, some Zainichi Koreans saw repatriation as the ultimate act of loyalty to the North Korean state and its leader, Kim Il-sung. But by no means were all those who emigrated staunch revolutionaries. For many prospective repatriates, leaving for North Korea meant taking a risk in an unknown land. In a sad irony, individuals who had been made painfully aware of their Korean identity in Japan were now considered too Japanese in the ethnic homeland.

The efforts of party cadres to mold new arrivals into compliance included discouraging them from acting in ways considered Japanese. Clothes, behavior, and language were all cause for concern since these features highlighted the newcomers' difference from native North Koreans. Even repatriates' comportment distinguished them from the locals. Kim Hyŏnjae told me that it was often possible to identify new arrivals by the way a person walked. Locals, for instance, walked quickly, bent over at the waist, and staring straight ahead. "There was no way of getting around, so they all had to powerwalk. And no one wanted to risk attracting the attention of state security, so they'd focus on the ground ahead of them." In contrast, repatriates walked in a relaxed fashion, as they had done in Japan. Kim Mi clarified these distinctions:

The Chae'il tongp'o [Koreans from Japan] sounded softer when they spoke, whereas the locals sounded harsher, tougher. Also, people who'd come from Japan, like my parents, had gentle faces and soft expressions, like Japanese people. This changed over time, however, and people started to look more like North Koreans. If you live in North Korea, you age quickly and look very tired [pulls down the skin on both sides of her face to emphasize a worn, hollow expression]. There's so much pressure from society, with everyone watching you, so you have to be cautious about who's watching and what you're saying. Anything can get you reported and land you in prison. In Japan, people don't worry about these kinds of things, so they walk about like this [her anxious expression changes to a relaxed face, her eyes looking around and her body moving in a slow, loping fashion]. You can just be yourself.

Pressure to conform started in childhood. State authorities directed repatriates to send their children to local schools, where they became targets for bullying from teachers and children. The Japanese language was forbidden in schools, in workplaces, and in public. Talking of Japan was also prohibited. Children who had gone to Ch'ongryŏn schools prior to leaving Japan could often speak a smattering of Korean, but most young repatriates spoke little or no Korean and struggled to understand what was happening during lessons. I interviewed Chang Michŏng over dinner in her Osaka home with her husband and two children; they were also returnees from North Korea. Michŏng told me that when she arrived in North Korea at seventeen years old she did not speak any Korean. She was sent to a school where she stayed in the dormitory, surrounded by native North Koreans. "I couldn't understand anything they said, but kept hearing the same vile words: 'Pig's trotters,' 'Bitch,' 'Son of a bitch,' and things like that. If we spoke Japanese, we'd be disciplined. They'd hit us. This was good to learn because later, if we spoke Japanese as adults, we'd have been seriously punished."

A fear of physical violence underlined North Korea's feeling code as it was transmitted to the new arrivals. It paid to learn the code as quickly as possible. Life for the first generation of repatriates in the DPRK was marked by constant reminders that they were outsiders. Repatriates often suspected local North Koreans of being agents of the state and, when possible, kept a distance from them. They learned from experience that the public sphere was for Korean behavior and the private could be for Japanese. On the surface, native North Koreans and repatriates were divided by language and daily habits. These differences were emphasized by the expressions used to refer to the other in each case. In an interesting reflection of how discrimination travels globally, repatriates referred to DPRK-born people as "Apache." This expression echoed the use of the term they had seen in American television shows and Japanese history books. It revealed their perceptions of locals' "savage manners and dress" that they equated to White North American depictions of Native Americans. Native North Koreans had their own pejorative terms for the newcomers–"Chaepo" became slang for a repatriate, and "pig's trotters" was another common insult, this one referencing a Japanese style of footwear that to locals resembled cloven hooves.[16] "They had lots of different names for us," recalled Kim Sŭngmi. "Chaepo, Chaeki, and *chokpal*; it all meant we were trash to them."

Sakamoto Mika, whose parents left for North Korea in 1960 and settled in Ch'ŏngjin, explained:

> As a child, I struggled to make friends. I took pride in wearing the clothes that my father's younger brother sent me from Japan. They were much nicer than North Korean clothes, but it also meant that local children could see that I was from Japan. They shouted "*chokpal*" and made fun of my family. . . . Generally, relations between repatriates and the Apache were troubled. Apache envied repatriates because we seemed so rich in comparison to them. The natives had nothing and really struggled, whereas we often had better food and clothes because we got these things from Japan. But our family had good relations with the locals. My mother helped the natives. She shared food and clothes with them and even invited them into our home.

Indeed, not all relations between Apache and Chaepo were hostile, particularly with the generations born in North Korea. Kim Sŏnjun escaped to South Korea from a small town on the North Korean side of the Sino-Korean border. Before he left North Korea he knew a number of families from Japan in his hometown. In school he was friendly with one boy in particular: "There were people from Japan in our town. It wasn't a secret. As a teenager, I had some Chaepo friends. It didn't seem like there was much difference between them and us, except they often had things they'd received from family in Japan, things we couldn't buy in North Korea. I remember once, my friend had a pornographic magazine that had arrived in one of the parcels from Japan. It was American, *Playboy* or *Penthouse*. That's something I'll never forget."

The second and third generations born to repatriate families did not always experience the same difficulties in relating to the host society as the first generation. Those born in North Korea had never known any alternative to the DPRK, and often their parents had impressed on them the importance of cultivating a separate inside and outside personality. Ko Hyerim was born in North Korea. Her father's family had emigrated from Fukuoka and her mother's family from Osaka in the early days of the repatriations. Over coffee in a Tokyo café, she explained her experiences in the North Korean education system:

> In high school we learnt that Japan is the enemy, and that they'd invaded and taken our country. Teachers told us that the Japanese are like animals, that they don't have any regard for human life, and that the Japanese police are evil. I learned this in school and then I'd go home and talk with my parents

Becoming a Foreigner in North Korea | 95

about it. My mother had never had bad experiences in Osaka. She told me that Japanese people are kind, and that life was better in Japan. But my father had little good to say about Japan; this was because he'd suffered racism prior to leaving for North Korea. Both my parents warned me that none of what we talked about at home should be discussed outside the house. In public we couldn't say what we thought, only inside the house.

Although Hyerim grew up in North Korea, she recalled the sense of frustration she often felt with the continuous cycle of political education:

> There are so many rules [in North Korea] and I could never adjust. Every week we had self-criticism sessions and struggle sessions.[17] I always found it so stressful. [After finishing high school] I went to film school, but we spent an unbelievable amount of time just reading about the Kims. When we weren't doing that, we had to practice our dance moves for the mass games. This was all instead of actually learning about plays and films. The government enforced group meetings were meant to promote unity, 'one mind,' but I couldn't see the point. I hated being told what to do and never felt like I fitted in North Korea.

Kin Work and North Korea's Economy

As encompassing as it seemed, Pyongyang's attempted transformation of repatriates–the exorcism of their Japanese past–was undermined by its reliance on goods and capital from Japan. Prior to the 1970s, aside from the repatriation project there had been little movement of goods or people between Japan and North Korea. Between 1963 and 1971, for example, the Japanese government granted only twenty-four Zainichi Koreans reentry permits allowing them to visit family in North Korea and return to Japan (Morris-Suzuki 2009, 9). This changed after 1979 when Tokyo eased restrictions on movement following Japan's signing of both the International Covenant on International Human Rights and the UN Refugee Convention. From this point on, Zainichi Koreans had both transport and permission to travel to and from North Korea to see family.[18]

The 1980s were subsequently a high point for some repatriates. Those with family in Japan enjoyed the advantages of a booming Japanese economy and an opening of informal trade between the two countries. It was not uncommon during this time to see the docks of Niigata cluttered with cars, motorbikes, refrigerators, and other items that had not found space on the ferry. Once such items arrived in North Korea, they were gifted to high-ranking cadres or sold to Korean-Chinese traders. Other times, entrepreneurial repatriates used imported goods for private enterprise. Japanese cars, for example, might be offered for hire or sold to North Koreans. Informal taxi services became a way for a few repatriates to make a living, although finding spare parts for ageing vehicles could be difficult.

The North Korean state recognized that repatriated Koreans had a distinct economic value and put enormous pressure on immigrants to extract as much from overseas kin as possible.[19] One the other side of the Sea of Japan/East Sea, in Japan, Ch'ongryŏn raised capital and procured items that contributed to sustaining the struggling North Korean economy and lining the pockets of the party elite. Although migrants from Japan were politically untrustworthy, local North Koreans coveted the products they imported. As a reward for contributing to the economy, the state allocated some repatriates high-status employment or the opportunity to join elite training programs in sports, culture, and medicine.[20] A select few were even able to join the Korean Workers' Party, thereby moving into the inner circles of the ruling elite.

Wealthy and politically connected families had a greater access to goods imported from Japan. Families with connections to the pachinko world, a form of gambling popular in Japan, for example, enjoyed regular economic remittances, sent by those who had stayed behind. But for the majority of repatriate families, those without political or economic capital, relationships to family in Japan were maintained by the work of women. Micaela di Leonardo argues that understanding kin work requires fusing domestic work and labor perspectives to recognize that maintaining broad kinship networks is also a socially necessary and economically pertinent form of labor. Kin work, and its role in the maintenance of kinship systems, can act as "vehicles for actual survival and/or political resistance" (di Leonardo 1987, 441), and neither legal nor political borders limit the significance of this work. The long-distance kin work of families divided by the repatriation project was gendered because Korean families regarded communicating with family in Japan as women's work, alongside other life-nurturing duties that fused activities inside and outside the home.[21] Existing outside the structures of state-level diplomatic relations, kin-based long-distance exchange was permitted to continue in spite of trade sanctions.[22]

Even in ordinary times, an emotional longing for loved ones left behind is enough of an impetus to encourage immigrants to foster long-distance relationships. These circumstances are magnified during times of crisis, for example when the support of family and friends in the homeland is required as a means of support. Such transnational practices include making phone calls, sending letters and packages, exchanging text messages and emails, and using web technology to establish a feeling of copresence (Baldassar 2008, 256). Repatriated families, however, had limited options at the time of their resettlement in North Korea. Families living in urban areas could send and receive mail, including parcels, and make telephone calls from workplaces or local calling centers, but the state attempted to monitor correspondence and often censored letters, and packages sometimes arrived missing items. State control, however, was always partial, undermined by officials' susceptibility to bribes and the government's inability to oversee all communication between citizens and outsiders. Those wishing to communicate without arousing the state's interest had to do so clandestinely. This might mean waiting for family to visit from Japan and orchestrating a moment out of the earshot of government minders. But, for most repatriates, reunions were infrequent, largely due to the difficulty and expense of traveling to meet family in North Korea.[23] Consequently, letters and parcels took on a heightened significance as a lifeline for families divided between Japan and North Korea.

Since the 1990s Zainichi Korean film director Yang Yŏnghŭi has made multiple visits to her family in Pyongyang, each time crossing the sea with armloads of gifts. Her three older brothers migrated to North Korea in 1971, leaving Yŏnghŭi and her parents in Osaka. Her mother regularly speaks with her sons by telephone and sends packages of food, clothes, and other supplies.[24] Once a parcel arrives in Pyongyang, the post office calls the registered recipients, and they go to pick it up. Recipients are required to open the package in front of postal officials, who check for illicit materials. Speaking to me in Osaka, Yŏnghŭi explained that her mother also sends money via the local post office in Tsuruhashi. "The process costs 10 percent of the money sent. In the early days, sending things this way wasn't reliable. The boxes would arrive with things missing. But it's gradually improved," she assured me.[25]

Letters and parcels, exchanged largely by women in North Korea and Japan, have been the primary means of communication for divided families such as Yŏnghŭi's. For families who were able to maintain them, letter writing and phone calls—the technologies of long-distance kin work—fostered a copresence with family in Japan, reminding those who had stayed behind of their obligation to needy kin in North Korea. In exchange, money, books, stationery, clothes, and luxury goods provided repatriates with items for personal use and trade.[26] Yujin remembered that when he was ten years old his father purchased a Seiko watch from a repatriate at a discounted rate. "It was the most expensive thing in our house," he recalled. "In my town, in North Hamgyŏng province, you could get anything you wanted from Japan, if you had money. Watches, television sets, electronic goods and lots of bicycles came from Japan. They were almost all second hand, but after arriving, they were refurbished and sold to North Koreans. Lots of people I knew had Japanese bicycles, never Chinese, because we thought they were low quality in comparison."

Once in North Korea, repatriate families might trade imported foodstuffs for local products, or distribute them strategically to gain favor with persons in power. Curry-rice flavoring, for example, was popular with both repatriate families and local North Koreans. Versions of Japanese curried dishes followed repatriates to North Korea, packed into the parcels sent by family who stayed in Japan. Curried foods were not the only cuisine to journey across the Sea of Japan/East Sea. Ramen and udon noodles were also a common item unloaded from the ferry. Japanese food products proved particularly useful, in terms of both their symbolic value for trading with local North Koreans, and for repatriate families as multisensory reminders of life before North Korea. One unintended effect of the goods exchanged between Japan and North Korea was that they contributed to cultivating, within repatriated families, favorable associations to Japan. Japanese food, foreign music records, and eye-catching clothes had an exotic allure. Furthermore, the quality of the products, as Yujin noted, was noticeably higher than North Korean– or Chinese-made goods. These items helped foster a positive image of Japan for the generations born to repatriates in North Korea.

Repatriates' letters also connected families across time and space.[27] A feeling of barely maintained restraint permeates some seventy such letters that I was permitted to read. Most were written in Korean, interspersed with the occasional Japanese and Chinese characters. Several themes recur throughout: death, the weather, and health concerns. Many included requests for financial support for medical expenses, weddings, funerals, and ancestor worship ceremonies. Almost all asked for items of economic value in North Korea, things like Japanese watches, nylon neckerchiefs, and soccer boots. Throughout the letters, repatriated women request very specific amounts of money, promising to meet again someday and repay all that had been taken. "My husband is dying," one woman pleads, before requesting Japanese yen from her kin. "I cry every day at the thought of losing him. We sold everything we own to pay for his treatment." Another such letter, from 1972, reads, "In July of this year, I suffered from many diseases. The rheumatism in my joints became serious. I felt severe pain in my hands and feet, enough that I wanted to cut them off. Please send me some medicine. I must survive until my son finishes school. If you cannot do that, at least write and encourage me."[28]

Long-Distance Survival

Among the tens of thousands of Koreans who migrated to the DPRK were several thousand Japanese women who followed their husbands. Their voices, although silenced in North Korea, would become prominent among a steady stream of letters sent to Japan speaking of the dire conditions in their new home. The Association for Human Rights of Japanese Wives of North Korean Repatriates, a Tokyo-based nongovernmental organization, collected correspondence sent from Japanese women to family in the homeland. The association used the letters as evidence of human rights violations in the DPRK. One particular bundle of letters collected and forwarded to the ICRC included two messages composed by the same woman, the first on 6 October 1960 and the second on 4 May 1972. In the letter dated prior to her emigration, the author, a Japanese woman who traveled to North Korea with her Zainichi Korean husband, writes that North Korean officials had promised Japanese wives they would be especially well looked after. As further assurance, Japanese making the trip were informed they would be permitted to visit Japan. In her second message, sent from North Korea, she pleads with her correspondents:

> My brother and sister, why should I live such an unhappy life? If I had no children, I might have already passed away like my husband. But I am a mother, and I am working hard for my children. I have been waiting for your letter since last autumn. . . . My brother and sister, please listen to my last request. I am very sad to tell you that you couldn't believe me even if I tried to tell you the truth. Oh. Oh! I really want to see you. If I had wings like a bird, I would fly across the sea.[29]

Such emotionally heavy correspondence alerted anxious family of the conditions in North Korea while underlining the limitations of state censorship. Throughout the late 1960s and early 1970s, Ikeda Fumiko, a representative of the association, translated the letters into English and included them with petitions from worried families as evidence of Japanese wives living in "miserable conditions, without freedom and in want of food and clothing."[30] Ikeda pleaded with the UN and the ICRC to carry out a fact-finding mission in North Korea and to demand free movement for Japanese wives.

Repatriates sent letters narrating their hardships over many years. But even the strongest of kinship ties strained under decades of pleas for help. The ongoing emotional and financial burden caused some family in Japan to sever contact with repatriated loved ones. Even after family in Japan ceased replying to their letters, it seems that many women in North Korea continued to write, hoping their voices would somehow reach the intended recipients.

Behind closed doors, in intimate spaces, repatriates embarked on a divergent kind of identity making. In their homes, families nurtured their own particular self-understanding in which long-distance relationships featured as a central aspect of what it now meant to belong. Such a reimagining of the self emerged through repatriates' relationships to kin and friends in localities throughout Japan, a country in which they had also been foreigners. "We'd get together with other repatriates, eat Japanese food and speak Japanese, talking about the life we'd left behind. We had to be careful, though, because if any of the natives heard us, we'd be reported and punished," Michŏng told me, making a gesture to demonstrate her wrists being bound together. During social gatherings, repatriates defied the state's insistence that they rid themselves of their Japanese cultural markers, instead surreptitiously drawing on Japanese cultural practices to foster a sense of solidarity with other immigrants from Japan.

As such, repatriates' home life became a space of knowledge regarding Zainichi Korean life in Japan. Following traditional child-rearing practices, children in North Korea were often raised under the watchful eye of grandparents. Most frequently, it was the grandmother's duty to supervise the household and its inhabitants while one or both parents were at work. The elderly thus became instrumental in nurturing group cohesion and maintaining emotional connections to the past. With mother and father working in a state factory or on a collective farm, returnees I spoke with recalled that it was usually grandmother who cooked for the family and disciplined the children. Many repatriates used imported ingredients and prepared food in the style they had learned in Japan. While cooking and in times of celebration, grandparents sang Japanese songs and retold folktales from southern Korea and Japan to their grandchildren. Pak Okcha recalled that her parents and grandparents sang Japanese songs to help her fall asleep. "And when there was a power shortage, which was often, my father got his guitar and we all sang together. I didn't always understand the meaning of the songs, but the sound was beautiful." In their homes, during gatherings with other repatriates, and with close family over meals, Japanese language became both a marker of their separate identity and a symbolic act of defiance. They used Japanese in private with other Zainichi Koreans while doing business, singing songs, recounting stories, and reminiscing about Japan. Hyerim explained, "My friends and I often mixed Korean and Japanese when we wanted to speak secretly. This was the case if we wanted to speak about the Kims [the ruling family of North Korea]. We had a way of speaking about political subjects if we thought there was a chance that the natives might overhear us. We'd drop the noun of the sentence and then mix Japanese and Korean. For example, 'Kim Jong-il' would become Musuko ['son' in Japanese] and we could say, 'Musuko is terrible.'"

Similarly, Kim Mi recalled, "Growing up in North Korea, I heard a lot about Japan. My parents and grandparents often spoke about how warm it is, how good and plentiful the food is, and how much they missed it there. They'd say, 'In Japan, you can do whatever you want. If you work hard, you can have whatever you desire.' Because my parents talked about life in Japan, I was curious about it and thought that one day, in the future, I'd go there."

Repatriates' homelife conveyed memories of a time and place outside of the towns and villages they had resettled in North Korea. Elderly repatriates who yearned for life in Japan passed on memories inflected with regret for leaving and nostalgia for the past to their grandchildren. Kim Mi's final comment hints at how these memories acted like a bridge, stirring desire and connecting the new generations to a life they had not themselves lived, yet to which they felt an intense pull. The DPRK state had represented North Korea to Koreans in Japan as heaven on earth. Over time, heaven on earth shifted in the minds of Zainichi Koreans from symbolizing North Korea to representing Korean community life in Japan.

The frictions that emerged between immigrant families and North Korean society compelled repatriates to adopt strategies of identity management that would protect them from state persecution. Individuals who had once identified with the DPRK's ethnic nationalism developed translocal identifications to kin and community in Japan.

Repatriates' long-distance relationships presented a means to survive the sporadic food shortages that characterized life outside the urban centers of North Korea. These long-distance kin relations were largely sustained by the work of women on both sides of the Sea of Japan/East Sea. Through letter writing, songs, stories, and socializing with others from Japan, repatriates fostered a different kind of belonging, one that resisted the DPRK state's efforts to erase their Zainichi Korean characteristics. In building a communal repository of translocal memories from which they could draw when in each other's company, repatriates shaped alternative identifications to those propagated by the state. But transnational kinship networks also reinforced their outsider status. Being Korean and being loyal to Kim Il-sung's North Korea, two aspects of an identity that had previously been conceived of as inseparable, started to unravel. Within the private sphere, it was now considered possible to be Korean while longing for a time and place outside of the Korean Peninsula.

Repatriates' translocal identification with the sights, sounds, and smells of Korean communities in Japan connected them to friends, family, and communities in Osaka, Tokyo, Kobe, and beyond. Many families had gone to North Korea with hopes that it would provide them with opportunities that had eluded them as former subjects of the Empire of Japan. But in North Korea the host society regarded Zainichi Koreans as little different from Japanese. The reality of life at the bottom of the DPRK's sociopolitical hierarchy further encouraged a shift in how repatriates identified with both the host society and with the communities they had left behind.

In escaping North Korea and emigrating to Japan, returnees are again required to renegotiate their ethnic and political selves, this time in the face of Japanese prejudice toward North Koreans. Many now ask similar questions to the ones their parents and grandparents asked after seeing the welcoming parties on the docks of Ch'ŏngjin for the first time: "Who are you? Who am I? Is this home?" In the following chapters, we answer the question of why people like Kim Mi, Ko Hyerim, and Chang Michŏng chose to return to Japan and how memories of multiple homes continue to shape their feelings of belonging.

Notes

A version of this chapter was first published as (2018) "Patriotic Revolutionaries and Imperial Sympathizers: Identity and Selfhood of Korean-Japanese Migrants from Japan to North Korea." *Cross-Currents: East Asian History and Culture Review* (e-journal) 27: 1–25.

1. JRC's guidebook instructs the prospective repatriate: "In this Center you will stay three nights and four days" (JRC 1959, 4).
2. Repatriates were not restricted on the amount of luggage they could take with them, but had to pay freight costs on anything over sixty kilograms of luggage (JRC 1959, 3).
3. ICRC records on the first fifty-one ships to leave Japan to North Korea (up until 16 December 1960) lists the range of occupations of the 12,021 adult males on board: 2,800 were classified as day laborers, 1,016 as factory workers, 469 as chauffeurs, 432 as farmers/fishers, 424 as clerks, 731 as workers in commerce and industry, and 4,476 as nonoccupation (B AG 232 105-019.01 "Monthly reports on the repatriation to North Korea, by the Immigration Bureau," Ministry of Justice, 18/03/1960-31/12/1960).
4. B AG 232 105-035. "Letter from DPRK Red Cross to the ICRC." 30 March 1965.
5. One interviewee and former member of Ch'ongryŏn told me that on Kim Il-sung's birthday the organization repatriated a group of young Zainichi Koreans as a gift to the leader, Kim Il-sung.
6. For a thorough treatment of the anthropology of emotions, see Leavitt (1996).
7. Chaepo is a contraction of the term "Chae'il tongp'o," meaning "Korean compatriot from Japan." It is another common term local North Koreans used to refer to repatriates.
8. *Sŏngbun* refers to the sociopolitical classification of citizens in North Korean society.
9. Yujin used the expression "Gam-jŏng nŭkkim" to refer to this feeling code.
10. According to the monthly reports by the Immigration Control Bureau of the Justice Ministry of Japan that recorded applications, detainees, and successful repatriates to North Korea, 189 individuals (166 Koreans and 23 Japanese) left for North Korea on board ship number 121 in December 1964. In total, by the end of 1964, 82,665 people had emigrated to the DPRK, constituting 88.6 percent of the total 93,340 who went to North Korea before the repatriation project was officially discontinued in 1984 (B AG 232 105-019.01, "Monthly reports on the repatriation to North Korea," 31/03/1961-31/12/1964, p. 5).
11. Robert Collins explains that this system, known as the *Ch'ulsin-sŏngbun* system, resembles the former apartheid race-based classification system of South Africa, since it divides the population into ranks of trustworthiness and loyalty to the state and Kim family. Individuals who can trace their family to revolutionary fighters or former poor peasants comprise the friendly class category and make up around 25 percent of the population; the wavering class comprises a further 55 percent; former landholders, pro-Americans or pro-Japanese, and Zainichi Koreans who arrived during the repatriations are included in the hostile class and comprise the remaining 20 percent of the population (Collins 2012, iii).

12. According to one interviewee, during Saturday political education sessions, participants learn about anti–United States social movements. Sunday is supposed to be a day of rest, but party members organize social mobilization political activities on farms and construction sites.
13. State agents monitor citizens suspected of having divided loyalties.
14. Morris-Suzuki notes that repatriates from Japan were disproportionately represented among the victims of the North Korean political purges. Large numbers of repatriates were sent to Yodŏk prison camp (Morris-Suzuki 2007, 239).
15. A report submitted by the JRC lists the following cargo on board ship number 108 to leave Niigata for North Korea in July 1963: 244 tons of baggage; 4 vehicles (2 small-sized cars, 1 light van, 1 Nissan Cedric, all used); 124 bicycles; 31 refrigerators; 42 washing machines; 12 stereos; 14 television sets; 83 electric lighting fixtures (B AG 105-030.01 "Monthly reports on the repatriation to North Korea," 31/03/1961-31/12/1964, p. 5).
16. The strap on Japanese traditional wooden sandals divides the big toe from the second toe, similar in appearance to the hooves of a pig. This is not only an insult used in North Korea, but is also used in South Korea to refer to Japanese or ostensibly Japanized individuals.
17. This is ideological training that North Koreans are required to join.
18. Sonia Ryang notes that from 1979 and 1994 a yearly average of almost four thousand Koreans left Japan to visit North Korea and that most of these were delegations from Ch'ongryŏn's Korean schools in Japan (Ryang 2000b, 40).
19. Nam Keun Woo (Nam 2012) describes the North Korean economy at this time as a "hostage economy," focused on extracting capital and goods through people with family in Japan.
20. During my research I met North Koreans who had represented the DPRK in a variety of sports including ice hockey, soccer, and baseball.
21. Di Leonardo makes this point explicit, saying that kin work is similar to housework and child care, and "men in the aggregate do not do it" (di Leonardo 1987, 443).
22. For more on the informal politics of exchange between families in North Korea and Japan, see Bell (2021).
23. Interlocutors told me that it could take up to five days to get from Niigata port to the home of family in North Korea. This included up to three days crossing the Sea of Japan/East Sea and one to two days of train travel within North Korea.
24. Over the years, her mother also sent items such as stationery, warm clothes, hand warmers, instant noodles, and money to family friends.
25. Interview with Yang Yŏnghŭi, July 2014. See Yang's documentary films (Yang 2005, 2009) for a detailed and touching exposition of the lives of families divided between Japan and North Korea.
26. A report by the Immigration Control Bureau of the Ministry of Justice of Japan lists the following items on board ship number 121 to leave for North Korea in December 1964: 160 bottles of ginseng wine, 47 kilograms (103.6 pounds) of dried sea cucumbers, 100 kilograms (220.5 pounds) of eggs, 26 cases of sugar, 338 cases of cigarettes, 7 cigarette cases, 26 cases of candies, and 29 cans of canned fish (B AG 232 105 030.01, "Monthly reports on the repatriation to North Korea," 31/03/1961-31/12/1964, p. 6).

27. Through an interlocutor in Osaka, I gained access to a cache of letters written between 1981 and 2014, sent from Ch'ŏngjin and Pyongyang to family in Japan. I located many more such letters, written in the 1960s–to 1970s, in the ICRC archives.

28. B AG 232 105-046. "Pétition mise en place par Mme Fumiko Ikeda, représentante de 'The Association for Human Rights of Japanese Wives of North Korean Repatriates,' pour l'organisation d'une mission d'enquéte en Corée du Nord et pour la libre circulation au Japon des éspouses Japonaises de rapatriés Nord Coréens: Correspondance." 21/06/1974-13/01/1975, "Miserable Daily Life in North Korea," number 1.

29. B AG 232 105-046. "Pétition mise en place par Mme Fumiko Ikeda, représentante de 'The Association for Human Rights of Japanese Wives of North Korean Repatriates,' pour l'organisation d'une mission d'enquéte en Corée du Nord et pour la libre circulation au Japon des éspouses Japonaises de rapatriés Nord Coréens: Correspondance." 21/06/1974-13/01/1975, "North Korea: The False Promise," number 2.

30. B AG 232 105-046. "Pétition mise en place par Mme Fumiko Ikeda, représentante de 'The Association for Human Rights of Japanese Wives of North Korean Repatriates,' pour l'organisation d'une mission d'enquéte en Corée du Nord et pour la libre circulation au Japon des éspouses Japonaises de rapatriés Nord Coréens: Correspondance." 21/06/1974-13/01/1975, "Miserable Daily Life in North Korea," number 1.

4

Choosing Japan

The biggest change I feel since coming to Japan is in human relations: the Japanese are so, so different. The Cheju grandmothers with whom I work [in Osaka] are warm and friendly, but these kinds of relationships don't exist with Japanese people. Japanese are cold and distant.
                              –Paek Kyŏngcha, born in North Korea, left in 2007

From my apartment overlooking Koreatown I observed the comings and goings of the Tsuruhashi residents. Over the months, I became a feature of Koreatown's eclectic scenery, sharing drinks with local handymen, invited to parties at the nearby language school, and commented on by curious Japanese tourists. Around eight o'clock each morning greetings in Korean floated up to my fourth-floor balcony as children on their way to school hailed the women charged with helping them across the road. In a quaint act of good manners, each child removed their yellow sun hat and performed a sweeping bow to the crosswalk supervisors, never breaking stride. In the evenings, rats emerged to scuttle along overhanging electricity cables, and mothers ferrying their children on the backs of bicycles weaved their way between the last remaining tourists of the day. It seemed as though the rhythms of a Koreatown day varied only according to the weather and the events happening in the nearby Miyukimoridai Park.

Many returnees in Osaka find work in warehouses, in factories, restaurant kitchens or in fresh food stalls on the main street of Koreatown. From the first time I met Paek Kyŏngcha outside one of Koreatown's fruit and vegetable stores, she insisted on slipping me apples, pears, and bananas from her stall. "It's fine, it's fine," she smiled, dismissing my concerns. "I'm allowed to give some away." In her early thirties when we met in 2014, Kyŏngcha had arrived in Japan in the late-2000s. In North Korea she had also worked in a market until the breakdown of her marriage and her family's increasing poverty propelled her across the border into China. Once in China, Kyŏngcha paid a people smuggler to take her to the Japanese consulate-general in Shenyang. She recalled, "I lived in the consulate for two and a half years before I was allowed to come to Japan. My family in North Korea had no idea what had happened to me. I was basically a prisoner. I had to stay indoors all the time while I waited. I spent my days staring out the window, just watching the guards. Eventually, the consulate employees located my aunt in Japan. I was put on a flight to Japan with a consulate employee."

For two and a half years, Kyŏngcha was not allowed outside the consulate grounds for fear that her arrest would spark a diplomatic incident between Japan and China.[1] As such, she spent her days living on takeout food and watching Japanese television shows, taking notes, and repeating unfamiliar phrases in preparation for her anticipated departure.

When she eventually arrived in Japan, Kyŏngcha struggled to find accommodation and employment. Although she had an aunt in Osaka, the relationship was distant and Kyŏngcha was reluctant to place a strain on her aunt's already stretched resources. Luckily for Kyŏngcha, Japanese activist Kawashima Akio encouraged her to start studying in Akiyama Ayako's language school. Shortly thereafter, a South Korean classmate introduced her to a Zainichi Korean businessman importing and selling fruit and vegetables. Kyŏngcha started work in the company's Tsuruhashi stall, alongside two elderly women. Her new work colleagues had immigrated from Cheju Island in the mid-1940s, entering Japan by fishing boat. Newly arrived, Kyŏngcha had no money and few connections, so the owner of the company allowed her to sleep on the floor of the distribution warehouse, also in Koreatown. In this way, working most of her waking hours and with few expenses, she saved enough money to rent an apartment near the fruit stall, on the main street of Koreatown.

Six days a week Kyŏngcha slipped on a red apron and elbow-length white rubber gloves and weighed out the produce for customers. In her own words, she was "always tired." Over dinner in a Tsuruhashi barbeque restaurant she reflected on her experiences in Japan. "When I first arrived, I didn't speak any Japanese, so I learnt everything I could from Akiyama sensei.[2] But, because I needed money so desperately, I had to stop studying so I could work full time. These days I work every day in Tsuruhashi, from 6:30 a.m. to 6:00 p.m. I eat my meals in the shop as well." Migration can be a freeing experience for some, offering a chance to reinvent oneself, while for others, especially refugees, it channels people into low-status, low-paid employment. The successful resettlement of refugees and displaced people often depend on their resilience and ability to exploit information and resources available in the host society. Kyŏngcha struggled to feel an affinity with Japanese people, as we heard in her opening quote to this chapter, but she had located alternative means for getting by in Japan. Her determination to succeed meant late nights studying Japanese, twelve-hour workdays, and the successful exploitation of her nascent social networks.

Return to Japan presents both opportunities and costs for new arrivals. Opportunities come in the form of freedom from the state scrutiny under which they lived while in North Korea, a chance to accumulate the economic capital required for succeeding in a consumer capitalist economy, and the possibility of renegotiating traditional gender relationships. The flip side to newfound freedoms is that they also present chances to fail, to live alone, to be exploited, and to toil for minimum wage. Why then, do individuals from North Korea choose Japan and not, for example, South Korea, where they would receive state benefits, and where shared linguistic and cultural practices ostensibly present a smoother path to resettlement? In this chapter, I show how both a real and, in some cases, an imagined familiarity with Japan contributes to returnees' migration strategies. Returnees' decision-making and migratory paths are part of a strategy in which emotional drivers direct people like Kyŏngcha back to Japan. Once in their new home, the dynamics of their successes and failures are shaped by echoes of life in North Korea, the opportunities that arise for cultivating social relationships, and distinctly gendered approaches to pursuing upward socioeconomic mobility—or succumbing to life on the margins.

Migration and the associated changes that occur in gender and labor relations both constrain and empower women, men, and the elderly in different ways. But the changes that transpire through migration and resettlement are unlikely to be a simple shift from unequal to equal gender relations. Rather, they represent instead a struggle over power, resources, and labor (Espiritu 2003, chap. 6; Levitt 2001, 106; Smith 2006, chap. 5). Within some families, migration offers opportunities to renegotiate patriarchal practices and to reshape the gender roles of the sending country. For others, the labor arrangements that emerge in the host country have the opposite effect, reinforcing traditional gendered practices.

In her ethnography of refugee families settling in the United States, anthropologist Nazli Kibria observed that Vietnamese couples experienced a shift in the balance of power due to changes in men's and women's relative degree of access to and control over social and economic resources (Kibria 1993, 108–44). Her male interlocutors, for instance, experienced largely unanticipated challenges to their power once in the United States, further aggravating feelings of loss and displacement. Similarly, changes in the gendered balance of power were a source of tension between men and women returning to Japan. Women gained new access to resources through their ability to successfully cultivate social networks, in addition to their willingness to accept financial support wherever it might be offered. In contrast, men appeared especially vulnerable to downward mobility, feelings of failure, and a resultant loss of status within the family. Men were often less willing to ask for help from Japanese civic groups, as they were unable to live with the loss of pride they associated with receiving such support. Consequently, they received less help and took fewer opportunities. Migration impoverished returnee men, both socially and economically, much more severely than it did returnee women.

This chapter examines how returnees' resettlement in Japan is directly influenced by the changes to labor and gender relations that took place in North Korea following the end of the Cold War. How have exiles from the DPRK been affected by the country's social and political fractures in the places they resettle? The ways in which returnee men and women respond to the demands of starting over in Japan's capitalist economy is directly influenced by their experience of the North Korean famine, and, specifically, the informal marketization of the North Korean economy and rise of the female capitalist that emerged as a result.

Echoes of the Arduous March

Following the 1991 dissolution of the Soviet Union, the DPRK's primary benefactor, North Korea experienced a series of calamities that devastated both economy and population. Pyongyang was not sufficiently prepared to manage either the fallout from the withdrawal of Soviet economic support nor the environmental crises that devastated food production in 1995 and 1996 (Haggard and Noland 2007, 33–35). As the state-coordinated rationing system ground to a halt, food shortages emerged across the country. The North Korean economy subsequently contracted by approximately 30 percent between 1991 and 1996 (Lee and Pollack 1999, xi).

Pyongyang was slow to respond to the humanitarian crisis. Even with aid from the international community, food shortages grew into a famine that led to the deaths of an estimated 3 to 5 percent of the precrisis population (Haggard and Noland 2011, 120). Without access to the resources required to live, hundreds of thousands of North Koreans were forced to leave for China in search of food and economic support. They carried with them news of widespread hunger and desperation (Robinson 2010; Schwekendiek 2009). The nationwide economic crisis and the resultant famine tore at the fabric of families and communities. This critical juncture would also have a dramatic impact on societal norms across the country.

Pyongyang had been especially efficient, among communist bloc members, in eliminating private commercial activities. The government achieved such successes by imposing obstacles to economic enterprise, including regulations on the size of private gardens, restrictions on unauthorized travel within the country, and a comprehensive rationing system (Lankov and Kim 2008, 55). In the years following the Korean War, the government extended the rationing system, so that by the 1970s almost all food and an increasing amount of consumer goods were state controlled. A person's occupation and age determined how much they received, with the elderly, children, and disabled people at the bottom of a hierarchy headed by high-ranking government officials (Haggard and Noland 2007, 53–54).[3] When the state rationing system broke down, subsequent attempts to apportion resources reflected the same political, age, and geographical determinants. As with other forms of crisis—war, economic depression, pandemic—the effects of the famine were mapped onto existing socioeconomic inequalities.

All North Koreans experienced, to various extents, the hardships of the famine. A number of my North Korean interlocutors in South Korea and Japan recalled being compelled by hunger to forage for resources. Those desperate enough to try and steal food from state-controlled collective farms risked being shot and killed. Without state support, survival was often determined by who could best navigate the shortages through illicit means. Subsequently, a coping response to the famine came not from the state, but from society, and it emerged in the form of a grassroots market economy in which women played a central role (Haggard and Noland 2005, 2012; Jung and Dalton 2006).

Legally, men and women in North Korea enjoy equal benefits and access to resources. The DPRK state boasts that North Korea is a "women's paradise" (Park 1992–93, 531), with women having been emancipated from the burdens of housework by the technological advancements of Kim Il-sung's revolutionary achievements. But the reality is that North Korean gender roles and the gendered distribution of resources are still rigidly imposed through traditional, patriarchal values.[4] Women's status, prior to the 1990s shrinking of the state's command economy, was primarily derived from their role as caregiver in the family—cooking, cleaning, child care—and, secondarily, their employment outside the home. The latter was not supposed to take priority over the former. In the 1980s up to 70 percent of North Korean women ended their participation in the formal workforce after marriage (Jung, Dalton, and Willis 2018). The work of women outside the home was thus regarded as temporary, contingent on family demands, and lower in social status than that of men (Park 2004). Although dismissed as peripheral, North Korean women's earning power has played an important function as a kind of economic backstop to their male counterparts' primary breadwinning status. Women's employment was not intended to usurp the man's role as primary earner. Rather, it was a useful stopgap during national labor shortages. Consequently, North Korean women have been doubly burdened by low status productive responsibilities in the workplace and unremunerated reproductive duties in the household (Ryang 2000a, 325–26).

As the national food crisis deepened, ordinary North Koreans' responses to the withering of state support were subsequently shaped by gendered expectations of the labor roles of men and women. Men often retained their state employment as a means of both fulfilling their nominal breadwinner role and for accessing residual social services provided by state work units (Haggard and Noland 2012, 5). In contrast, many women left financially unrewarding, low-status state employment to pursue emergent market opportunities.

The Rise of the Female Capitalist

Gender roles in the DPRK shifted during the famine years. Prior to the economic crisis, North Korean men worked outside the home, accumulating social capital through their modest earning power and their proximity to state institutions. The majority of commercial production in North Korea is state owned, and workplaces throughout the country are a highly politicized site of party messaging. Party ideology frames hard work and sacrifice as honorable activities through which ordinary citizens can achieve heroic status. From the lowest factory worker to the highest levels of government every citizen has had a role to play in exceeding production goals and creating the surplus needed for industrial growth (see Kim 2018). The North Korean state thus maximizes productive labor by glorifying in particular the man's role in the political community, as proletarian nation builder, Labor Hero, and head of the family.

The economic collapse stripped ordinary workers of their earning power, but the state demanded that people continue to work. North Korean men were compelled to attend the workplace, whether there was work to be done or not. By leaving the house each morning for the collective farm, factory, hospital, or company offices, men held on to their positions of symbolic importance. Their reward was not an income that could be spent in the markets. Instead, men's proximity to the workings of the state provided them with social capital to prop up their position in the patriarchal order. North Korean men's socioeconomic standing was emptied of the modest financial and material benefits that were once accorded positions in state-operated enterprises, and were undermined by the impossibility of fulfilling a breadwinning status in the family. Recalling the gendered shift in labor roles during the famine, one of anthropologist Sandra Fahy's respondents joked that North Korean men were "like daytime light bulbs," essentially useless (Fahy 2015, 149). Men became virtual figureheads in a gutted economy. Despite this, they held onto their positions of symbolic power in North Korean society, even while women assumed more-direct roles in the family's economic survival.

Even as the command economy retreated, the parameters of masculinity—a man's obligations with regard to work and society—remained rigid. In contrast, the range of invisible, low-status work that many women had previously performed to subsidize state provisions, such as brewing rice wine or making rice snacks for sale, moved outside the home and into market-places. The markets that sprang up across the country consisted primar-ily of farmers' markets, roadside stalls, and black and gray (semi-official) markets (Smith 2015, 2; Tudor and Pearson 2015, 25). The North Korean women with whom I worked in South Korea and Japan felt that they had no choice but to work in these unofficial markets or to trade across the Sino-Korean border if they were to feed themselves and their family. As the fam-ine deepened, women's informal work became the difference between life and death for many families, but without the attendant social recognition of their increasingly vital status.

It was primarily young mothers who bore the brunt of work in the domestic sphere, while they were also expected to provide for the family through market participation.[5] Informal markets became the primary source of income for many North Korean families, with women making drastically more money through trade and barter than ordinary workers earned in par-alyzed state enterprises (Park 2010, 105).[6] Interviewees told me that women working in informal commercial spaces in the 1990s–2000s largely traded for foreign currency. Specifically, Chinese RMB and US dollars have been the preferred currency of exchange. Traders sold a range of cooked and raw food, as well as basic household items and medicines. Kyŏngcha confirmed this:

> When I was younger, I had dreams of becoming a professional baseball player, but then the Arduous March [the famine] happened and I needed to make money to help my family. So, I started working at a small stall in my town, not too different to what I'm doing now. I'd sell anything I could–clothes, food, CDs, whatever there was. A lot of it was smuggled in from China and we sold it at the market. As things got harder [and my family came to rely solely on my income], I brought in my younger sister, Yumi, to work with me.

Some repatriates relied on family in Japan to send them items for con-sumption or trade. But many, such as Kyŏngcha and Yumi, had lost contact with family and instead sought an income elsewhere. Such demands meant putting aside aspirations for careers or education, and instead entering into private commerce at a high personal risk. As the North Korean economy re-configured from a planned state economy to a hybrid economy with a mod-icum of private commerce, North Korean women carved for themselves a space in the changing socioeconomic landscape, gravitating toward mar-ket-oriented employment. Although commercial enterprise in North Korea has commonly been regarded as ethically suspect work (Lankov and Kim 2008, 57), the role of women in the shadow economy has been vital for the survival of both ordinary citizens and the state.

The rise of the female capitalist provoked further social changes in North Korean society. Women's increasing economic power is eroding a patriarchal culture in which the ideal woman is a stay-at-home wife. Divorce is on the rise, and daughters are favored over sons for their earning potential in the markets (Jung, Dalton, and Willis 2018, 24). But whether participation in North Korea's emergent grassroots economy offers broader freedoms for women remains to be seen. Although such newfound freedoms have not translated into increased economic, social, or political status, women's informal economic activities mean that they travel, assemble in groups, and learn how to negotiate with state and non-state actors. In short, women have gained skills and practices that have translated into "increased flexibility in personal decision making and diminished state control of family life" (Smith 2015, 229).

But greater freedoms and a breadwinning role in the family also made female entrepreneurs vulnerable to state reprisals. With women providing the family with resources that the government could not, their participation in the black markets created a tension with party cadres. Such a strained relationship is evidenced by recurrent state crackdowns on markets and traders (see Park 2011, 172). Provincial and local cadres, often the same people listlessly occupying decaying state enterprises, tolerated women's involvement in the marketization of the economy insofar as it could be dismissed as temporary, informal, peripheral, and a feminized appendage to the role of the man and, by extension, the state. Once the economy started to recover from the meltdown of the 1990s, the government responded to the growing importance of feminized commercial spaces by trying to shut them down and punish women working in the stalls. Haggard and Noland understand the regime's attitude toward market activities as shifting between a mild to severe hostility: "Oscillating between grudging tolerance during periods of severe shortage and harsh crackdowns during periods when it seeks to reconstitute the state sector" (Haggard and Noland 2012, 11). Whatever the case may be, the country's grassroots markets had become too important, both in the lives of ordinary North Koreans and as a means of supporting the state apparatus when it was on the brink of collapse. Subsequently, black markets continue to exist in an uneasy relationship with the government.

The reimagining of women's work, as extending beyond the home and into marketplaces, has taken on transnational dimensions for women such as Kyŏngcha and Yumi. As with most returnees I spoke with in Japan, Kyŏngcha had not severed her relationships to family in North Korea. On the contrary, she now justified her long, demanding working hours by saying that it ensured that her family in North Korea could live a better life. She sent as much of her pay as she could afford to her family in North Korea. Kyŏngcha told me that her ex-husband uses the benefits of her long-distance kin work to pay for their daughter's education and the rest for everyday necessities. In working twelve-hour days, six and sometimes seven days a week, and by allowing herself few luxuries, Kyŏngcha had managed to save enough to pay back the debts she owed to her aunt. At the same time, she fulfilled her caregiving duties by sending remittances to her daughter, her former partner, and her parents in North Korea. In this sense, Kyŏngcha's ability to support her family was sustainable only as long as she did not return to North Korea, as long as she remained physically absent from her family.

Kyŏngcha was not the only one of my interlocutors to have reconfigured gendered notions of labor in the informal economy. The marketization of the North Korean economy and the role of women in leading the socioeconomic changes therein has, to varying extents, contributed to preparing North Korean men and women for the demands of the Japanese labor market.

Gendered Notions of Labor

Men's social and political advantages in North Korea placed them in positions of power relative to women, despite their inability to earn. But in Japan, these same men find themselves to be supplicants to state officials and to the benevolence of civic organizations managed primarily by Japanese men. Although unable to regain their former status, the ideology of the breadwinning Korean man features prominently in their approach to resettlement, and their efforts to reestablish their traditional role in the family. The experiences of two couples with whom I worked exemplify how returnees respond to the shifting gendered notions of labor that emerge through immigration to and resettlement in Japan.

When Oh Sŏngmin and Yumi arrived in Osaka in early 2014, they both moved in with Kyŏngcha, Yumi's older sister. But three adults sharing a one-room apartment quickly became untenable. "Too many people under the same roof. It's just stressful," Kyŏngcha agonized. The living situation was further strained as Sŏngmin became increasingly unhappy with Yumi's emerging independence. The couple argued heatedly about whether Yumi should be working and studying Japanese. Sŏngmin felt it would be better if she remained at home, preparing meals and keeping house. Making matters worse, Sŏngmin was struggling to find employment. He hesitated to take help from Japanese civic groups and balked at the idea of attending Japanese lessons with a class full of women.

A few weeks after the couple's arrival, Yumi's Japanese teacher, Akiyama Ayako, organized a barbecue party, inviting me along with several South Korean students in addition to Kyŏngcha, Yumi, and Sŏngmin. Over dinner, Sŏngmin announced that he had found a job in a Tsuruhashi kimchi factory. He felt like he was starting to get back on his feet. A South Korean lay monk from the local Buddhist temple was perched on the other side of the sizzling barbecue: "Of course you feel better now that you're working," he opined, in between mouthfuls of marinated pork. "It's the role of the Korean man to work." Sŏngmin nodded in agreement. "I've always worked. When I was younger, I could have gone to college, but we were too poor. So, I worked every night until midnight to make money for my family. This kind of work–long, hard hours–it's always been like that."

The monk's comments linked Korean masculinity to economic ability. Sŏngmin had found it difficult to reconcile his experiences of economic dependence on Kyŏngcha with his picture of what a man should do. He imagined his masculinity through idealized Korean gender roles, specifically by understanding manhood as a fulfilment of the economic imperative to accumulate enough capital that his wife could stay at home and take care of the family. His determination to avoid depending on others–including his wife–and to find any kind of work available meant that he sacrificed opportunities for self-improvement, such as learning Japanese or obtaining a qualification, for immediate pecuniary reward. His understanding of gendered labor roles compelled him to find employment that he believed would provide the basic necessities for himself and Yumi. In doing so, he attempted to reassert his masculinity and his dominant position in his family. But Sŏngmin's conception of masculinity, devoid as it now was of DPRK state legitimacy and shorn of social networks, had less value as an immigrant in Japan.

Kyŏngcha and Yumi had also experienced changes in how they understood their roles in the family. For Yumi in particular, arrival in Japan had opened up a world of possibilities. Her new clothes, her enthusiasm about learning Japanese, and her desire to experience life outside of North Korea reflected her eagerness to explore and capitalize on what lay before her. In North Korea Yumi had felt little choice but to work in the markets, to marry, and to raise children. She had little control over her education, her marriage partner, or her career. But now she looked to the future and saw her new beginnings in Japan as a chance to change her life trajectory. In Japan she could make money, go to school, and, if she desired, go on to higher education–she had even started studying for college with the hope of qualifying as a nurse.

The experiences of another couple I met in Osaka, Minji and Pyŏngchŏl, reveal similar shifts in gendered labor roles through migration to Japan. The Chŏng/Han family's attempts to escape North Korea had not been without a great deal of hardship. In North Korea Chŏng Minji finished high school and studied design at college. Graduating in the mid-1990s, she worked as a tailor before marrying Han Pyŏngchŏl in an arranged marriage. But Pyŏngchŏl, frustrated by the corruption and inequality around him, was determined to get out of North Korea. Feeling that their family had no future in the DPRK, Pyŏngchŏl crossed the border into China in 2007. The plan was to smuggle his wife and son out immediately after. But the plan failed when Minji was arrested and interrogated. With the help of a Japanese activist group with contacts in North Korea, Pyŏngchŏl tried again in 2012. The second attempt succeeded, with Minji and their son traveling for a week through China to Thailand, guided by a family friend.

Once they arrived in Japan, Minji threw herself into studying Japanese. Within a year, she was taking night classes for her Japanese elementary school certificate. Once she passed her exams, she studied for her high school qualifications. During this time, civic group leader Kawashima Akio found her work as a hospital orderly in Yao city, just outside of Osaka. Minji's studies gave her hope that she would find work as a designer, something that she had been unable to do while in North Korea, since her career choices had been determined by the state.

In contrast, Pyŏngchŏl felt the effects of a dramatic downward social mobility in his new home. In North Korea Pyŏngchŏl was part of the country's elite. He had lived in Pyongyang and was employed as a high school teacher. His elevated status had protected Pyŏngchŏl and his family from the worst of the famine. Although he had lived in Japan some five years longer than his wife, he told me that he had been forced, out of economic desperation, to work from the first week of his arrival. He now held two jobs, one as a day laborer and another with an activist group. Both jobs paid poorly, and he lamented his inability to provide for his family. His commitment to earning money meant that he had not had the chance to take language classes, nor did he hold any Japanese educational qualifications. Furthermore, the majority of the jobs he had worked required little to no Japanese language, meaning that, even after ten years in Osaka, Pyŏngchŏl struggled to communicate comfortably in Japanese. Pyŏngchŏl's lack of qualifications and his poor language skills meant his prospects to improve his earning power were limited.

Further complicating matters, since starting Japanese primary school his son had been reluctant to speak Korean at home. Without a common language, Pyŏngchŏl was talking with him less and less. "I speak Korean to him, and he answers in Japanese or some mix of the two languages," he told me. Pyŏngchŏl was trying to remedy this problem by taking his son to taekwondo classes at a church run by South Korean immigrants in downtown Osaka. "But I hate church. I'm North Korean, how can I believe in God? What's the difference between Kim Il-sung and the Christian God?" he asked rhetorically. "I said goodbye to one and now I have to deal with another for the sake of getting my son to speak Korean." His frustration at being unable to communicate with his son added to feelings of isolation and impotence at failing to provide for his family.

Does migration to Japan offer returnee men and women the chance for greater freedoms than they had in North Korea? Certainly, returnees live in Japan comparatively free of fear for their lives and without the stresses associated with state surveillance and insecure access to essential resources. But returnees' experiences in Japan diverge in a number of ways. The women with whom I worked, such as Kyŏngcha and Yumi, pursued a measured strategy to fulfil their immediate economic needs such as renting private accommodation, and purchasing everyday necessities and some luxury items, while gaining skills and qualifications that would open possibilities for upward mobility in the long term. In contrast, Sŏngmin and other returnee men I worked with were constrained by a sense of manhood "bound up by autonomy and activity" (Chamberlain [1997] 2017, 108), limited by a conception of masculinity that hinged on exchanging labor for money. Such a strategy, however, provided immediate gains in exchange for long-term loss: in the short term they were able to accumulate a modest amount of capital and develop basic social networks through their paid employment. In the long term, however, income levels for these men remained low, and were contingent on their ability to develop skills relevant to the Japanese labor market. Furthermore, they were often subject to losses of esteem, since their wives' earnings gradually outstripped their own.

One consequence of the grassroots marketization of North Korea's economy and the associated reconfiguration of the relationship of gender to labor has been how this period differently prepared men and women to survive in Japan's consumer capitalist economy. With few exceptions, returnee men now toiling in factories and warehouses felt that they were no better off, in terms of financial security, social position, and feelings of self-worth, than when they first arrived in Japan. So, why would any anyone fleeing North Korea, man or woman, choose Japan?

"I Chose Japan"

For new arrivals from North Korea, Japan feels both familiar and strange. It presents elements of the known and yet, to most returnees, it is completely alien. Unlike North Koreans who escape to South Korea, returnees to Japan do not receive any kind of financial resettlement package. In the words of a Japanese government official I interviewed in 2014 who wished to remain anonymous, "There are simply no taxes set aside to support these individuals." Tokyo uses taxpayer money to fly returnees to Japan. But they do not travel as refugees–officially Tokyo does not accept any refugees from the DPRK. Instead, according to activists who have spoken to Japanese officials on this topic, the government regards returnees from North Korea, individuals who repatriated to North Korea and their family, not as North Korean refugees, but as Japanese citizens who have found themselves in trouble while overseas. According to this logic, taxpayers are not helping North Koreans, but they are instead aiding Japanese who request emergency support, albeit people who might not identify as Japanese and who might never have previously visited Japan.

Interviewees recalled that the first contact they had with the Japanese state occurred in China. In many cases, they had used a broker to smuggle them across the Sino-Korean border. Once in China, they met Japanese activists in a safe house established by a Japanese civic organization (see chapter 5). The activists smuggled them either to the Japanese consulate-general in Shenyang, or to a safe third country such as Thailand. For people like Kyŏngcha who made contact with Japanese government employees, once their story was deemed credible, they were given a bed in the consulate. From this point on, according to interviewees, Japanese government employees lightly question the new arrival, attempting to confirm their story prior to taking further action.

The confirmation process requires establishing a link between the interviewee and family living in Japan. If kin ties have been severed, this can be impossible, and their claims may be regarded as suspect. An interviewee explained that the Japanese government requires a DNA sample from prospective returnees to Japan. This sample is purportedly matched with individuals in Japan whom the returnee claims as kin. Only people who can prove that they, or their family members, were part of the repatriation project are permitted to continue to Japan.[7] If the DNA sample confirms the applicant's story, the government issues the applicant with a one-time-only travel visa and flies them to Japan, accompanied by a member of Japan's Foreign Service. One interviewee told me that, at the moment of arrival, a government official told her, "Welcome to Japan. Go and live quietly." She felt that it was a polite warning not to ask for more from the state. Once arrived in Tokyo or Osaka, the consulate employee transfers responsibility of the new arrival to waiting family or to a civic organization representative. After registering at a local government office, returnees can apply for social security.[8] Unless someone is working full time, social security payments are unlimited. The recipient is allowed to work part time, but has to declare their earnings and the state will reduce their payments accordingly.[9]

In contrast, due to the wording of the South Korean constitution, all asylum claimants from North Korea are regarded as ROK citizens. This legal obligation compels the government to offer financial and educational support that is not available for returnees to Japan.[10] For example, the South Korean government gives each new arrival from North Korea a one-time resettlement benefit, including housing subsidies and educational support in the form of tuition waivers and vocational training (ROK Ministry of Unification 2018). Considering the benefits available to North Koreans in South Korea, the bright lights of Seoul would seem an obvious choice for resettlement. But economic incentives are not always the most important feature guiding decision-making. Imagined familiarity can be enough of a pull factor to convince a prospective migrant that they will be better off moving to where they have kinship ties and friends than to a destination that may be more economically lucrative. Certainly, this has been the case among Israeli and Irish migrants (Gmelch 1980, 139–40) and Newfoundlanders (Gmelch 1983, 50–51), where economic incentives were not considered as important as either patriotic-social motivators or familial-personal or emotional motivators.

Noneconomic factors played a central role in my interlocutors' migration decisions. Sŏn Donghyŏn, who lived in North Korea for thirty-five years and left in 2008, told me that he knew about the South Korea resettlement package, but was equally aware of South Korean prejudice toward North Koreans. "North Koreans are treated badly in South Korea. Don't come here," his friend in Seoul had warned. Convinced that Japan offered more opportunities for success, he decided to migrate to the country his parents had left a generation earlier. Donghyŏn explained his rationale:

> Life in North Korea is so constricting. You can't say what you want, and you can't do what you want. I couldn't live there. So, with my wife and son, I left with nothing and went to China. Living in China meant being invisible and living in fear of the police, because the Chinese state sends back North Koreans they find. I had to decide, do we go to South Korea or to Japan? Several things influenced my decision: First, I had friends in Japan from my school days. I was confident they would help me. Also, I calculated what a North Korean defector gets in South Korea, in terms of the settlement money. I compared it to how much we'd get in social security from the Japanese government. If we'd gone to South Korea, we would have ended up getting about 5 million yen [US$45,650 in March 2020]. In Japan, we were going to get about four and a half million yen [US$41,100 in March 2020]. It's almost the same. Knowing that I'd get help from my friends, I chose Japan.

At face value, the ROK's resettlement package for North Koreans appears a tempting prospect. But emotions play a significant role in influencing the migration decisions of returnees from North Korea. Donghyŏn calculated that his family would be better off in the long term going to Japan, in terms of the ongoing social security payments. But a further pull factor compelling Donghyŏn to choose Japan was the expectation that his social networks—comprised of Zainichi Koreans with whom he had stayed in contact—would help with his family's resettlement. His calculations proved correct. With the help of friends he had known prior to going to North Korea, he found work for himself and schools for his children. Donghyŏn's planning resonated in the experiences of other returnees with whom I spoke.

I met twenty-five-year-old Ko Hyerim in Tokyo, where she was studying to become a nurse. Hyerim's parents migrated separately from Japan to Hamhŭng city in the early 1960s. They later met at medical school and married. Hyerim was born in North Korea and had never herself been to Japan, yet she only briefly considered emigrating to South Korea. Even before she secreted herself across the border and into China, she had decided to go to Japan. In Fukuoka, her parents told her, she had family with whom she could stay. Hyerim explained, "South Korea is a foreign country to me, I know nothing about it. We all know that in South Korea, North Koreans get money from the government. But my parents had always talked about my uncle in Japan. So, although I'd watched lots of South Korean dramas while in North Korea, I never felt that I wanted to go there."

Hyerim and her family knew that moving to South Korea guaranteed access to educational and financial support. But similar to Donghyŏn, she considered the material rewards less significant than the kinship ties that existed in Japan. The familial-personal motivators of Japan, as tenuous as they might have become over the years, presented a greater pull for Donghyŏn and Hyerim than both the patriotic-social and economic motivators of South Korea. Although, in many cases, emotional ties have withered over the decades, the pull offered by intimate relationships are powerful enough to inform a returnees' migratory choices.

Striking a Balance

In early 2014 Kyŏngcha took a second job, as a shift manager in a downtown Osaka bar. While she felt as though she had been "working like an ant" since she came to Japan, she reflected, "Japan is a good place. If you work hard here, you can survive." She added, "What I really want is for my daughter to join me. If I make enough money, maybe that can happen." Her frustration with the demands of her life seemed tempered by the comfort she drew from imagining that her sacrifices brought her closer to reuniting with her family.

For the majority of the men and women who escape from North Korea, often forced to leave under life-threatening circumstances, South Korea presents the most logical option as a country in which to seek asylum. Despite more than half a century of division, North and South Korea share linguistic and cultural practices that should allow new arrivals from North Korea to assimilate without great difficulty. The men and women from North Korea with whom I worked in Japan had seemingly chosen the more challenging destination. But the decision to choose Japan rather than South Korea is informed by the influence of familial-personal pull factors and the potential for converting these relationships into economic gain. Those who choose to migrate to Japan regard the connections to kin and friends as more significant than the socioeconomic benefits promised in South Korea.

Similar to North Koreans in South Korea, returnees lack skills and qualifications suitable for Japan.[11] Unprepared for finding skilled work in their new home, both men and women often have little choice other than to work in low-skilled positions. Men and women's previous relationships to labor and political status in North Korea circumscribes their willingness and capacity to earn capital, nurture social relationships, and plan for the future.

In the transnational space of Tsuruhashi, a working-class area of Osaka that has for more than a century been home to immigrants from across East Asia, echoes of the Arduous March resonate in the responses of returnees from North Korea to the challenges of the Japanese labor market. Newly arrived returnee men secure a working wage as the primary means of reestablishing their position in the gendered hierarchy of the family. But, with few exceptions, men such as Sŏngmin and Pyŏngchŏl are unlikely to regain their former breadwinner role since their contributions are no longer framed by the same social and political prestige they enjoyed in North Korea.

In contrast, during the worst food crisis of North Korea's turbulent history, women like Kyŏngcha learned the value of adapting to the demands of the country's emergent capitalist market. Individuals who came of age during the famine have spent their lives practicing a form of survival capitalism and, in some cases, have learned how to prosper in the most adverse of circumstances. As a result, they are often more capable and willing to rise to the challenges of the host society. While men who lack the necessary skills, linguistic capacity, and social networks struggle with the economic stresses of their new home, women recognize the importance of developing skills and networks as a long-term investment. The strategy pursued by these women is to strike a balance between immediate pecuniary accumulation and developing skills and social and educational capital required for upward mobility in Japan.

In my final conversation with Kyŏngcha before I left Tsuruhashi, she appeared melancholic. Over dinner in her Koreatown apartment, she spoke to me about her family in North Korea and what it meant to be working without an end in sight: "Every day is the same and it's not how I imagined my life would be. It helps me that I don't think about the past. I can't think about it. So, I just look to the future, to save money and send it back to my family. I miss my home and my friends in North Korea. That's where all my memories are. Here, in Japan, there are no memories for me. This place feels empty and I don't have time to make any new memories because all I do is work."

The past troubled Kyŏngcha. Memories of her life in North Korea were an important part of her self-narrative, connecting her to family she left behind when she crossed into China. But these recollections also appeared to cause her distress, inflected as they were by experiences of hunger, family disintegration, and feelings of helplessness. The future also troubled her, because she saw few options other than working to save money. Yet, while constantly working, it seemed she was unable to foster a sense of attachment to her new home.

New arrivals' difficulties resettling in Japan are exacerbated by limited state support and the atrophied nature of family and friendship networks. As a result, they come to depend on Japanese civic groups for support. In the next chapter, I explore how returnees from North Korea strategically engage the support of civic groups following their arrival in Japan. Specifically, I show that feelings of guilt and indebtedness have become defining features of a relationship founded on a moral economy of emotional exchange and characterized by a symbolic violence that emerges from a gift that can never be repaid.

Notes

1. In May 2002 a diplomatic dispute of this nature arose regarding an incident in the Japanese consulate general in Shenyang, China. Chinese police chased five North Korean asylum seekers into the consulate, violating Japanese sovereignty and international law on the Convention on Diplomatic Relations. The Japanese government later released a statement in which it claimed that it had not given consent for the Chinese police to enter its consulate and demanding that China return the five North Koreans to Japanese custody (MOFA-Japan 2002).
2. Kyŏngcha referred to Akiyama Ayako as her Japanese mother when telling me, for example, that Ayako always buys her a cake on her birthday.
3. For a comprehensive account of state rationing in North Korea, see Haggard and Noland (2007, 51–76).
4. For a historical overview of North Korea's early socialism see Kim (2010).
5. Hazel Smith further notes that women experienced a more rapid reduction in life expectancy: "A major cause of poor health in women was marketization that meant that women worked hard to earn income and had also to carry out physically onerous domestic functions to support the family" (Smith 2015, 267).
6. Haggard and Noland (2012, 10) recorded the responses of three hundred North Korean interviewees demonstrating an overwhelming dependence on private business activities at the time they left North Korea. Specifically, nearly half the sample indicated that they received all their income from private business, and 69 percent said that half or more of their income came from the markets.
7. An activist in Japan told me that the government refuses North Koreans who cannot prove they are Koreans from Japan, subsequently passing them on to the South Korean government.
8. Social security payments generally come to 80,000 yen per month for daily living and 40,000 yen for housing, in total 120,000 yen per month (US$1,100 per month, as of March 2020.)
9. There are further restrictions on receiving these benefits; for example the state does not permit the claimant to possess a car, nor to travel overseas. If authorities discover the claimant has traveled outside of Japan, they deduct money from their monthly payment.

10. For more on how South Korean law shapes and circumscribes the relationship of the South Korean state to North Koreans who leave their country see the work of Andrew Wolman (2011, 2012).
11. For more on the difficulties facing North Koreans who flee their country and resettle in South Korea, see International Crisis Group (2011).

5

Freedom, the Impossible Gift

A man possesses in order to give. But he also possesses by giving. A gift that is not returned can become a debt, a lasting obligation; and the only recognized power—recognition, personal loyalty or prestige—is the one that is obtained by giving.

—Bourdieu [1980] 1990, 126

Yi Sunhyŏng appeared anxious. Her speech was jittery, and she fidgeted nervously as we spoke. A petite woman in her mid-fifties, she spoke loudly in Korean, drawing stares from nearby Japanese in the Osaka coffee shop where we sat. She became animated when talking about her escape from North Korea and her desire to punish Ch'ongryŏn for convincing her family to go to the DPRK years earlier.

Sunhyŏng's family had experienced the extremes of minority life in both Japan and North Korea. In the years before the repatriations, her parents and grandparents had staunchly supported the Kim Il-sung regime. They campaigned for the repatriations, propagating the moral and material virtues of Kim's revolutionary state to Koreans in the ghettos of Osaka. Sunhyŏng was only three years old when she arrived in North Korea. The state rewarded her family with membership in the Korean Workers' Party and an apartment in Sinŭiju, across the Yalu River from Dandong, China. Her brother lived in Pyongyang and Sunhyŏng moved back and forth between the capital and her home. Her family appeared to be one of the lucky ones, trading across the border and mingling in Pyongyang's inner circles.

During times of hardship, Sunhyŏng was largely sheltered from the food shortages and state purges that ruined so many repatriate families. But in the early-1990s, when North Korea's spluttering economy ground to a halt, her parents had to rely even more on their overseas business connections. They traded stolen machine parts from the factory where her husband worked, and tools that had been sent from Japan with Chinese merchants. But pressure was building. Local party cadres, also feeling the pinch of hunger in their bellies, nurtured their jealousy of her family's wealth. Sunhyŏng's worst fears were realized with the arrest of her uncle on a charge of fraud. Sunhyŏng and her entire family were immediately blacklisted from the Korean Workers' Party. A few days later, a knock on her door brought news that the state was relocating her family to the mountains of North P'yŏng'an Province. "In North Korea," Sunhyŏng told me, "everybody knows that there is no returning from exile." Sunhyŏng decided that she had no other choice than to plan her family's escape. "I prepared for a year to leave. It was never going to be easy because we were always being watched," she recalled, detailing the many bribes she had distributed. One night in 2002, close to the deadline for her exile, Sunhyŏng and her children crossed into China.

Life in China would be little better than it had been during their final months in North Korea. She was unable to speak Mandarin and so relied on Chosŏnjok (Korean-Chinese) to help her find work in a Korean restaurant. Laying low was also tricky, since the influx of North Korean refugees into the area had attracted both Chinese police and North Korean agents tasked with catching and forcibly returning escapees. But Sunhyŏng's luck was about to turn. In Dandong she met a South Korean pastor at a church she had been attending. On hearing her story, the pastor contacted a Japanese activist who was secretly working in the area, sheltering and smuggling North Koreans out of China. The activist introduced Sunhyŏng to employees of the Japanese consulate-general. After two and a half years in China, with the assistance of the consulate, Sunhyŏng boarded a plane bound for Japan.

For more than ten years in Japan, three organizations in particular have made a name for themselves on North Korean humanitarian issues: Save Repatriates to North Korea, started in 1994 and headed by Kawashima Akio, Providing for North Korean Refugees, established in 2002 and led by human rights campaigner, Hayashi Isamu, and No Camps in North Korea, founded in 2008 and led by Funai Kichiro and Hattori Masanori. The agenda of each organization converges on the issue of human rights in North Korea.

All of the returnees with whom I worked had experience with these groups, either while in China or immediately following their arrival in Japan. Each organization is comprised largely of elderly Japanese men who speak openly about the need for regime change in the DPRK. The leaders of these groups often played a central role in supporting the repatriation project in the 1960s and 1970s. As such, it is perhaps unsurprising that guilt is a trope driving members to actions that include daring rescue operations in China and funding returnees' employment and educational opportunities in Japan.

Many returnees find that the assistance from these organizations is the difference between living alone on state welfare and feeling a sense of community in their new home. Elderly new arrivals in particular struggle to find employment when they are considered too old or weak to work, and incapable of learning new skills. As part of these groups, some older returnees participate in protests outside Ch'ongryŏn buildings in Tokyo and Osaka, demanding compensation for the organization's role in the repatriation project. Others volunteer translating textbooks used in Ch'ongryŏn schools to assist the Japanese government in monitoring these institutions. These same individuals are also regulars at civic group meetings. Civic groups are particularly important for elderly returnees deemed unemployable in the Japanese labor market.

In 2013 Kawashima Akio's Save Repatriates to North Korea organization started a project offering employment for elderly returnees. The idea was that, if some returnees were struggling to find jobs, work would have to be created specifically for them. Given that most elderly returnees lack skills applicable to Japan, the work would have to be simple to learn, but rewarding enough to maintain interest. Accordingly, money was raised from civic group members and several hectares of land were purchased on the outskirts of Kyoto. The land was registered under the name British Gardens.

British Gardens became an agricultural project through which returnees learn to grow strawberries, tomatoes, and whatever else they can produce on the land. The farm is a gift for returnees, and operates as a self-sustaining community, offering Japanese language and culture classes, as well as employment. In British Gardens returnees earn a monthly salary and have the option of living in nearby accommodation. Early one June morning I joined a group of returnees on a trip to visit the Gardens. One of the participants I recognized as Watanabe Mei, whom I had recently visited in the hospital where she was recovering from a broken ankle. She appeared in good spirits as she introduced me to her companions, Azuma Chika and Mrs. Nakamura.

Our van pulled into a dirt road outside of Kyoto and continued until it reached a cluster of fields next to a river. Two blocks of arable land under transparent plastic tents housed row after row of strawberries. Another tent hosted several batches of cherry tomatoes. Inside, the sweet scent of strawberries mixed with the pungent sweat of fertilized soil. The four of us ambled up and down the rows, picking off the choicest fruits. Most went straight into our mouths, the survivors ended up in the basket for later.

On the day that Chika, now in her early fifties, arrived in Japan in 2002 she felt extremely unwell. Barely able to stand, she was taken to a Tokyo hospital where a panel of tests revealed that what was thought to be airsickness were actually the symptoms of a degenerative nerve disease. The doctor told her she needed to take medication on a daily basis if she was to lead a pain-free life, but this has not prevented her severe migraines. As a result, she is unable to work. "I get free health care in Japan and I enjoy the freedom here, but I can't earn money and that's why I've come to Osaka," she explained. Chika was living with her elderly mother, Mrs. Nakamura. Together, they barely scraped by on social security. "It's simply not enough money if I'm to pay for a broker to bring my daughter here," she told me. Unable to work a regular job because of her illness, she had come to see if she could work on the strawberry farm. If she could put away enough money, she reasoned, she might also be able to pay for her daughter to join her in Japan.[1]

Not all returnees welcome the opportunity to work on a farm. As we saw with Sunhyŏng at the beginning of this chapter, the North Korean state is known to internally exile people for crimes against the government. Exile is permanent. The stigma of agricultural work and lingering memories of rural hardship among returnees lead some to associate living and working in the countryside as a form of punishment. For men and women who imagined life in Japan as a chance for a better life, there is a possibility that agricultural work will be associated with the North Korean penal system. This was not the case for Chika and her mother, however. They had calculated, "There are five people in our family. We want to save money to bring them from North Korea to Japan as soon as possible. To do that we need one million yen per person." In their case, British Gardens represented opportunities for family reunification.

This chapter explores how people like Chika and Sunhyŏng strategically engage with civic groups in Japan, and the moral economy that subsequently emerges between returnees and activists. Despite the best interests of the men and women who assist returnees, feelings of guilt and indebtedness are defining features of a relationship built on a gift that can never be repaid, what I call an impossible gift. I explore three questions with regard to this relationship: Why do civic organizations feel compelled to help people escape from North Korea? How does the debt that permeates the relationship between returnees and activists shape returnees' resettlement in their new home? And how does a relationship that is supposed to free individuals from persecution instead endanger them further?

A Crisis of Political Faith

Japan's economic recovery in the 1950s saw deep class and ideological divisions emerge as Prime Minister Yoshida Shigeru negotiated Japan's security arrangements with the United States (Jansen 2002, 704–5). In the years following the 1960 renewal of the Security Treaty, signed between the two allies, student activists and intellectuals dissatisfied with Washington,

DC's influence on Japan looked to their neighbors and saw two Koreas, one seemingly independent and united under socialism. The other, in contrast, appeared to be an overpopulated, agricultural backwater, led by an anti-democratic government and propped up by the United States. In the early years of East Asia's Cold War, the DPRK seemed to be forging a genuinely autonomous path, all the more impressive given the destruction wrought by the Korean War (1950–53).[2]

This was the climate in which young Japanese ideologues joined South Korean students in protesting the ROK's Rhee government, while at the same time lobbying for the repatriation of Koreans to the North. In the years leading up to the repatriation, North Korean propaganda had been especially effective in appealing to Japanese government and public alike. Lawmakers, students, and supporters of the DPRK rallied to the socialist cause, and by October 1958 "twenty-two 'democratic organizations and groups' manifested in public their willingness to support and promote the repatriation movement" (Lee 1981c, 100–101).

More than half a century after the social unrest and political division that characterized Japan's postwar recovery, the students who became politically conscious in that time are approaching the end of their working lives. Age, however, has not dampened their activist spirit, and men who have spent a lifetime building political networks are now rallying support to a new cause. This time they have positioned themselves in opposition to the North Korean government.

One young man to become politically active during Japan's road to economic prosperity was Kawashima Akio, now a teaching professor at an Osaka university. As a student in the 1960s, he became captivated by socialist ideology, thinking that encouraged him to take an interest in North Korea. Over coffee in a campus cafeteria, he told me this:

> I was gazing across the sea at North Korea and I thought that it looked like a bold, young country with an impressive new leader, Kim Il-sung. On the other hand, South Korea had a terrible image as a powerful dictatorship. So, my sympathies lay with North Korea. When I look back at that time, I think that, if I were a Korean resident in Japan, I would also have returned to North Korea. But after a while, the power moved entirely to Kim Il-sung and I questioned my compassion towards North Korea. Zainichi Koreans in Osaka told me stories of family members and friends who had gone to North Korea and subsequently been victimized by the state. This was a country I had put hope in. I had to do something. Since then, I've been involved in movements to help these people [in North Korea].

Akio's view had changed over time, a change provoked by developments in North Korea, including rumors of repatriates being disappeared into the country's prison network, the elevation of Kim Il-sung to deific status, and the tightening of state control over North Korean citizens. Akio's politics shifted from a point at which, had he been Zainichi Korean, he would have left for North Korea, to a position critical of socialism and critical of the North Korean leadership. At this ideological crossroads, his activism also changed focus. It is with a sense of sorrow regarding his initial support of North Korea and the repatriations that he now spends so much of his own money and time making amends for the actions of his younger, idealistic self.

Akio is not alone in having weathered a crisis of political faith leading him to his role as civic leader and political activist. Hayashi Isamu, the director of the Tokyo-based Providing for North Korean Refugees organization, expressed similar reasons for supporting North Koreans in exile:

When I was a high school student, one of my friends was a Zainichi Korean. My friend was highly talented and capable but couldn't get a job at a major company. Nor as a teacher at a primary school, although he fully deserved employment. In those days, Japanese society had severe racial discrimination against Korean people, so Koreans in Japan found it extremely hard to get work even if they were well qualified. Believing North Korean propaganda, I encouraged him to go, telling him that he would even be able to go to Moscow State University. He and his family went to North Korea in 1960. The advice I gave him back then still tortures me. It's my mission to help as many North Korean refugees as possible. ("I Believed North Korea's Propaganda" 2003)

The messaging coming out of North Korea during the 1960s and 1970s impacted Japanese politics at the national and local levels. In particular, Japanese left-wing politicians' communist and socialist associations with the DPRK were undermined by Kim Il-sung's emergent cult of personality. Local activists like Akio and Isamu went from sympathizing with the North Korean government and supporting the repatriation of Koreans to a position critical of socialist ideology as it became a reality in the DPRK. Through correspondence sent back from people who emigrated to North Korea, young Japanese and Zainichi Koreans alike learned of repatriates living in poverty, ubiquitous state surveillance, and shortages of food and medicine.

Akio and Isamu's explanations of how they became involved in civic group-coordinated activism reveals tropes common to participants I met at seminars and meetings in Osaka and Tokyo. One afternoon in mid-2014, for example, I joined the annual meeting of an activist organization in Tokyo. During a break, deputy leader of the No Camp organization, Okuda Haruhisa, explained that he and other members of the organization had believed that sending people to North Korea was the right thing to do. "We contributed to the repatriations. Now we feel responsible for those who went to North Korea." Haruhisa's comments reflect the feelings of guilt that are woven into the moral fabric of organizations working with returnees. The meeting was followed by dinner, attended by several former Ch'ongryŏn schoolteachers, men once responsible for recruiting students to send to North Korea. "Now, they regret their actions deeply and they work hard for our organization, writing thousands of letters to the North Korean government, telling them to return the people back to Japan," Haruhisa told me.

The narratives produced and reproduced within these organizations echo biblical tales of trial and redemption. These men regard their younger selves as having been hoodwinked by North Korean propaganda. They carry a weight of concern that their enthusiasm for the repatriations contributed to destroying the lives of the people who set sail from Niigata. In their twilight years, they seek redemption for supporting an ideology and a social project that time has since proven to be deeply flawed. The immediate problem that now faces these organizations is that young Japanese people cannot relate to their cause. Public opinion in Japan regards North Korea and the North Korean people as a threat to national security. As such, North Korea is more likely to induce antipathy rather than a will to volunteer in the resettlement of returnees. Japanese ambivalence is a challenge for the group, as it attempts to avoid dying out with its members.

Facing a crisis in terms of an ageing membership, the groups are changing how they engage with North Korean human rights issues to better appeal to the younger generation. In particular, activists argue that the Japanese wives and children of Korean repatriates are, in fact, Pyongyang's hostages. As hostages, the repatriation project is thus reimagined as a large-scale kidnapping. Civic organization members believe that because the North Korean government has never permitted repatriates to leave North Korea, the Japanese government should consider the repatriation issue as one and the same as the DPRK's 1970s abductions of Japanese citizens.[3] The organizations clarified their position in an open letter from "Five Japanese and Korean NPOs [nonprofit organizations] to Prime Minister Abe." The letter requests the permanent resettlement in Japan of all Japanese spouses and family (including grandchildren) of Zainichi Koreans repatriated to North Korea, "After 2–3 years they can expect to live full and enriching lives in Japan. Therefore, in order to facilitate their smooth integration into Japanese society, we ask you to use the former facilities for the Japanese orphans left behind in China to provide a minimum level of Japanese language instruction and job training in preparation for their settlement in Japan."[4]

The letter shows how Japanese activist groups link the repatriation to matters of contemporary geopolitical import, in this case North Korea's abductions of Japanese. Furthermore, it shifts the focus of their mission, making it more topical and, they believe, more palatable to young Japanese.

The leaders of the groups believe that they have a special connection to the lives of the people they encouraged to migrate to North Korea. Their historically rooted, imagined intimacy with returnees from North Korea subsequently justifies their heavy-handed approach to addressing North Korea's human rights violations.

Legal Activism

The work of Japanese activist groups has evolved over the past twenty years, from dramatic and risky embassy crashing (charging the gates of foreign embassies in China with North Korean asylum seekers) to using the Japanese courts to raise awareness of North Korean human rights issues.[5] Specifically, in addition to aiding returnees in their immigration to Japan, Akio and the Save Repatriates to North Korea organization have been at the forefront of two lawsuits taking legal action against Ch'ongryŏn. Akio explained, "Our experiences working with defectors who returned to Japan convinced us that the repatriation project, led by Ch'ongryŏn, was a large-scale kidnapping case. It was certainly a criminal activity."

The first returnee enlisted in these organizations' battle with Ch'ongryŏn was Kim Kwangmin. Kim arrived in North Korea in 1964 and, in an extraordinary and daring escape, crossed the DMZ separating the two Koreas soon after. The South Korean government was incredulous when they heard about Kim's story, but also recognized the repatriate-defector as a rare source of information. Kim was permitted to go to Japan, making him the first repatriate to return. Akio explained, "When Kim arrived in North Korea, he realized that he'd made a mistake. In 1966, he fled to South Korea, crossing the 38th parallel through the snow and land mines. In total, he'd spent 575 days in North Korea."

Encouraged by Kim's testimony and his willingness to join them in open court, Akio and a team of volunteers built a case against Ch'ongryŏn. The crux of their lawsuit rested on the claim that North Korea's representation in Japan had knowingly lured Japanese and Koreans to North Korea, where they had been persecuted because of their relationship to Japan. Despite the plaintiff's best efforts, the court ruled against Kim. The ruling explained that Kim's lawsuit was outside of a three-year statute of limitations. Akio and others were not to be deterred: "The next case we put together was with Yi Sunhyŏng, in 2006. We were determined to learn from our mistakes and worked hard to present the case to the courts within three years of Yi entering Japan. The trial was different from the last one in that we aggressively pursued our claim that North Korea forbidding Yi from returning to Japan was a hostage case."

The second time, although the lawsuit was put to the court within three years, the judge again dismissed it, Akio told me. Akio and his supporters were back at square one. But public opinion in Japan had since shifted in the organizations' favor. As a consequence of the 2014 publication of the UN commission of inquiry into human rights violations in North Korea (OHCHR 2014), during which several Japanese and Korean organizations presented testimony, the issue of North Korean refugees has entered the public discourse in Japan. Although both attempts at suing Ch'ongryŏn have ended in failure, Akio and his organization are steadfast in their commitment to finding a returnee to champion their cause. As of this writing Akio is waiting for a newly arrived returnee who can lead their next lawsuit. On the heels of the international community's condemnation of the DPRK for crimes against humanity, Akio intends on prosecuting not only Ch'ongryŏn, but also the North Korean government. He realizes that taking such high-profile actions comes with risks: "The hardest thing of all is finding a person who's willing to do this, as all the case records and everything during the legal process has to be done using real names. A defector who enters Japan has to be willing to be at the head of a case presented within six months of their arrival. That's a completely new arrival to Japan and they'll probably still have family in North Korea. They'll need a strong will to make a strong case."

Such high-profile activism also places a significant psychological strain on an escapee from North Korea. It is well known, among North Koreans in exile, that Pyongyang keeps a watch on its fugitive citizens through spy networks in communities where they resettle. A returnee who agrees to be the figurehead of a lawsuit against Ch'ongryŏn risks the lives of family still in North Korea by publicly exposing herself. Given the dangers, why would such a person risk everything for what might amount to little more than attention-grabbing ventures?

"A lot of people have asked me, 'What's the point of it all?' Why did I want to sue Ch'ongryŏn for the repatriations?" Sunhyŏng asked, clutching her stomach with one hand while picking at her napkin with the other. Since her court case she had suffered from a number of anxiety-related health problems, including insomnia, and had become estranged from her children. Sunhyŏng's deteriorating health was the price that she had paid for joining the fight against Ch'ongryŏn. She recalled that in 2006 there had been rumors of Ch'ongryŏn merging with Mindan to represent all Zainichi Koreans in Japan. The thought had both infuriated and terrified Sunhyŏng, who firmly believed that Ch'ongryŏn was responsible for sending tens of thousands of people, including her own family, to North Korea. She also believed that Ch'ongryŏn passed on all information about escapees from North Korea to the DPRK government. Sunhyŏng explained,

> I can't forgive them for their actions. I can't forgive them for sending people to North Korea. So, with Akio, we decided to take them to court. Before we did that, we approached the United Nations to put a case together. I went to Washington, DC, and testified about life in North Korea. I explained to them why people went to North Korea, why I decided to leave, and the role of Ch'ongryŏn in all of it. The point was to inform the Japanese people, to

tell them about North Korea and Ch'ongryŏn through the United Nations. It wasn't possible to speak directly to the Japanese public; people still believed that Ch'ongryŏn had done a good thing in organizing the repatriations. We had to go through the United Nations so the world, and Japan, would know what really happened.

Sunhyŏng and Akio believed that using the UN as a platform for their testimonies would amplify and lend authority to their claims, convincing an apathetic Japanese public that Ch'ongryŏn was not the benevolent protector of Koreans that it claimed to be. Echoing Akio's determination, Sunhyŏng told me that they were waiting for a new arrival from North Korea who would take the lead on the next lawsuit. Even without the required new arrival, some returnees had gone ahead with legal action. On 12 August 2018, for example, five returnees filed a lawsuit against Pyongyang for luring them to North Korea under false pretenses. The plaintiffs asked for 500 million yen (US$4.52 million) in compensation ("In first, five defectors in Japan sue North Korea for ¥500 million over rights abuses" 2018). As with previous efforts, this lawsuit would also end in failure because of the statute of limitations on such litigation.

The stakes are high for North Koreans in exile, and high-profile activism is pursued by only a few individuals, usually those without loved ones in North Korea. Sunhyŏng was aware of the consequences an escapee faces for stepping into the public eye. "There's a law in North Korea that states that the whole family is punished for the mistakes of one person.[6] Many of my family are still in North Korea. Because of what I did [taking legal action against Ch'ongryŏn], the government sent them to state labor camps. My children can't forgive me for getting involved and causing so much trouble for everyone. They think I was being selfish and didn't consider how it might affect their lives."

Despite the cost to her health and her family relationships, Sunhyŏng felt compelled to do everything she could to support the groups that had aided her in her escape. Since Sunhyŏng's arrival in Japan, Akio's organization had helped her find work and accommodation in Osaka. The groups also invite Sunhyŏng to their meetings, sometimes to testify to the suffering she had endured, other times simply to share a meal. Sunhyŏng's personal desire for retribution dovetailed with activists' aims to raise public awareness of their mission, but it was also a means for her to repay the groups' support.

The Grateful Migrant

Refugees are required to continuously perform their gratitude to the host society. Gratitude for rescue. Gratitude for support. Gratitude for the gifts of freedom, security, and opportunity. On the "grateful refugee," Nayeri writes

"As for volunteers, even the most good-hearted want to *feel* thanked. They have come for that silent look of admiration that's free to most, but so costly if you're tapped for gratitude by everyone you meet" (Nayeri 2019, 98). Like refugees the world over, Nayeri lamented the anguish of having to reproduce narratives of suffering and gratitude for the community in which her family resettled after fleeing Iran, and the expectation that her family would shed their past like an old skin. Constantly accepting charity, constantly being tapped for gratitude, and having to retell rescue stories eat away at a person, eroding their dignity and sense of pride.

When Kim Hyŏnjae arrived in Tokyo in 2007, he had neither money nor a place to stay. He had been in contact with Hayashi Isamu's organization while he hid in China, and again looked to Isamu for help in Japan. Isamu invited Hyŏnjae into the organization's offices, situated in Isamu's home. For several weeks, until Isamu helped him find a place of his own, Hyŏnjae slept in Isamu's spare bedroom. Hyŏnjae explained, "When I arrived in Tokyo, I couldn't do anything–eat, make money, or even speak without their help. Hayashi-sensei was like a father, telling me to do this and to do that. He was quite stern, but he helped with everything, finding a place to live and with matters of everyday life. He's helped my family and many others to get out of North Korea. If it weren't for Hayashi-sensei, I wouldn't be here; my family wouldn't have been able to survive."

Hyŏnjae invoked kinship terminology in describing Isamu's role in helping his family resettle in Japan. The use of familial language highlighted the intimacy he feels toward Isamu and the significance of Isamu's organization in teaching Hyŏnjae "how to speak" in Japan. He had learned how to express himself, how to make money, and the importance of swift adaptation to his new life. Isamu later used his networks to help Hyŏnjae move to Osaka, to find work, and to connect with Akio. Akio's organization in turn helped smuggle Hyŏnjae's wife out of North Korea. Once his wife arrived in Japan, Akio found her work in Osaka. The work was menial, but with Hyŏnjae's income the couple had enough money to move into their own apartment.

Learning Japanese is also a necessary part of resettlement in Japan. Again, civic groups play a central role in facilitating this process. Akio and Isamu, for example, usually introduce new arrivals in Kansai to Ayako's Japanese school, located in Ikuno ward, Osaka. "The language school is my space and I make it so that students from North Korea are away from the politics and the political noise that surrounds them," Ayako explained. "In the classes they can meet people from South Korea and Japan who help them find work."

Ayako was always conscientious in her relationships with returnees. She showed a sensitivity to the traumatic experiences that some returnees had endured, calling students regularly and remembering each current and former student's birthday. She avoided using honorific titles in class and used Korean names for the Korean students. This was in contrast to some of the group leaders, who referred to returnees using the Japanese pronunciation of their names, a practice that caused annoyance among returnees. If a returnee cannot afford the tuition, Akio might pay it for them. "I thought the lessons were free until my friend told me otherwise," explained one new arrival. "I found out that [Akio] Kawashima-sensei had been paying my tuition without telling me."

Civic organization members help returnees like Hyŏnjae find their balance in Japan. In return, they ask that returnees attend organization meetings and contribute to the groups' activities. This could mean finding work in Koreatown for other newly arrived returnees. It could also mean contributing to activities such as telling their stories to an audience of curious Japanese and contributing testimonies on DPRK human rights violations.

Returnees' inclusion in Japan is contingent on their presenting the right kind of behavior. Demonstrating appreciation in these cases requires not just learning "how to speak" but learning how to speak in a language of gratitude. The narratives of North Korean refugees who publicly reproduce their personal stories illuminate the particular conditions required for belonging in Japan. Gaining acceptance requires that a returnee identify as North Korean while earnestly condemning Pyongyang's human rights abuses. Such condemnation is produced through stories aligning the narrator with a "good" discourse of anticommunism, freedom, and human rights. The media, activist groups, and international organizations reward testimonies that both highlight suffering in the DPRK and present a narrative of salvation in the places they resettle (Han 2013; Hough and Bell 2020). But by producing and reproducing a narrative in which the DPRK is a monolithic entity associated only with suffering and political oppression, these organizations contribute to a powerful, singular narrative of victimization in which North Koreans are turned into "speechless emissaries" for human rights movements (Malkki 1996).

Not everyone who leaves North Korea is a political dissident. Not all North Koreans are victims. North Koreans now living in exile in places like Seoul, Tokyo, London, and Los Angeles have responded to a variety of pressures and an equally compelling range of desires before taking their chances in China and beyond. The families who repatriated to North Korea and those who have since returned to Japan often did so out of desperation, but to regard them simply as victims is to discount the many decisions that culminated in the act of migration. A singular master narrative of suffering, struggle, and redemption devalues returnees' memories. Even for families in exile, people who felt compelled to leave their home, life in North Korea was more than a life of suffering and struggle. As we saw in previous chapters, returnees' voices–their vernacular memories–are testimonies that can be harnessed for ideological purposes. But selecting, refining, and staging North Korean refugees' memories for the purpose of attacking the DPRK stigmatizes the past. The underlying message becomes that a person's past has value, but only when it fits within a narrow humanitarian narrative.

Stigmatizing the memories that contribute to a person's self-understanding exacerbates an existential crisis that arises from displacement. I often heard members of civic organizations try to make sense of returnees' temporal disorder saying, for example, that North Korean refugees need to move on from the past and instead focus on the future. "They have had such hard lives," commented one well-meaning activist over dinner at a Japanese Izakaya restaurant. "They need to look forward, not back." Well-intentioned activists in South Korea and Japan seem to have reached a consensus that it is better to forget North Korea, because the past is synonymous with suffering. Except, however, when a North Korean's suffering can be channeled to their cause. For the North Korean refugee, gratitude is not only offered through public performance. A North Korean is encouraged to give their voice, their micro-histories, everything that came before salvation, and be thankful as their memories are flattened into a political critique. But erasing and manipulating aspects of an individual's biography robs them of the cognitive tools needed to reconfigure traumatic episodes into "sanitized impressions of the past" (Hirsch 1992, 390), in which negative memories are combined, filtered, and renegotiated into a form in which a person might be able to make sense.

Returnees offer up stories of struggle and redemption to repay the people who shepherded them to freedom. One of the ways they do this is by joining activist groups in condemning North Korea. Indeed, the gift is never free.

The Violence of the Gift

The gift is not free. Receiving a gift comes with an obligation to reciprocate. We feel it when we give someone a birthday present, when we send a postcard from vacation, or when we invite someone for dinner. We rarely give a gift without giving a little of ourselves; there is a spirit that accompanies goods and gift giving (Mauss [1925] 2002, 13–16). The act of giving, something that may seem little more than an innocuous pleasantry or a common cultural practice, has a distinct social function and, sometimes, even a dark side. A gift creates and renews bonds between people by reminding the recipient of the relationship that exists between them and the giver. Furthermore, a gift requires that the recipient offer something in return—a postcard, a return dinner invite and so forth. In this sense, a gift creates a debt, and the debt follows the person wherever they go. The only way to remove oneself from this cycle of obligation is to destroy the debt, but with the destruction of the debt, the relationship also vanishes (Graeber 2011, 266).

Indeed, whether tribes exchanging ornamental shells in the Western Pacific (Malinowski [1922] 2014; Mauss [1925] 2002), or friends sending postcards while on summer break, there is a pattern of reciprocity that gifting must follow, and there are distinct, often unspoken, rules of conduct. The cycle of reciprocity, at its most basic, is made up of a triple obligation: to give, to receive, and to reciprocate the gift. Accordingly, there are three possible outcomes to the obligation: a refusal of the gift, incapacity to respond to the gift, or an offer of a counter gift (Bourdieu [1980] 1990, 98). The first two options are unfavorable in the moral economy of gift giving. To refuse the gift invites discord within the relationship, because to reject a gift is to say no to the person making the offer and to deny the relationship. The value, timing, and handling of the gift are thus significant factors in a relationship perpetuated by an obligation to reciprocate. A gift repaid too early has the same effect as refusing the gift entirely, threatening to destroy the social relationship. A gift repaid too late is a comparable denial of the relationship. Similarly, an incapacity to reciprocate indicates that either the giver has committed an act of "symbolic violence" (Bourdieu [1980] 1990, 126–27) by giving something that causes anxiety with regard to the size, expense, or emotional value of the object, or that the relationship is unsustainable, based as it is on an inequitable distribution of power, wealth, or resources.

This is not to say that the gift is always accepted nor that refusing the gift always leads to a breakdown of social relations. In his rethinking of gifting in ancient societies, anthropologist James Laidlaw showed that gifts do not always encourage the emergence of a reciprocal bond between the giver and the receiver. Laidlaw examines how alms givers and Shvetambar Jain renouncers in India avoid moral entanglement with each other (Laidlaw 2000, 630). In this instance, giver and receiver behave as strangers toward one another to mitigate the obligation that gift giving produces. Furthermore, the givers try to consciously distance themselves from the alms they provide in order to fulfill their spiritual obligation to give freely without thanks or reward. In creating distance between the giver and the gift, they try to nullify the obligation and destroy the social bond between giver and receiver.

Most people have at least a subconscious awareness of the rules of gift giving and try to offer something that best represents the occasion of giving and the recipient's ability to return the gift. Of course, there are times when the gift is beyond a person's capacity to reciprocate: perhaps an uncle pays off his nephew's student loan, or a friend pays for a group vacation. On these occasions, it is imperative that the giver minimize the symbolic violence imparted by a gift the receiver can never repay. A person might do this by telling herself that, for example, because her uncle is wealthy the money does not mean as much to him. Or, because the friend recently received a promotion, she can afford the gift and, after all, everyone deserves a vacation. On these occasions, people justify their worthiness and minimize the debt to the gift giver. Nevertheless, there is always something uncomfortable about these situations, a voice that inquires, "Is this really OK?" Exchange ideally takes place between equals, the cycle of giving and receiving highlighting and reinforcing the relationship between participants. When exchange takes place between individuals for whom there is a power differential, such as the wealthy uncle and his student niece, it is impossible to repay the gift and the closest the recipient can come to doing so is to simply recognize the impossibility of the gift. Recognizing that there is no way of repaying the debt, Graeber says, is the true meaning of sacrifice, since in doing so you concede that you and the giver of the impossible gift are simply not equivalents (Graeber 2011, 266–76).

Consequently, the path of least resistance, when possible, is to offer a counter gift in due course. Counter gifts are usually of similar pecuniary value or emotional investment. On occasions when this is also not possible, it might be feasible to present a symbolic gift of thanks that demonstrates gratitude and indebtedness to the benefactor. Such a symbolic gift might comprise inviting the loan-clearing uncle for a home-cooked dinner or buying the vacation-giving friend a nice bottle of wine. Either way, offering a counter gift perpetuates a cycle of gift giving that obligates people to one other, that keeps friends and family talking with each other, and that ensures each person's embeddedness within an invisible network of social relations.

Things become further complicated when the gift is not an item imbued with economic or social value, like money or a new car, but an abstract concept, such as the gift of time, respect, or freedom. Intangible gifts also come with an obligation to reciprocate, but it can be much harder for participants to determine an equitable back and forth. The giver of the gift may be convinced of her generosity in dispensing largesse without expectations, but the spirit of the gift, especially with unquantifiable exchangeables, is prone to changing its meaning. Again, this is exemplified when there is a power imbalance between giver and receiver and when the giver believes that their gift consolidates a position on the moral high ground. A transaction of this nature is present in the transferal of the "gift of civilization" from imperial powers to a colonized people. In regard to gift giving between European colonizers and native peoples, Ferguson explains, "Poison has long been indistinguishable from the gift. These presents were freely given, and sometimes freely received, but they often built relationships that were lethal to the recipients" (Ferguson 2007, 50).

The gift of charity and the moral imperative to repay the giver contributes to informing an inequitable relationship, especially when it is clear to both parties that the receiver is unable to repay the gift. Such inequalities force recipients into alternative forms of reciprocity, such as giving to a third party or conspicuously performing submissive behavior that publicly

demonstrates the hierarchy of the relationship (Kowalski 2011, 195). Ultimately, when the gift is of such immense significance and the relationship
between giver and receiver is inherently inequitable, the obligation of the
gift becomes a form of symbolic violence. A troubled transactional element
of this nature characterizes the relationships of North Korean returnees to
activist groups in Japan.

Symbolic Family

Everyday acts of collaboration with group members were a means by which
returnees attempted to transform their relationship from one of transactions
to an intimacy approaching pseudo-kinship. On occasion, North Korean
exiles performed such a pseudo-kinship relationship in a more conspicuous
manner. As a young man, Kim Sŏngkwan, for example, was a homeless
orphan prior to escaping North Korea. He was without family and without
hope that his life would improve if he stayed in North Korea. After escaping
to China, Isamu's organization helped Sŏngkwan emigrate to South Korea
in 2009. In South Korea, he met and fell in love with a young woman who
had also escaped from North Korea. Soon after, they arranged to marry and
invited Isamu to the ceremony. During the wedding, conducted in Seoul,
Isamu performed the role of father to Sŏngkwan. In an act of filial piety,
Sŏngkwan deferentially poured a cup of *soju* for Isamu, his symbolic father,
and his bride fed Isamu traditional Korean candy. By conspicuously performing familial roles, group members and North Korean escapees seek to
cleanse the relationship of its economic underpinnings.

Returnees' intimacy with activists such as Isamu at times compelled them
to open up the details of their lives to the scrutiny of organizations. The Japanese government requires that organization members act as guarantors for
the safety and conduct of returnees who are without family support in Japan.
As part of their guardianship, group leaders asked that their charge keep
them regularly updated as to their personal progress in Japan. One young
returnee, Ko Hyerim, arrived in Fukuoka, where her uncle subsequently introduced her to Isamu. Although Hyerim receives no financial support from
Providing for North Korean Refugees, Isamu receives her college updates
through the mail. "So, I have to study hard because he sees my grades before I do." Her progress, since arriving in Japan, had also been tracked and
publicly reported on the organization's website. The organization claimed
her assimilation was a successful litmus test for the future resettlement of
returnees in Japan.

Exchange creates debt and debt in turn facilitates further exchange. To ignore the obligation to repay the debt is to ignore the social relationship. "Even
acts of charity and self-sacrifice are not purely generous," Graeber argues,

noting that in Buddhism, bodhisattvas accumulate merit through their social contributions (Graeber 2011, 267). The debt lingers in the background of social relationships, manifesting itself within exchanges between the giver and receiver, for example, in the favors that returnees completed for members, and in public declarations of gratitude. Within these debt-derived interactions, returnees are infantilized, encouraged to perform the symbolic position of a child with the attendant obligations to their fictive parents, the organization leaders.[7] But returnees are not helpless within these relationships.

My interlocutors strategically performed their fictive filial duties, demonstrating agency in opting out of the relationship, if and when they found an alternative way of supporting themselves. It was not unusual for individuals to disappear entirely from the sphere of activities organized by the groups. One young returnee I spoke with explained that she cut off all contact with the organizations once the obligation of constant meetings became too much. In such cases, it is possible that the spirit of the impossible gift had become toxic, and the recipient was prepared to annihilate the social relationship by ignoring the debt. Instead of continuing to perform the role of grateful child, it was easier to cut off all ties in a very real attempt to annul the bond. For most returnees, however, opting out of the pseudo-kinship relationship is more difficult, because of the importance of the organizations as a social network hub.

The Poison of the Gift

The obligation of the gift, as Sunhyŏng and other returnees experience it, is enough that they are willing to risk their lives and the lives of their family to support local civic groups. But it is the nature of the debt, wrapped up in the idiom and performance of kinship relations that gives it such an enduring power. The gift that Japanese activists bestow on returnees carries with it a heavy burden. Freedom comes with the chance to begin a new life, away from the oppressive state apparatus of the DPRK. Bondage, on the other hand, is the inevitable result of the symbolic violence imparted by a gift that can never be repaid. In an effort to renegotiate this debt, returnees' engagement with activists is characterized by continuously doing small favors for the groups. Returnees' participation in their benefactors' organizations is a way to express gratitude for their freedom. But their efforts to balance the scales will never succeed. Instead, frequent interactions and exchanges lock returnees into a relationship with civic organizations. Over time, the relationship thickens, as strands of trust reach out and wrap around the initial bond of obligation. But instead of the relationship becoming durable and robust, the relationship infantilizes the debtor and endangers their family who remain in the DPRK.

In nurturing pseudo-kinship relationships with activists, returnees from North Korea risk breaking their blood-based kinship relations. The poison of the gift creeps outwards along returnees' kinship networks, threatening to rupture familial ties. In her foreword to Mauss's *The Gift*, Mary Douglas eloquently claimed, "Charity is meant to be a free gift, a voluntary, unrequited surrender of resources. Though we laud charity as a Christian virtue we know that it wounds" (Mauss [1925] 2002). Decades ago, the best intentions of men such as Kawashima Akio and Hayashi Isamu contributed to a large-scale migration project that sent tens of thousands of people to North Korea. In North Korea many of these so-called repatriates were subject to social discrimination and state persecution. The best intentions of the same men are again driving the return of these families back to Japan. But their efforts to assist returnees and bring the North Korean government to justice risks harming the people who have become central to their lives as activists.

In Japan, civic organizations are prone to constructing the figure of the returnee as either a mute victim without a political, historical, or cultural past, or as a morally suspect figure who struggles to evolve beyond "being from North Korea." As a consequence, returnees' resettlement in Japan is conditional on their willingness to barter their memories of life in North Korea for the support of activist groups. Memories of North Korea, of traveling through China, and remaking home in Japan are the price a returnee pays for their new life. They trade their stories with activists and researchers who use these micro-histories to attack the DPRK government, while at the same time conspicuously performing gratitude for people who desire affirmation of their generosity. "The refugee has to be less capable than the native, needier; he must stay in his place. That's the only way gratitude will be accepted," writes Nayeri (2017). But politicizing and weaponizing the intimate narratives of people to have escaped the DPRK risks further stigmatizing their past and condemning them to forever perform the role of grateful–damaged–refugee. Returnees unable or unwilling to trade their narratives instead offer their silence in exchange for freedom and acceptance in their new home. They participate in the erasure of aspects of their own selves by a communal forgetting of the past. Their erasure within a singular narrative of suffering is the poison of the gift.

In the next chapter I go beyond the debt relationship of returnees to activist groups, exploring how returnees imagine their new lives in Japan.

Notes

1. The British Gardens agricultural project makes sense in the context of Japan's demographic crisis. The Japanese population is rapidly ageing, especially in rural areas, where the average Japanese farmer is in his late sixties. As a result,

the price of land is decreasing, and more land is becoming vacant. With more land available, civic organizations working with returnees from North Korea could expand their agricultural project. "Using water drainage techniques even old people are able to work on the strawberry farm. Potentially, returnees from North Korea could contribute to the revitalization of Japanese agriculture," an interviewee explained.

2. Inoue Masutarô, director of the Foreign Affairs Department of the JRC, quoted a delegation from the JRC returning from the DPRK as offering a positively glowing report on conditions as of the late 1950s: "The underground resources and electric power are in North Korea [rather] than in South Korea. The capital and technics are also introduced from the Soviet Union. Industrialization of North Korea is far advanced and North Korea lacks manpower. South Korea is an agricultural country and is suffering from overpopulation. The life is very hard in South Korea" (Inoue 1960, 8).

3. There have been some exceptions to the DPRK's no-returns policy, but these are usually individuals who have family remaining in North Korea and thus have a reason not to defect. For example, Yang Yŏnghŭi's *Our Homeland* (2012) is based on her brother's temporary return from North Korea for medical treatment.

4. Thousands of Japanese civilians were left behind in Manchuria following the Japanese defeat and withdrawal from Northeast China. Some of these individuals have since returned to Japan. For more on Japanese war orphans in China, see Chan (2011).

5. Kelly Greenhill explains that South Korean and Japanese civic groups pursued these methods both as a means of drawing international attention to North Korean human rights violations and as an attempt to provoke regime change via the mass emigration of North Korean refugees (Greenhill 2011, chap. 5).

6. This is a "guilt by association" policy, whereby three generations of a family are punished for the political crimes of a family member. This practice is applied inconsistently, dependent on such factors as the ability of a family to pay bribes, the crimes of the person arrested, and the standing of the accused in the community.

7. Filial piety has long been at the center of both Korean and Japanese child-parent relations (Hashimoto 2004; Sorensen and Kim 2004). The dynamics of filial piety orders the relationship of child to parent. A child is in its parents' debt from birth. The magnitude of this debt means that the child is required to spend the entirety of its life obligated to its parents. A life of obligation is spent demonstrating indebtedness through acts that reflect well on the individual and the family and that demonstrate obedience to the parents' authority.

6

Mobility, Memory, and the Fractured Self

Nowadays, I feel like I'm split three ways, between North Korea, South Korea, and Japan.

–Yi Misŏn, born in North Korea

We have a complex, my daughter and me. We both have South Korean citizenship but when we meet South Koreans, they don't believe that we're South Korean. My daughter has always felt anxiety at having to hide her background; to the point that she had to take time off work because of the stress of living so close to North Korea while pretending to be someone she isn't.

–Kang Sŏnok (Yi Misŏn's mother) emigrated from South Korea to North Korea as a child

Misŏn grew up among the elites of North Korea. She had family in the Korean Workers' Party and both parents had graduated from college. Her family's elevated political status derived from her grandparents' fervent support for North Korea–affiliated organization, Ch'ongryŏn, while in Japan. Like so many other Zainichi Korean families, they immigrated to Japan from the southern half of the Korean Peninsula during the colonial period. Misŏn was thus raised on a diet of rich family stories on both the vicissitudes of life in 1950s Osaka, and tales of the famous Chŏnju Yi clan, of which she was the newest generation.

Sitting in her Osaka apartment, she described feeling pulled between North Korea which was the place of her birth, South Korea which was her ancestral home, and Japan which was her home now and for the foreseeable future. In each of these places, she felt her migrant status on display, marking her as conspicuously different. For Misŏn and her mother, Sŏnok, a family history of mobility was also a history of pretending to be someone else, and of searching for belonging wherever they went.

So often, a migrant expects to feel an emotional connection to the ethnic homeland. This might be the case when Celtic-Americans cross the Atlantic in search of Scottish roots, or when Korean-Canadians arrive in Seoul to connect with estranged cousins, aunts, and uncles. But disappointment so often awaits. "Beware o wanderer, the road is walking too," writes poet Jim Harrison to the traveler who strays too far and for too long (Rilke, quoted in Harrison 1996, 37). A returnee's hope that she will be received as a compatriot, or feel a deep connection to ancestral lands, fails to materialize when confronted by the reality that long periods outside of the homeland transforms both person and place.[1] Indeed, the road changes as does the person traveling it. Ethnic Germans returning to Germany from the former Soviet Union in the 1990s, for example, responded to increasingly negative public criticism by viewing themselves as neither German nor Russian, but as a group with distinct cultural practices and histories (Klekowski von Koppenfels 2009, 104–5). Similarly, *nikkeijin* (ethnic Japanese born overseas) found that Japanese regarded them as little different to other foreigners arriving to work low-status jobs. Some ethnic Japanese born in Brazil, for instance, responded to societal pressures to assimilate by conspicuously performing a Brazilian nationalist identity as a form of autonomous ethnic resistance (Tsuda 2000). In such cases, when reality fails to live up to expectations, returned ethnic migrants have responded to unexpected social pressures by finding new ways with which to express their hybrid cultural identities.

Returnees from North Korea also often expected to feel an emotional connection to Japan. As we see, those born in Japan, such as Sŏnok, seek out physical reminders of life before their emigration to North Korea. Relics of the past may emerge in the form of recognizable buildings and scenery, familiar smells, sounds, and faces. Others, like Misŏn, search for connections to memories inherited from their parents and grandparents. Whether trying to externalize personal or inherited memories, it is possible for a person to imagine themselves at home in the host society by identifying material and emotional points of familiarity. But how does a displaced person foster emotional connections to a place where no obvious connections exist? How does a returned migrant feel at home when home has changed beyond recognition?

Roots and Soil

There is a preference for us to connect family narratives to official country histories as a means of establishing entitlement to land and deservedness to national resources. Some Australians, for instance, claim to be descended from those who were part of the first fleet to arrive in 1788. In this case, time-passed is used as evidence of ownership of the country, with obvious disregard for indigenous Australians' occupation and use of the land long before the eighteenth century. Similarly, it is common for ethnic Japanese to point to the longevity of the Yamato people on the Japanese archipelago to justify exclusionary policies against ethnic minorities who have, in the case of indigenous Ainu or Ryūkyūans, lived on the archipelago for as long or perhaps longer than the Yamato ethnic majority. In Japan ethnic identity is conceived of in such a way that it is difficult to separate from national identity. Specifically, "being Japanese" unofficially requires speaking perfect Japanese, being able to physically pass as Japanese, having a "pure" bloodline (evidenced in family genealogies)–without mixing with non-Yamato people–and holding Japanese citizenship. In effect, this cultural and political checklist ensures that the majority society will always consider ethnic Koreans, for example, as outsiders, no matter how long they live in Japan or how well they speak the language (see Chapman 2008). It also means that the ethnic Japanese who joined husbands and children emigrating to North Korea may also feel a need to reassert their ethnic Japanese identity upon their return. Proving their right to be considered Japanese could be challenging when, in this case, belonging to the national community is contingent on reversing the effects of decades in North Korea obscuring Japanese characteristics.

The preference for connecting family origins to a country's history is further evident in, for example, the idioms widely used to describe belonging to a place. Expressions that refer to a person's origins as their "roots," or their ancestral lineage in soil-related metaphors, appear in European languages and, to various extents, in East Asian languages, too.[2] Nation-centric thinking in this case equates having roots with having a community–a place in which to belong.[3] The flip side of a sedentary bias, as Misŏn and her mother, Sŏnok have found, is that lacking obvious roots in a place is regarded as a form of deviance. If a person appears to lack connections to the soil, if they are immigrants and without the social and economic capital required to move seamlessly from one country to another, they are more likely to be imagined as without community. A lack of community suggests an absence of accountability for a person's actions. And if a person cannot be held to account, there is no means of distinguishing them as either friend or foe. In this way, a refugee–someone forced out of their community–is positioned in opposition to the nation and pathologized as homeless and without community, as deviant.

As in many places, mobility in East Asia has historically been regarded as emblematic of a social failure, and indicative of something pathologically problematic (see Tsuda 1998). The mobile person–whether trader, wandering sword for hire, or vagabond–has been socially construed as a person outside of a specific community, without obvious ties of kinship, locality, or occupation. With no recognized position in the social system, the unmoored person provokes anxiety as a kind of "matter out of place" (Douglas 1969, 35), meaning that they do not fit neatly into any one social category. Such a multiplicity of belonging and identity is at odds with dominant narratives of bordered sovereignty and rooted ancestry.

Displacement is not only a matter of geographic dislocation. Migration also unsettles a person's linear sense of time, as families displaced by conflict, poverty, or persecution are caught between worlds, existing concurrently in places they have left behind and places where they have arrived. The experience of feeling trapped in time is common among refugees: "The future brings anxiety because you don't belong and can't move forward," writes Nayeri. "The past brings depression, because you can't go home, your memories fade and everything you know is gone" (Nayeri 2019, 173). For displacement to give way to some sense of belonging requires a person to construct cognitive links with which to imagine his or her place within the social and physical space of the host society. But without reference to past objects and events, it is difficult to understand one's self in the present (Connerton 1989, 2). The conscious actions of imagining a transnational belonging, with links to multiple spaces, requires a balance of strategic forgetting and creative remembering (Halbwachs 1992; Hobsbawn and Ranger [1983] 2003). Refugees forget and remember individually, in concert with their material surroundings, and communally, with others, through practices like storytelling, sharing food, and religious rituals. In such ways, displaced people who share elements of the same narrative have the ability to contribute to building a common past, which in turn informs their present. The ethnographic examples in this chapter illustrate the importance of memories and remembering for displaced people, suggesting that forced migrants consciously remember and forget as a means of psychologically connecting themselves to both places they leave behind and those in which they resettle.

Koreans on both sides of the DMZ share ethnic, cultural, and linguistic ties. Despite common cultural markers, North Korean refugees arriving in South Korea exist in an ambivalent relationship with their southern brethren. While enjoying the privileges of citizenship, they are nonetheless treated as a suspect community (Hough and Bell 2020, 3). Subsequently, North Korean refugees often find themselves experiencing a liminal existence, living as an outcast of the homeland–the DPRK–but not as a full member of the host society. But a time of uncertainly can also be a period imbued with the potential for creativity, and an opportunity for a person to shape new self-understandings. Misŏn's feelings of being pulled between Japan and the two Koreas was common to other returnees with whom I worked. While in Japan and during visits to South Korea, the stigma associated with being from North Korea threatened to rupture her kinship ties and fragment Misŏn's sense of self identity. The difficulty she experienced with referencing the past as part of her self-narrative provoked her complete withdrawal from public life.

The Fractured Self

It was approaching the end of winter and Misŏn had not been seen nor heard from for several months. She had ceased answering her telephone and stopped opening the door of her one-room apartment to concerned friends and family. Over dinner at a civic group meeting her friend worried, "She hasn't talked to me in months. It's like she's just disappeared."

In her late twenties, Misŏn's youth, diminutive frame, and gentle mannerisms gave no hint of the challenges she had already overcome. These included escaping across the Sino-Korean border under the cover of darkness, and working illegally in a Korean restaurant while in constant fear of arrest and deportation back to the DPRK. Misŏn had spent hours studying how to act Japanese. Her cheeks had a permanently flushed appearance, the result of her extensive use of pink blush. Her eyes were lined with deep black eye shadow, giving her a *kawa'ii* (cute) look popular with young Japanese women. She wore smart clothes and her comportment and mannerisms reflected idealized characteristics of Japanese femininity. Her tone of voice, in Japanese and in Korean, was frequently an octave higher than most of the Korean women I have spoken with over the years, emulating a manner of speaking commonly adopted by young Japanese women. Her head nodded up and down as she spoke, appearing to seek confirmation for what she was saying, and her right hand would sweep across her face on the rare occasion that she would refute something. Misŏn was also a meticulous timekeeper, being the first of my North Korean interlocutors to arrive on time to our appointments. Her seemingly flawless adoption of Japanese mannerisms drew compliments from the Japanese she met. In spite of her impressive ethnic and gendered performance, Misŏn felt she was failing to fit in. "People can tell that I'm not Japanese," she mourned. "It never takes long before they ask where I'm from." If a person asked after her origins, Misŏn would resist telling them that she had immigrated from North Korea, instead relying on a fictional past that she had created for herself. She explained, "In Japan, the image of North Korea is really bad and, when I first arrived here, I was met with lots of prejudice. People reacted to me in a way that showed they were shocked that I'm from North Korea. They either pitied me or they feared me. That's when I decided to stop telling people. I'd just make up a different story, tell them I'm from somewhere in South Korea. But I'm so tired by all the lies."

Her performance was manicured enough to draw praise but never enough to pass as Japanese. While she had become skilled at managing her performance during limited interactions, extended discussions tended to end with a questioning of her origins, questions that forced Misŏn to reproduce her fictional life. It was this discovery that prompted Misŏn to further explore herself. "I was curious if South Korea would be a better fit. I watched South Korean dramas constantly, imitating the accent so I could sound more like a Seoul person. But then I went to South Korea and everyone there asked me where I'm from. I told them, 'Here's my [South] Korean passport. I'm [South] Korean. I'm from here.' They replied, 'No. You can't be. You're Zainichi Korean.'"

A week in Seoul was enough to foster the same sense of disappointment with her apparent inability to perform South Korean-ness as she had experienced while trying to pass as Japanese. Misŏn had a finely tuned ear for languages and was skilled at embodying and replicating the symbolic aspects of both Japanese and South Korean identity. Nevertheless, she was unable to switch entirely between one and the other. When in Japan, her Japanese performance was held together with threads of her Korean identity that would, on occasion, begin to unravel.

In South Korea, Misŏn experienced similar challenges to her personal biography. Her accent, learned and refined from studiously watching South Korean television, was peppered with Japanese mannerisms that she had adopted as a façade to hide her (North) Korean behavior. In Japan, her bodily performance was betrayed by mistakes in her Japanese. While she was in South Korea, her Korean may have been flawless, but her personal presentation, gestures, her fashion aesthetics, and her accent projected what locals perceived as foreignness. Misŏn often reflected on her difficulties hiding her incongruous mannerisms. Her comments indicated that her failure to feel at home in Japan had led her to feeling cast adrift, lacking a cognitive mooring and an attendant feeling of belonging. Echoing her family's experiences of forced migration and displacement in China, her self-narrative had also shifted markedly over the years and she struggled to locate herself in any one place. Continuous movement appeared to have unbalanced her sense of self. Misŏn's feelings of dislocation were further evident in how she represented her relationships with family and friends.

For migrant communities, material memory aids assist with the creation of a social field, imagined as extending between the migrant and the community in the sending country (Basch, Schiller, and Blanc [1994] (2000; Glick Schiller, Basch, and Blanc 1999). The home, in particular, becomes a site of significance linking the world of the past and the world of the present (Levin and Fincher 2010, 401–2). Within the home, items of emotional value–photographs, documents, and keepsakes–reflect connections to people and places important to the biography of the occupant. Such intimate connections are not defined by co-temporality, meaning that a person does not have to be alive for an object to create a feeling of copresence with a loved one.

The idealized Japanese home is characterized by an atmosphere of brightness in which social heat is generated by activities between family members. These activities consist of communal times of bodily contact, such as co-sleeping and co-bathing (Daniels 2015). The bodily activities of family and the material reminders of kin and community generate a continuity of narrative with absent family. In contrast to the brightness of the idealized Japanese home, Misŏn's apartment felt stark, dull, and lacking in the intimacy needed to yield connectivity and foster feelings of belonging to family and friends. Her home was devoid of family photographs, graduation certificates, or the keepsakes that might connect her with loved ones. She stored her few photos and official documents hidden from sight, inside a set of drawers. Items initially imbued with possibility had also taken on new meaning. Shortly after arriving in Japan, Misŏn had successfully applied for a South Korean passport. Where initially this travel document had been for her a symbol of membership within the South Korean community and an opportunity for freedom of movement, it had since become a further marker of her failure to belong and a reminder of her inability to be recognized in the way she desired. Within her home, there were no objects for Misŏn to claim authority over her past, just as there were none to establish a connection with her present. Misŏn had no means of indexing herself in Japan and no window with which to positively reference her life in North Korea. Furthermore, her experiences in South Korea had made her sensitive to her ambiguous ethnic and cultural positioning. Since returning from Seoul, her carefully crafted bodily comportment and her performance of both South Korean and Japanese identities felt clumsy and flawed. Misŏn's withdrawal and isolation was compounded by the absence of material memory aids to support a process of self-referencing. Her past and her being from North Korea had become a pathological state that affected her relationships and everyday life in both Japan and South Korea.

While in Japan and during visits to South Korea, the stigma that Misŏn associated with being from North Korea threatened to rupture her kinship ties and fracture her sense of self, eventually provoking her complete withdrawal from community and public life. Misŏn told me she was unhappy living in Japan but could not imagine returning to South Korea. In our last conversation before she disappeared, she told me, "I have no memories in Japan, and I can't seem to make new ones. I don't think about the past, either. I'm unable to think about life in North Korea or my time in China and there's nothing here to bring back those old memories. I need to leave Japan. It's too close to North Korea. I'll never fit in anywhere and people will always care that I'm from North Korea. It always hangs over me. I need to go to the US or somewhere, anywhere else."

Neither the Japanese landscape nor the people embraced Misŏn or reflected the history and sense of belonging that she had inherited from her mother and grandparents. Furthermore, because Misŏn had become isolated, she lacked community with which to reconstruct and repopulate a shared past and a self-narrative in which to situate herself in the present. She felt caught between worlds and outside of time. Her past was simultaneously near and far in that, although she had tried to block out her life in North Korea, its absence had created a vacuum in her self-identity. Misŏn perceived that she had failed at passing as Japanese or South Korean. She also understood her North Korean origins as a taboo aspect of her identity. Despite this, she felt she had exhausted all possibilities for creating a self-biography without reference to life before leaving North Korea. Consequently, she had been unable to conceive of belonging anywhere. Her proposed solution to her predicament, similar to a growing number of North Koreans in South Korea (Song and Bell 2018), was to leave East Asia and move to a place in which she imagined neither her foreignness nor her association with North Korea would define her.

Landscapes for Remembering Japan

Reading the physical landscape is a means of interpreting people's historically, politically, and socially specific actions. But landscapes are constantly changing, shifting with the imprint of people and ideas. In such a way, material reminders of the self are shaped and reshaped by those who use and pass through a place Remembering the past and the self within a place is a creative process, requiring a person to locate multiple threads of narrative to build a communally agreed on history and a shared sense of belonging. The shifting physical environment circumscribes such a communal remembering. Physical objects such as statues, monuments, and places of spiritual or political importance are touchstones in the memories shared by groups. A person who returns to the group after a long time away will try to reconnect with family and friends through these objects (Halbwachs 1992, 204). But, just as time cannot be rolled back, the landscape resists a simplistic reading, sometimes changing during a person's absence to the extent that it yields little of familiarity upon return. When markers of a group's identity have disappeared, perhaps through the destruction of war, or by design through the planned obsolescence built into the consumer capitalist economy (Connerton 2008, 66), how does a person recreate emotional connections to the group and to the land? If familiarity is nowhere to be found and, like the bare walls of Misŏn's apartment, if there is nothing to speak to social connections beyond the self, does a person exist at all?

Not all returnees find themselves cast adrift in the manner of Misŏn. Unlike imagined returnees such as Misŏn, who arrive in Japan for the first time, birth returnees–returned migrants from North Korea who were born in Japan–arrive in a country where they once lived. Subsequently, birth returnees are likely to hope for some sense of belonging to emerge following their return. Since her arrival, a month prior to our first meeting in Spring 2014, Kim Sŭngmi had been rediscovering herself. Her Japanese language was gradually returning, and she was venturing farther outside of Tsuruhashi in an effort to explore Osaka city. In spite of offers from Ayako, Sŭngmi stayed away from the Japanese language school. She was also unenthusiastic about the prospect of working on the British Gardens strawberry farm. Reflecting on the prospect of growing and selling strawberries, Sŭngmi had likened it to state-enforced exile in the North Korean countryside. She had also quit her part-time position in a Korean restaurant only a week after starting. Sŭngmi blamed sore feet for her inability to work, although she later told me that her South Korean colleagues had been bullying her and that she struggled to understand what they were saying. "They use so much English in their Korean," she complained.

Kim Sŭngmi is a birth returnee to Japan, having migrated to North Korea from Japan in the 1960s and only recently returned. Over dinner with Osaka activist Matsumoto Tadashi, Akiyama Ayako, and several South Korean students from Ayako's language school, Sŭngmi reminisced about the home she had left behind when her family moved to North Korea in the early 1960s. "I wonder if it's still there?" she pondered, as Tadashi topped up her glass with beer. "I heard from a friend, before I left North Korea, that it's there and that the area isn't that different. But it's been so long. I was just a child when I left, so I guess I'm just curious," she continued. "There's nothing else here that feels like home. Japan's another world now," she lamented. Tadashi did not miss a beat, "Why don't we go and find it?" he suggested. "It's your hometown. It's where you're from and it's a part of you." Two weeks later, the three of us set out in the direction of Wakayama, to the south of Osaka, on the Kii Peninsula in search of Sŭngmi's hometown.

From Umeda's Osaka station to our destination took two hours and four train changes. The muggy June weather had made everyone drowsy. The only saving grace was that the windows on the slow-moving rural train could be opened wide, allowing for a generous breeze to sweep through the wagon. "I used to ride this train as a child," Sŭngmi announced, emerging from a meditative state. "Fifty-three years ago, every day I took this same line to the Korean school. The trip took hours. It's all coming back to me," she declared, with an expression halfway between a smile and a frown. "My friends and I used to run around the neighborhood trying to convince the housewives to give us snacks. Sometimes we'd tangle with Japanese children, call each other names and maybe even fight. They'd yell things at us, and we'd yell things right back. Just kid stuff."

The two-carriage train rumbled lazily along the tracks, rocking gently from side to side, the same tracks that Sŭngmi had ridden more than a half a century earlier. The rhythmic vibrations, moving up through the metalwork and into the seats, had a languorous effect on the few remaining passengers to make it to the end of the line. For Sŭngmi, it was stirring memories of her childhood: a child born in postwar Japan to working-class, Korean immigrant parents. Despite her family's outsider status, Japan had been the only home she had known. The train came to a standstill at the final station, where the Pacific Ocean meets the jagged edges of Honshu Island. The environment had changed dramatically since we departed from Osaka. We found ourselves surrounded by emerald green mountains on one side and ocean on the other.

Alighting from the train, Sŭngmi and Tadashi sought out shade under the cover of the single-room station and entered into conference. "What can you remember? What did your friend tell you?" Tadashi probed for a clue that might take the investigation further. Sŭngmi appeared flustered. She could not recall where her childhood home was located. Referencing the train station map yielded nothing, so she called a friend in Osaka. After a great deal of nodding into the mobile phone we had a plan and the three of us started in the direction of the closest hill. Sŭngmi led the charge.

With the midday sun beating down, we walked up and down the empty streets, hunting for a building that had existed in Sŭngmi's imagination since her childhood. Although the elevated position afforded us a pleasing view of the sparkling Pacific, Sŭngmi's confidence was clearly flagging. "It was so different back then. Nothing looks familiar now," she exclaimed, scanning the landscape. "I remember our neighbors. Like many of the families in this area they were Korean, too. They lived in an old-fashioned house, wooden slats and straw roof. The grandfather in that family wore traditional Korean clothes and had a long white beard. I remember that. But I don't know where it is."

It is through the landscape that people who have been absent are able to reconnect with the past and imagine belonging to a community in the present. But in half a century, Sŭngmi's hometown had changed markedly: factories had sprung up alongside the main road, and the traditional wooden houses, so impractical for the biting Japanese winters, had been replaced by modern, earthquake-resistant homes. The characters from Sŭngmi's past, Japanese children with whom she had often quarreled and the elderly pipe-smoking Korean scholar, had long vanished. Sŭngmi could not relate to the landscape, nor did the landscape speak to her. The emptiness she felt contrasted starkly with her recollections of playing with Korean friends and of sharing the tasty treats that neighborhood mothers lavished on them. Instead, an absence now characterized the landscape around her, a silence that threatened to unhinge the search for her past and her tenuous link to Japan.

Sŭngmi was in the grips of an existential crisis–if she could not find her childhood home, had it ever existed? If she could not locate herself within this space, how reliable were her faded memories of life before emigration to North Korea? The dissonance of her memories to the contemporary Japanese landscape unsettled Sŭngmi. Aspects of how she understood herself, of the world constructed and reconstructed over the years, were on the verge of disappearing.

We headed back down the hill, toward the main road from where we had started our search. As a last resort, Tadashi suggested we knock on a door. The whitewashed wooden door creaked open slowly and an elderly woman gingerly poked her head out. "Hello. Can I help you?"

"Ah yes. We have an unusual inquiry that perhaps you can help us with," Tadashi gently explained. "This lady here," he continued, gesturing to Sŭngmi, "used to live in this neighborhood. She left when she was a child and we've come back today to help her find her old home." Having opened the way for the women to talk, Tadashi withdrew.

Separated in age by only a few years, the two strangers started to piece together Sŭngmi's childhood. As they spoke, the enthusiasm returned to Sŭngmi's face. Her back straightened and her eyes lit up. Her hands darted this way and that, gesturing in concert with the Japanese woman to the geography around her. Her Japanese also returned and, for perhaps the first time since arriving in Japan, she appeared to speak with confidence. The Japanese woman, oblivious to the presence of anyone except Sŭngmi, was equally engrossed in the conversation and seemed to draw pleasure from adding fragments of her own recollections to what Sŭngmi could remember. Through a dialectic process, they gradually rebuilt the space around them from their shared memories, reimagining the past and overlaying the 1960s neighborhood onto their contemporary surroundings. The longer they spoke, the more textured the picture they painted, oscillating back and forth in time. Together, they drew deeply and creatively from a communal palette of memory, one that had remained dormant for decades.

As if experiencing an epiphany, the elderly woman unexpectedly recalled, "In those days there were a lot of Koreans in this neighborhood. Most of them left for North Korea, but I'm sure I remember your family. It was a long time ago. But yes, your house was nearby." With her adult son now at her side, she recalled her memories of Sŭngmi's family home. But there was bad news. Hesitating to tell us right away, she instead pointed across the street, "Over there," she said. "Let's go over there." We followed her out of the shade and across the street onto a vacant parking lot. The elderly Japanese woman paused and turned again to Sŭngmi, "It was here. Your family house was right here," she announced, gesturing around the empty lot. "It was pulled down years ago and now, well, you can see. In those days there were several houses around here. The town has grown and changed. Some things have gone." Everyone was quiet, contemplating the anticlimactic ending to our search for Sŭngmi's past.

"Let's take a picture," said Tadashi, trying to salvage the moment. We gathered together in the middle of the parking lot and Tadashi photographed the group. Eager to return to the shade, we started back across the road. Sŭngmi lingered a few moments more, casting her gaze here and there. Without saying anything further, she followed the elderly Japanese woman across the road, and they said goodbye like old friends.

Their memories of the village some fifty years earlier may have been imprecise, and they had not led to Sŭngmi finding her former family home, but in those moments the two collaborators in memory had shared a feeling of kinship. They had been partners in facilitating a communal return to the past, to a point in time and in space that, while profoundly mediated, had allowed Sŭngmi to feel a sense of belonging to a place that was otherwise entirely foreign.

After parting ways with the elderly Japanese lady, we walked down to the shoreline, to a place where Sŭngmi recalled playing as a child. The coastal area had been subject to the same industrial makeover as the rest of the village. Giant cement tetrapods lined the seawall, built to defend against the encroaching waves. Along the edge of the coast, not more than a few kilometers away, an expansive cluster of rusting factory buildings loomed over the nearby village. "I'm not sad that I couldn't find my childhood house. I understand that it's gone," Sŭngmi said. "I'm just happy to be back where I was born," she continued, affirming to herself her historical existence in Japan.

Because of Sŭngmi's difficulties in relating to the environment around her, she initially expressed a sense of ambivalence at the idea of returning to her birthplace. But, as our sun-weary group wandered farther around the sea wall, Sŭngmi smiled and chatted to Tadashi. "All of this is new," she explained, motioning to the factories and two-storied homes. In narrating the changes, Sŭngmi was claiming authority over the landscape, incorporating the village, with all its new buildings, roads, and restaurants, into her own self-narrative. While living in North Korea, her parents had idealized Japan. Sŭngmi was possibly too young to remember the difficult circumstances in which many Korean families had lived prior to repatriation. Her parents' nostalgia and the struggles their family subsequently endured in North Korea had added a rosy tint to her childhood memories of this small, seaside village. Although Sŭngmi did not find her hometown as she left it, she managed to piece together fragments of her past through a collaborative resuscitation of memory. She had located her former self within Japan, confirming her existence among the murky memories of the past and giving herself a starting point from which her new life might begin.

Nostalgia as Creation

Memories are inherently unstable reproductions of the past. Each time we go in search of them, they emerge in a slightly different form. Sŭngmi's return to her village showed how episodic memory—recollections of events rather than facts—are creative explorations in which the person remembering has some control over shaping the raw material into a pleasurable nostalgia. But just as nostalgia can foster beneficial experiences, futile attempts to return to the past can also provoke a chronological homesickness (McDonald 2017).

I met Yi Chihu in Osaka, through a Japanese journalist who invited me to dinner on a snowy mid-winter's evening. Over the course of my research for this book Chihu became both an invaluable guide into repatriate life in North Korea and a close friend, educating me on the finer points of Japanese Izakaya culture. Chihu was a taciturn man. He kept his feelings to himself, except when the conversation turned to sports. Rugby, basketball, and ice hockey—each brought forth reels of commentary from an otherwise stoic individual.

Chihu arrived in Tokyo with his father in late 2008. Like Misŏn, he was born in North Korea to parents who had immigrated from Japan. And, like so many people to have fled the country in the past twenty years, he left North Korea seeking a better life, something similar, he told me, to the South Korean dramas he had furtively watched at home. Chihu's family was not wealthy; they were, in his words, "Just an ordinary Korean family." Nevertheless, his childhood was largely carefree. He spent his time between school and his favorite pastime, skating. "My parents aren't from privileged families. They weren't rich, nor did they have political connections. They didn't even speak Korean when they arrived in North Korea. So, they were sent to the northern rural areas, near the Chinese border. But we had family in Japan who supported us by sending money, food, and clothes. It's so cold in the northern provinces, so all I did was play ice hockey. I became really good, too. When I was twelve, the state selected me for the national development program and I moved to Pyongyang for training."

North Korea's athletics training was hard on new recruits. The older athletes treated the younger boys like their personal butlers. Chihu was bullied mercilessly. Despite years of hard regimen—early starts, long runs in the snow, broken fingers, and cracked ribs—he recalled these times fondly, romanticizing the casual violence that was a part of his childhood. "I've good memories of being a kid in North Korea. Sometimes the boys' hockey team played the girls and that was always an opportunity to fool around. The girls were tough. They'd whack us with their sticks and it always hurt like hell. The problem for everyone was that our equipment was really old, and we didn't have plastic on our helmets or padding or mouth guards, so a lot of the players were seriously injured–lost eyes and broken bones. It wasn't until we got to the top level that they gave us better equipment."

Chihu recalled the thrill of playing against international teams and the bitterness that followed a loss to a better-equipped side. Ice hockey and the fraternity of elite athletes shaped his life world from an early age, offering him opportunities not available to ordinary North Koreans. In the Pyongyang dormitory where he lived, the state ensured that all athletes could eat as much as they wanted, so much so that Chihu and his teammates smuggled the surplus out of the dorm and traded it on the streets. "We always had rice and meat, even when most people had nothing. When things were particularly difficult, we hid the food we couldn't eat under our clothes and sold it outside. Whatever we made we gave to our families."

After ten years playing ice hockey, Chihu was permitted to go to college, and in 1999 he graduated as a physical education teacher. Shortly thereafter, a matchmaker specializing in matching families from Japan introduced him to his wife. "After we married," he recalled, "we moved into an apartment that was next door to a shop selling beer. It's a kind of open secret in North Korea that places like this exist. As long as no one makes a big deal out of it, police and state officials turn a blind eye to the private commerce and general drunken behavior. There were always people coming and going, getting drunk and having a good time. It was a really fun time for me, because there was always someone to talk to and with whom to share a beer. My wife wasn't so happy with the situation, though."

Chihu's memories are steeped in nostalgia for his life in North Korea, where he enjoyed job security, social standing, community, and friendship. Central to his memories of the life he left behind is a longing for a sociality that he has not found in Japan. Chihu recalled a canteen set-up by a repatriated Korean in a nearby apartment block, cooking Japanese food, and his neighbor's speakeasy serving beer and snacks until the small hours. Over lunch in his Osaka apartment he explained, "Most of the houses in North Korea are very close together and everyone knows everyone. There's a real sense of community. People are always doing favors for each other. We all knew who to talk to and where to go to get whatever we needed–food, alcohol, whatever. If you wanted *soju*, you'd go to the home of the person who makes it. You'd explain what you need, and he'd sell you some. If you're sick, of course there's no ambulance. Instead, you got a neighbor to carry you to the hospital on their back."

Crises do not affect populations equally. The North Korean famine was no different, since national food shortages had impacts on existing socioeconomic inequalities (Fahy 2015, 24). Consequently, during the years of the Arduous March, families with established social and kinship networks and access to resources, within and outside of the country, were more likely to survive than those who were isolated. As a member of the nation's elite,

Chihu was largely insulated from the dire situation facing many North Koreans, as the effects of the economic meltdown took their toll.

Unable, perhaps unwilling, to manage the crisis, Pyongyang encouraged citizens to fend for themselves during the famine years. Sharing resources was just one way that ordinary people dealt with the shortages characterizing everyday life at that time. Chihu was aware of the depth of the suffering around him. He described beggars in the streets and the women who gathered at the train station to sell their bodies for food. Yet his recollections of the busy years, as anthropologist Sandra Fahy's (2015) respondents referred to the famine, emphasized not the desperation of the times, but a longing for the community that had rallied during a time of shared hardship.

Chihu's nostalgia at times appeared to empower him. His nostalgia was a creative force shaping his memories of North Korea into a narrative in which people had little of material value, but were nevertheless caring and generous. In contrast, Chihu felt that all the modern conveniences and wealth of Japan could not compensate for a loss of sociality or sense of shared purpose. Chihu had lost his public life, and what remained was a sense of emptiness: "In Japan no one knows anyone. You never meet your neighbors. There's no community life. Sure, North Korea is a backward country in many ways, but as in other underdeveloped countries, people rely on each other for help with things. It's like during the Stone Age when people needed other people to help them hunt their prey. In North Korea, people still need each other to survive, but not in Japan."

After five years in Japan, Chihu was sensitive to feeling like nobody needed him. Although his family were now with him in Japan, his former teammates remained in North Korea. His loneliness was exacerbated by the everyday difficulties that he still experienced. Yet, only once did I see him let his frustration show. "How is it that I've lived here so long and still can't speak Japanese?" he had growled, after struggling through a phone call.

In contrast to Misŏn, whose fractured sense of self derived from a denial of the past and her perceived failure to locate herself in the present, Chihu could not help but feel pulled back to life in North Korea, to a time when he was an important athlete and when he was embedded within community and commonality. Chihu felt that his life had had value in North Korea, first as an athlete and then as an educator. Since coming to Japan, however, he had experienced the effects of downward social mobility, in terms of both low-status employment and the loss of social capital that resulted from his inability to negotiate aspects of the everyday. He told me that he no longer has dreams for his own future. As is the case for so many first-generation immigrants, he instead deferred his ambitions to his children, "I want my son to study hard so he can live well. His mother has had a difficult life, too. So, all we want is for him to do better." Chihu continued to remember his life in North Korea fondly, but he was always mindful to conclude recollections of former glories with reference to the present and to his family, "I have my wife and my son here now," he emphasized. "It's enough."

A Longing for Home

In early spring, Misŏn reappeared. She had quit her job and was spending her days learning English by watching episodes of the US sitcom *Friends*. Despite her fragility, she appeared happier than she had prior to her disappearance. She had few plans for the future, she said, but hoped that she might leave Japan, perhaps to lose herself in Europe or North America.

Whether they are refugees returning to the homeland for the first time since their displacement, or migrant workers who have been away longer than intended, returning migrants often fail to account for specific transformations that have occurred in their absence. Changes that might include new roads, buildings, and businesses in the villages and towns they once called home; new trends within the religious and ethnic demographics of a society; and unexpected shifts in the language and behaviors of communities once so familiar. Confronting such dramatic changes unsettles a person's sense of self and gives rise to feelings of displacement while supposedly at home. Further overlooked, among the tangible unfamiliarity that renders a returnee disoriented in their erstwhile home, are the changes that have taken place within themselves. Such changes might run only skin deep: a person might have learned to move differently, developed an accent when they speak, or a palate for unusual foods. But for migrants returning to the ethnic homeland after so many years away—or arriving for the first time, in the case of the second generation born outside the homeland—they may discover that a longing for home and for people with whom they were once so familiar has in fact been a longing for a time and place that no longer exists. In this case, when displacement and multiple migrations have shaped personal histories marked by dislocation, the creative acts of forgetting and remembering may contribute to fostering a renewed sense of belonging in the host society.

Men and women who return from North Korea experience varying successes with strategically and actively connecting themselves to both places they leave behind and those in which they resettle. Their ability to feel at home in a society that feels alien reflects complex and often ambivalent relationships to both the sending and receiving countries. Misŏn, for example, had worked hard on how she presented herself when in public, initially refining her Korean accent to sound like a Seoulite, and subsequently dressing and acting in what she saw as a Japanese manner once in Osaka. Her carefully curated ethnic performances reflected a cosmopolitan South Korean identity when in South Korea and an idealized female manner when in Japan. But so often her accent or the wrong choice of words would give her away. As a consequence of failing to pass for a local in both South Korea and Japan, Misŏn struggled to identify a home for herself. Her feeling trapped in time and unable to comfortably discuss her life in North Korea was manifest in the austere nature of her apartment, a place in which the material reminders of kin and community were kept out of sight.

Sŭngmi's relationship to the country to which she returned was very different to imagined returnees, such as Misŏn. Sŭngmi returned to her rural Japanese hometown after fifty years in North Korea and was distraught that the landscape had changed beyond recognition during her time away. The town in which she was born no longer presented her with objects or images through which she could claim a sense of familiarity and belonging. But even without prompts from her surroundings, she was able to reposition herself in the landscape by means of a communal act of remembering. Although her memories were fragmented and her surroundings largely unfamiliar, through selectively remembering and forgetting she edited the past into the present to locate herself in the village that she left as a child.

Sŭngmi used her memories to remember her past in a way that appeared to bring her a sense of peace. Chihu, however, returned time and again to a nostalgic version of events prior to his escaping North Korea. His disappointment with life in Japan when compared to his near-celebrity status as a DPRK elite athlete provoked in him a chronological homesickness in which the present held scant joy in comparison to the triumphs of the past. Chihu's romanticizing of the famine years, and his longing for the kinds of friendship and sociality that had existed when he lived near a speakeasy suggested that he felt he had lost something important since coming to Japan: he had lost community. Consequently, North Korea, a place where he felt his life had value, continued to tug at Chihu's sense of self, beckoning him back across the Sea of Japan/East Sea.

Memory and the intricacies of remembering and forgetting play a significant role in enabling and directing a refugee's resettlement in their new home. Memories of life prior to migration both help and hinder moving beyond a sense of homelessness for individuals who perhaps feel that they should not talk about their past. The resettlement process and the accompanied shock of an imagined life world falling apart leads some returnees to reconnect with the past by recalling themselves in the landscapes of the host society. For others, nostalgic recollections bring as much pain as they do pleasure, discouraging lingering too long in the past. Returnees arriving in Japan as children will likely inherit their parents' complex and conflicted memories of life in North Korea. A desire to revisit a particular emotional state, rather than a specific moment, means that the stories the generation born to returnees may hear are not limited to tales of struggle and forced exodus. Chihu's son, already asking questions, gives audience to his father's yearning for caring neighbors, drinking buddies, and long winters spent on the ice. This version of the past may one day beckon his son to return across the sea, back to North Korea.

Notes

1. Stuart Hall put it in more pointed terms when he said, "Migration is a one-way trip. There is no 'home' to go back to" (Hall 1996, 115).
2. The characters for *furusato* (hometown/ancestral village), for example, feature the radicals for soil and rice paddy. The term of *sokoku* (motherland) is also used for ancestral home, and features the radical that represents one family, implying the nation is a large family.
3. The expression "falling leaves return to their roots" is used in Chinese and in Japanese to refer to a person who returns to their hometown or family after a period of time away. In this case, the falling leaf refers to a person who leaves and the roots to a person's origins.

CONCLUSION

Reimagining Refugees

From Crisis to Solution in Modern Japan

Hong Hŭiŭn had a plan. Since the day she pulled shut the door to her North Korean home and crossed the Yalu, she had felt pursued by something she could not define, "It's like my feet don't touch the ground," she pondered. She had not stayed long at Akiyama Ayako's Japanese language school. She had had too much to do and not enough time to do it: late nights cramming for her high school certificate, struggling with math problems on the last subway home. Not long after arriving in Osaka, Hŭiŭn had found work as a professional massage therapist. "But my hands always ached, so I started waiting tables in a Sichuan Ramen restaurant. Finally, the Chinese I picked up in Shenyang is useful for something," she mused. Earning just enough to cover rent in her one-room apartment, she watched online makeup tutorials on her days off. "I've never liked studying. But for the first time I can see a way forward–get Japanese qualifications, join a beautician, and improve my Japanese. Then, open my own nail and hair shop," she explained. "My aunt already introduced me to a South Korean woman who runs a hairdresser. I can probably start there."

Like many of the returnees with whom I shared evenings and insights, Hŭiŭn arrived in Japan with little other than the clothes she wore and a sprinkling of Japanese vocabulary. But the same determination that carried her through China to Japan supported her through the hardships of resettling in her new home. "I'm even dating," she told me with a grin. "My aunt says it's fine to date Japanese guys. But only if they eat kimchi."

* * *

Many of the migrations examined in this book started in the first half of the twentieth century and set in motion a pattern of intergenerational movements across East Asia. Human displacement will become more common throughout the twenty-first century and the vignettes of returnees from North Korea offer important lessons as to what happens when people are compelled to move again and again, sometimes without the ability to return. For those who are able to do so, often the place to which they return has changed beyond recognition.

For the families in this book, mobility has been both a logical and a necessary response to exclusionary national narratives that designate them as outsiders, to limited life opportunities, and even to state-sanctioned persecution. Their experiences demonstrate the resilience of people managing often-desperate circumstances of poverty, discrimination, conflict, and violent political persecution. But this is not merely a story of loss, nor of individuals being crushed under the wheels of history. Rather, even when it seems as if there is nothing left, the voices of the families moving back and forth between Japan and the two Koreas have shown the ways in which people like Hŭiŭn are able to reinvent themselves through distinct strategies, and how the transformations taking places in individuals, families, and minority communities reshape the places in which they resettle. Hence this is as much a story of reinvention as it is dislocation: for the host societies as much as for the migrants. How will the arrival of these people remake societies, such as Japanese society, that are experiencing unprecedented social and demographic changes?

The Migrant's Path

The migratory histories and demographic imaginings of the countries of East Asia have contributed to very different paths toward modernity. Japan, for example, shifted from the extractive economic practices of empire building to a Western-style liberal democracy. It was traveling the road that would culminate in it becoming an economic powerhouse and key US ally in the containment of communism. North Korea on the other hand, emerged from decades of colonial subjugation as an autocratic command economy, structured along socialist lines. As different as the modern iterations of the two countries became, reimagining the nation in both cases required the state to draw boundaries of belonging and identity. And in both cases, an ethno-nationalist ideology positioned racial purity and blood lines as crucial to deciding who would belong and who would not.

In imperial Japan, a state-sanctioned set of memories was central to nation building, as the histories, languages, and cultural practices of the indigenous communities, of Koreans, Chinese, and others, were subsumed into a broader history of the Japanese people. But Japan's surrender and occupation shattered the expansive empire. In the aftermath, people previously regarded as part of the empire—Koreans and other former colonial subjects—became aliens in the new Japan as the country sought to rebuild, protect, and reconstitute itself. A person could be born in Japan, speak perfect Japanese, and be culturally indistinguishable from Japanese, but still not be Japanese. North Korea pursued a similar race-based nationalism, with one important difference, the political lineage—*sŏngbun*—of its citizens would further determine their life opportunities and relationship to the state.

The Japanese state had used colonized Koreans as labor in factories or disposable shock troops on the battlefield. Similarly, North Koreans tolerated ethnic Korean immigrants and their spouses from Japan insofar as they supplied the state with human capital, economic sustenance, and political legitimacy. In each case, the host state imbued the families in this book with an almost magical capacity to unsettle the national community. Within the Japanese, the North Korean, and the South Korean contexts, people like Hŭiŭn have been variously viewed as criminals, social and political deviants, and enemies of the state. Once reduced to a lower form of human life it became easier for the Japanese government to argue for the repatriation of Koreans, for the South Korean government to torture and incarcerate Koreans from Japan who were suspected of harboring communist sympathies, and for North Korea to punish so-called political reactionaries for speaking Japanese, criticizing the regime, or trying to escape. A nation is a community in which imagined commonalities foster a sense of belonging to something that is greater than the individual parts. In Japan, in South Korea, and in North Korea the people in this book were cast as a virus, threatening to destroy the imagined community from the inside out.

In the postwar world the Japanese reimagined social and ethnic divisions and redrew borders of national sovereignty to reinvent themselves along racial lines. Consequently, the newly imagined ethnically homogenous Japanese people have interpreted the momentous events of the twentieth century that impacted Japan as either moments when the national community was led astray by duplicitous leaders, or when the community was subject to the machinations of outside—foreign—forces. The Japanese framing of the repatriation of tens of thousands of Koreans similarly depicts both the Japanese public and the political class as doing their best to help struggling Korean families return to their homeland. Indeed, the intentions of many of the people who supported sending Koreans to North Korea were surely good. But just as the ICRC failed to understand the web of geopolitical tension and pressure that characterized Cold War geo-politics, ordinary Japanese who supported the repatriations were equally naïve with regard to the broader forces at play.

Returnees from North Korea bring the human feature of what really happened before, during, and after the reparations back to the country they left more than sixty years ago. Their vernacular memories of tenuous belonging, exclusion, and discrimination sit uncomfortably alongside Japanese histories of humanitarianism undone. Returnees' bitter recollections of life in postwar Japan frustrate claims that the Japanese government was acting out of humanitarian concern for its ethnic minorities. Instead, their experiences of social, political, and economic marginalization suggest that they emigrated in response to both the Japanese state's racialization and criminalization of people it deemed expendable and inassimilable, and North Korean propaganda disseminated by Zainichi Koreans and Japanese sympathetic to Pyongyang.

Micro-Transformations

People like Donghyŏn, Sŏnok, and Sŭngmi, described in the preceding chapters, moved to North Korea to escape discrimination and poverty in Japan. Many subsequently left North Korea for similar reasons. During their moments of decision-making, as they moved and resettled in new homes, found work, married, and had children, they consciously and unconsciously deployed particular strategies to negotiate and overcome the challenges they faced. The vernacular histories in this book have highlighted five key strategies commonly used by migrants around the world to ensure their economic, physical, and emotional survival: intramarriage for alliance building, identity management, emotionally directed mobility, activist engagement, and imagined belonging.

Intramarriage

Arriving in North Korea, repatriates' ethnic identity and sense of belonging were destabilized by both real and imagined differences between them and local Koreans. Treated as suspect by the state and subsequently persecuted during Kim Il-sung's political purges, repatriate families experienced their identity as being simultaneously on display and on trial by the host society. To the locals, the families that moved into apartments and houses in towns and cities throughout the country appeared little different from recently departed Japanese colonial administrators—the way they moved, their difficulty speaking Korean, the expensive clothes they wore, and the unusual smells drifting from their kitchens. So often, to local Koreans, it seemed that the people disembarking in Ch'ŏngjin acted, looked, and spoke like strangers, and not like Korean compatriots. Compounding their foreignness, local North Koreans avoided marrying repatriates out of fear of what would happen to their own sociopolitical position. As such, repatriates tended to marry each other. As they had done in Japan, they used matchmakers to introduce families sharing similar ethnic and geographical backgrounds. Repatriated Zainichi Korean matchmakers knew the histories, the economic and political status, and the social standing of the repatriate families in their town or village. Repatriate families called on these matchmakers to help them build kinship alliances in response to social marginalization in North Korean society. The alliances that repatriate families subsequently created exacerbated extant social distance from the broader society, while incubating a transnational, Zainichi Korean identity that connected these families back to Japan. Echoing their experiences in Japan, the relationship between immigrant Koreans and the locals was fraught from the beginning.

Identity Management

The friction between repatriates and locals manifested itself in both structural and direct violence and subtle forms of resistance. Agents of the state targeted repatriates during political purges, imprisoning men and women, confiscating wealth, and banishing families to the hinterlands. But repatriates were not passive victims in their relationship to the mechanics of power. Repatriate families became the locus of decision-making on how to negotiate and in some cases how to resist attempts by the state to monitor and discipline new arrivals. Resistance took the form not of explicit antistate protest, but everyday acts like speaking Japanese, writing letters to family in Japan, and consuming Japanese foods. These ordinary practices contributed to the careful management and subsequent transmission of a group character to the next generation. Not an ethno-nationalist, revolutionary socialist identity, but a transnational, trans-local identity.

Within repatriates' homes, seemingly mundane acts shaped the identities of their children, fostering a sense of familiarity in the new generation to places in Japan they had never been to. While Pyongyang encouraged the inflow of capital and goods as a revenue stream benefitting the state, those very same items and the relationships that sustained them also allowed for the emergence in repatriate families of diverging imaginaries of self and belonging, not to North Korea, but to communities in Japan.

Emotionally Directed Mobility

Refugees are sometimes presented as cheating migration systems, using fake stories and false identities to exploit the generosity of unwitting, wealthy countries. The processes engaged in by international refugee agencies and national immigration departments are designed to uncover just these falsehoods. But the queue jumper narrative commonly ignores two important realities. First, the majority of refugees do not flee to wealthy Western countries–they instead seek shelter in countries geographically close and culturally similar to their home country. The reason for such proximate migrations is that it benefits a refugee to remain close to the homeland while sheltering in a place as culturally familiar as possible; it takes much greater economic investment to travel farther away. The majority of refugees fleeing Syria, for example, have found safety in neighboring countries: as of 2020, Turkey alone hosts more than 3.5 million Syrians (UNHCR 2021). Second, the decision to leave home is never taken lightly. Instead, for those who must leave everything they have, much more goes into thinking through migration strategies than simply the financial benefits offered by receiving countries.

People fleeing North Korea know about the South Korean government's resettlement packages: information on financial and material assistance not limited to a cash gift, housing benefits, and discounts on tertiary education are channeled back to North Korea. Yet, although these benefits should make South Korea the logical destination for a refugee from North Korea, returnees like Donghyŏn and Hyerim cite a fear of South Korean prejudice as a reason not to go there. Instead, the people in this book are pulled to cities like Osaka and Tokyo by emotional drivers. In chapter 4 I showed that both real and inherited memories of life in Japan—of family, friends, and community—are enough of a reason to migrate to places they either left as a child or only heard about in stories told by parents and grandparents. Choosing personal familiarity over immediate economic reward is a strategy that directs Donghyŏn, Hyerim, and others to Japan rather than to South Korea.

Migration is often thought of as a kind of reset button for the distribution of power, resources, and labor in a family. In some families, distance from the homeland offers the freedom to challenge assumed norms of gender roles and patriarchal practices. Certainly, men and women returnees' experiences differ according to their age, skills, and experience in the North Korean labor market. But usually returnees' social and political capital—specifically their technical skills and standing in North Korea's political economy—are of little value in Japan. Instead, their participation in North Korean black markets, particularly women's contributions to the informal capitalist economy, are a significant factor contributing to their resilience in the places they resettle. The informal marketization of the DPRK economy has had a ripple effect in the lives of North Koreans in exile. And, just as women were at the forefront of North Korea's marketization that arguably prevented the country's economy from entirely collapsing, returnee women again take the lead in supporting both family in Japan and those still in the DPRK.

In this sense, migration to Japan is an empowering process for women like Kyŏngcha, Yumi, and Hyerim as they develop new skills, gain new qualifications, and build social networks within and beyond ethnic Korean communities. In contrast, returnee men commonly find low-skilled work through the Zainichi Korean and South Korean communities. While employment satisfies their need to be the family breadwinner, they often forgo opportunities for other forms of self-development that would likely lead to economic and social upward mobility in the long term, such as learning Japanese and studying for educational qualifications. Consequently, few returnee men I knew had enjoyed the successes of Donghyŏn, working as a math teacher, or Minch'ŏl, employed in a trading company. Many, like Chihu, felt they were failing to live up to their family's expectations.

Activist Engagement

As of this writing in 2021 there are only a few hundred returnees in Japan, a small enough number for the Japanese government to abdicate responsibility for them to civic groups. The groups that assist returnees are often comprised of people who contributed to their exodus years earlier. But, as discussed in chapter 5, the emergent relationship is not one built on mutual understanding, nor on an equitable balance of power. Instead, returnees find themselves pulled into the humanitarian activism of Japanese civic organizations.

The activists who work with returnees have become proficient at managing individuals unwanted by the countries of East Asia. Coopted in the late 1950s–1960s into facilitating and documenting the outmigration of Japan's ethnic minorities, elderly members of these groups now participate in returning the human vestiges of the country's reconfiguration from empire to nation-state. But the groups' mission goes beyond helping with returnees' resettlement, to collaborating with new arrivals to prosecute the North Korean government. For activists who campaign for human rights in the DPRK, a North Korean in exile is a living condemnation of North Korea's leader, Kim Jong-un. To speak out against North Korea becomes a returnee's duty, an obligation generated by the need to demonstrate gratitude and to settle a debt. As a result, their freedom unintentionally exacerbates their liminality, ensuring they are "never to be free from the knowing sense of transience, indefiniteness, and provisional nature of any settlement" (Bauman 2004, 76). Having depended on activist groups for both their escape from North Korea and their subsequent access to resources in Japan, returnees are trapped by the violence of the gift.

The problem is one of choice. Returnees working with Japanese civic groups often feel they cannot refuse to help, even if their participation in high-profile attacks on the DPRK risks their own life. Just as the gift of freedom can offer a person endless benefits, the poison of this impossible gift also inflicts ongoing harm on the recipient. Returnees thus find themselves infantilized under the stewardship of humanitarian groups and harmed by the very thing that offers new life.

An imagined familiarity to Japan directs returnees back to the communities they left decades earlier, while echoes of life in North Korea shape the resettlement of men and women following their return. Their "being from North Korea" subsequently provides civic groups with evidence of the Kim family's disregard for its people. As the leftovers of contracting empires and communities reimagined along nationalist lines, families for whom migration and displacement have become central to their self-understanding are forced to choose between state-sanctioned invisibility or activist-supported hyper-visibility. Both choices perpetuate regimes of violence.

Imagined Belonging

Displacement is not only a matter of geographic dislocation. It also unsettles a person's linear sense of time. People who are forced to leave their homes because of critical junctures like war, famine, persecution, and increasingly by the effects of climate change, can become emotionally unsettled as they are caught in between worlds. The feeling of being neither here nor there follows a displaced person long after they arrive in their new home. The means by which the displaced tries to imagine a place in the host society, attempting to move beyond the liminality of displacement, depends on how they understand their relationship to both the sending and receiving societies.

Returnees' personal narratives and family stories challenge the idea that stasis within political borders is the only way of belonging. Mobility across time and space has encouraged the people in this book to develop a sense of attachment to multiple places, not just one. Families forced to leave Cheju Island in the early days of the Cold War, for example, remember kinship connections to what has since become one of South Korea's premier tourist destinations. The same people who subsequently traveled to North Korea drew on memories of family and community in both Japan and Cheju in order to ground themselves during dark times.

Without memories of life in the sending community, it is difficult for a refugee to locate himself in the present, to make sense of how and why he came to be where he stands. Resettlement thus also requires building and rebuilding memories to the country left behind, however bittersweet these recollections may be. Sŭngmi consciously sought to connect to Japan by remembering and recreating the built environment around her (described in chapter 6). For Misŏn, a search for familiarity took her to South Korea and to Japan as she attempted to locate a place where she could belong.

Rootedness is not required for belonging. Nor is home limited to four walls and a roof. Migrations reshape connectedness to home, but they do not erase those relationships. Instead of home comprising physical structures, instead of belonging being defined by political markers like a passport, or cultural markers like language ability, or even along racial lines through ancestral lineages, home and the associated feelings of belonging are inwardly projected to family and the individual. Home becomes a portable abstract that can be projected onto new spaces when required. Home becomes a malleable sense of belonging to multiple places, resurrected in family stories and the taste of food from lands since departed. Chihu's nostalgic recollections of life in North Korea pulled him into the past, back to his life as a famous athlete, back to times when he was surrounded by friends and admirers. His cherished memories, however, mean he may never fully imagine himself as belonging in Japan. Instead, Chihu has transferred his hopes for finding home in Japan onto his two children, doing everything he can to make sure they speak both Korean and Japanese, know their North Korean family history, but still manage to succeed in their Japanese home.

In an age of hyper-connectivity, assertions over who belongs and who does not, based on differences of color, sexuality, language, religion, and cultural practices, have made national borders and nationalist attitudes increasingly salient the world over. The prominence of nationalism benefits only those who count. And those who count are most commonly citizens of communities rooted in sovereign territory and immersed in the myths of founding fathers and hero warriors. Expectations that globalization would erode national borders have been found premature at best (cf. Kearney 1991). Instead of migrants, forced or otherwise, precipitating the dissolution of borders, transnational flows are currently provoking walls to rise higher and our tolerance for people treated as the outcasts of modernity to grow thinner (Bauman 2004). The strategies used by forced migrants are a way to survive these rising walls and growing intolerance. Through intramarriage and managing identities, by migrating somewhere because of both a real and an imagined familiarity, by advantageously engaging with civic groups and by drawing on memories to seek out and create a sense of belonging in the host society, displaced people demonstrate resilience in the face of seemingly overwhelming odds.

From Crisis to Solution

The twentieth century produced the largest flows of refugees in recorded history, but it also saw, for the first time, the creation of a system of global governance in the UN that offered new ways of understanding, assisting, and protecting forced migrants. At the time of this writing, migration has become a topic of global political import. But instead of governments coming together to provide an updated framework for how to manage a migration crisis, nations are turning in on themselves as migrants and asylum seekers become the kindling to rising nationalist sentiments, increasingly insular thinking, and a shift to the political right on a global scale. "National borders," writes anthropologist Hans Lucht, "rather than being contested and transgressed, are being reified in the form of lethal traps from which migrants barely escape alive" (Lucht 2012, 17).

In a number of Asian countries, including Japan, South Korea, Myanmar, the Philippines, and Indonesia, immigrants are pointed to as a source of racial pollution, political insecurity, and economic instability. But politicking over migration and scapegoating asylum seekers for wins at the ballot box ignores the reality that migration, specifically the forced displacement of people from their homes, is only going to become more common in the coming decades. With the exception of 2020–21–a period characterized by a global pandemic, local lockdowns, and closed borders–the tally of displaced people and refugees grows each year as families resort to emigration in response to conflicts new and old and the worsening effects of climate change impacting food supplies and livelihoods.

Globally, the number of people on the move is growing alongside dramatic demographic shifts and an economic atrophying of some of the wealthiest countries in the world. The global population is forecast to peak at 9.73 billion in 2064, while the age structure in many parts of the world will shift, with 2.37 billion people older than sixty-five years by 2100 (Vollset et al. 2020). The world is experiencing a dramatic decline in fertility and population growth while trending toward an older global population. In the United States, China, South Korea, and Japan, for instance, a combination of an ageing population; more women having access to education, entering the workforce, and using contraception to have fewer children; and increasingly frequent economic shocks are contributing to rapidly dwindling populations, and impending socioeconomic challenges for health care, labor markets, and the environment.

These trends are prominent in Japan. Behind only the United States and China, Japan is the world's third largest economy. Since the 1990s, however, when land and stock prices collapsed, the country has struggled with sluggish economic growth, large fiscal deficits, and near zero inflation. More pointedly, Japan is experiencing demographic changes that threaten an existential crisis within our lifetimes, including a fast-ageing population and declining fertility. Japan's population is the oldest in the world, with a median age of 48.4 years (International Monetary Fund [IMF] 2020). While the population is ageing, it is also shrinking. More people ageing and fewer births means that Japan is forecast to have population declines greater than 50 percent from 2020 until 2100, by which time the entire population will have fallen to around 53 million from its current level of 126 million (Vollset et al. 2020). Consequently, fewer Japanese will be able and willing to work. Those who continue in the workforce will be older, less productive, and more likely to hold on to positions that would otherwise be filled by younger workers. Broader societal burdens will emerge to further hamper economic growth, in terms of the financial and infrastructural demands of directly and indirectly supporting an ageing population. More elderly people will mean more private capital spent on age-related insurance programs and pensions, and more public funds channeled toward specialist geriatric health care. Finding people to work in the Japanese health sector, in positions often regarded as undesirable or 3-K–*kitanai, kiken,* and *kitsui* (dirty, dangerous, and demanding)–presents further challenges. More semi- and high-skilled caregivers will be needed for homes and hospitals across the country, a skills gap that policymakers and private enterprise are currently trying to resolve with technology, specifically with artificial intelligence and robot care workers.

Further efforts are being taken to tackle these momentous impacts. Former prime minister Shinzō Abe introduced policies encouraging Japanese women to enter the workforce in greater numbers ("Economic Challenge of Japan's Aging Crisis" 2019). The hope is that more women working will boost tax income, increase spending, and encourage sustainable economic growth. The fear, however, is that more women leaving for the office each day will further exacerbate the country's low fertility rate, meaning fewer workers to grow the economy. Despite Japan's clear and immediate economic, demographic, and public health crises and an associated skills gap in key industries needed for the country's graying population, the most obvious solution is the one perhaps least likely to gain public acceptance– employing immigrant workers. The problem, even for societies that do not pride themselves on being culturally and ethnically homogenous, is that there is a fine, yet unknown tipping point between having just the right number of foreigners that they remain useful but out of sight, and so many foreigners that they need to be politically and economically accounted for.

Currently in Japan, there appears to be a gradual yet reluctant reliance on immigrant workers in service sectors struggling with employment gaps. Although existing in the shadows of public life, returnees from North Korea work in wet markets and restaurants, ethnic Japanese from South America assemble car parts in factories, Nepalis staff the sweltering kitchens of South Asian restaurants, Filipinas care for elderly Japanese, and Chinese plant and pick crops consumed by Japanese families. These often-invisible groups are already helping the country navigate the cliff face presented by an ageing society and an economy ever-threatening to slip into recession. In mid-2019 the government announced policy changes that may see 345,000 more foreigners employed in mainly rural areas of Japan (Toshihiro 2019). In an effort to address the country's demographic shortfall, Tokyo is also trying to attract low-skilled and semi-skilled workers to agriculture, construction, manufacturing, and hospitality, sectors that have hitherto found workers through a much-criticized Technical Intern Training Program. Cracking the door open to desperately needed migrant workers is a litmus test for both the people who arrive to take up jobs across the country and the willingness of the Japanese public to tolerate, perhaps for the first time, close and frequent proximity to foreigners.

Future social tensions emerging from more foreign workers in Japan will manifest themselves in familiar questions of rights and belonging. Questions such as, What makes a person "Japanese"? What kind of society is Japan's? And, what kind of society do the Japanese want? How the government and public helps to answer these problems will have a profound impact on Japan's ability to navigate the economic, social, and geopolitical future of the country as Japanese society is visibly reorganized by anticipated endogenous and external demographic shifts.

The age of migration has opened up enormous opportunities for new ideas, entrepreneurship, collaboration, and understandings of human existence. In an increasingly precarious world, the global movement of people will continue to reshape national cultures, attitudes, and economies. The micro-histories of the families that have moved back and forth between the two Koreas and Japan tell us that people transform nations as much as nations transform people. In the coming decades, the world will look to Japan and South Korea for how to manage the inevitable patterns of social and demographic change, especially how they answer questions of identity and belonging. Perhaps, more than ever before, migration will be a strategy for survival, not only for the people who move, but also for societies on the brink of unprecedented economic and demographic upheaval.

Return to Tsuruhashi

In late winter of 2015, several months after I had concluded the initial research for this book, I flew into Narita airport and caught the bullet train west to Osaka. On my second evening in Tsuruhashi I caught up with three returnees whose lives I had shared during a year in Japan. Kyŏngcha, Yumi, Misŏn and I met in a brightly lit Korean restaurant on the fringes of one of the city's many canals. The neon lights of Dōtonbori's Glico Running Man splashed the oily black water a shimmering red, blue, and white.

We ordered round after round of beer and fried snacks as we caught up on the time apart. My compliments on Yumi's improved Japanese language skills were reciprocated with surprise at how poor my own had become in such a short time. As the evening wore on, Misŏn proffered advice on life in Japan, "Study Japanese, make as much money as you can, and respect your sister," she commanded an attentive Yumi. "You'll do well here." She added, "Think about starting a business. You're young. You have time, unlike us," her furrowed brow nodding to Kyŏngcha and me.

Yumi's life lesson was interrupted by the arrival of more food, served by a weathered man in jeans and a t-shirt. "I own this restaurant," he announced, shunting a huge plate of garlic fried chicken onto the table. Uninvited, he pulled up a chair and ordered another round of beer. "Are you all Korean?" he asked in Korean, apparently oblivious to my presence. Kyŏngcha nodded, hesitantly.

"Seoul?" he brusquely inquired. "Nope. Think farther north," Kyŏngcha encouraged. "What's farther north than Seoul?" the owner considered. "Ch'unch'ŏn?" he guessed, referencing a city in a northern province of South Korea.

"Farther north than that," Kyŏngcha teased, causing everyone at the table to snigger. "There's nothing beyond that," he scoffed. "China? Are you Chinese?" Taking mercy on the confused man, Kyŏngcha leaned closer and whispered, "We're from North Korea." The man paused, mouth agape. "North Korea?" he exclaimed, reaching for his beer, eyes bulging. "I didn't see that coming." Perhaps out of politeness, perhaps surprise, the restaurant owner finished his drink, ordered another round for the table, and disappeared back into the kitchen.

Things had changed for each of my friends in the months since we had last met. Kyŏngcha had moved out of Koreatown, and into an apartment owned by a South Korean church group. The one-room apartment was fully furnished. The rent, she told me, was cheap and the pastor did not make her attend Sunday services. She still worked six days a week at the fruit stall, handing out free samples at every chance. "My best friends are all ninety years old," she joked, talking about the Cheju Island grandmothers who worked alongside her. But she now worked with a clear focus—to get her daughter, Sojin, out of North Korea. With family reunion in mind, she had taken a second job, as a hostess in a Nipponbashi whiskey bar. Growing her savings, she almost had enough money for bribes to pay DPRK border guards and to hire a broker to take Sojin from the border to a safe house in China. The toughest part, though, would be convincing her ex-husband that their daughter leaving for Japan would not spell the end of Kyŏngcha's remittances—she worried that he was keeping Sojin as a way to guarantee the flow of money from Japan.

Anticipating her daughter's arrival, Kyŏngcha had spent her evenings studying for a driver's license. "I've never had time to travel outside of Osaka. I've never seen Japan. But when she gets here, we can be tourists together," she beamed, imagining road trips to Kyoto and Nara. But Kyŏngcha was not limiting herself to dreaming of visits to Japanese temples. "Perhaps, one day, I'll visit South Korea," she pondered. "That's where my grandmother came from, in a city called Ulsan. She came to Japan during the colonial time and lived right here, in Osaka. I'd like to see where she grew up, maybe even meet some of my relatives," she said.

Where Kyŏngcha's world was on the verge of expanding, with new free-doms and family, Misŏn was only just emerging from her self-imposed exile. After several months, she had traded her full-time accounting job for part time administrative work in a Zainichi Korean company. The work was less stressful, and she had more time to study English. "It's the only way I'll leave Japan, if I speak English. I can travel, maybe meet a nice guy, but only if I can say more than, 'It's cold today,'" she added, straight-faced. Gone, it seemed, were her hopes of moving to South Korea. "I'm a foreigner there, too," she reminded me. But there were signs that she had found peace. "It doesn't bother me, you know? Frankly, I feel citizenship is like clothing: you change it when you feel like it or when you need to. So, I'm not wor-ried about my nationality; it's not me." Misŏn continued to avoid returnee events hosted by South Korea–affiliated Mindan, and her relationship with her family remained strained. But this evening she seemed in her element, scattering pearls of wisdom for Yumi to follow.

Not long after Yumi arrived in Osaka, she and her husband permanently split up. "Everyone heard them," Kyŏngcha chuckled, remembering the fight that had precipitated their divorce. "They woke up the whole of Koreatown. That was the night Sŏngmin moved out." Separating had been a straightfor-ward process, Yumi explained. Neither Yumi nor Sŏngmin had evidence of their marriage, so there was no need to inform anyone or do anything. They just stopped seeing each other. Meeting Yumi again, the changes in her life were evident. Gone were the purple high heels, her dyed red hair, and blue jeans with sparkling English script over the pockets. Sitting at the table now with her straight, shoulder-length black hair, knee-length skirt, and light blue blouse, it would be hard to distinguish her from any Japanese woman in the street. Her language skills had also noticeably improved. Taking pity on me, she did her best to stick to Korean, but as the beer flowed the con-versation muddied into a Korean-Japanese-English soup. Yumi's other big news was that she was preparing to move to Tokyo. With the help of Ayako, her former Japanese teacher, she had found work in a restaurant in Shin-Ōkubo, home of Tokyo's Koreatown. Kyŏngcha planned to rent a car and drive her sister to the capital using her new license.

Returnees from North Korea have been displaced and resettled many times. A sense of belonging to multiple places, while also belonging no-where is a trope fitting to many of the people described in this book. Return-ees look for ways to reconnect to Japan, but not by losing their attachments to the two Koreas. Individuals like Donghyŏn feel comfortable identifying as Zainichi Korean. Others, like Misŏn, have difficulty finding their place, feeling, as they do, the threads of history tugging uncomfortably at their sense of self. But their stories speak to alternative ways of belonging and new understandings of home. Tied up in communal stories of mobility, resilience, displacement and community-disrupted, home has become as much a portable and abstract concept as it is a tangible connection to soil, bricks, and mortar. Zainichi returnees' family narratives are evidence that rootedness within a nation is just one way of forming community, of creating home, and of belonging. Migration is not evidence of failing, but is a means of surviving and remaking family, community, and belonging in the modern world.

APPENDIX

Notes on Methodology

There is no publicly available record on how many returnees from North Korea currently reside in Japan. Nor is there publicly accessible data on the demographics of returnees. Members of the various civic organizations working with returnees agreed that there are around three hundred returnees in Japan. With such a small research group it was unlikely that I would create a sample representative of broader migration trends. Subsequently, I met with whoever was willing: men, women, former elite athletes, factory workers, teachers, students, former party members, and activists spoke with me about their migration experiences and of life in both North Korea and in Japan. Over a year I interviewed and informally spoke with a little more than fifty individuals, thirty of whom had emigrated from North Korea, and twenty of whom were part of civil society organizations. Interviewees included Zainichi Koreans with family in North Korea, and South Korean immigrants working with returnees from North Korea. Interviews lasted between one and two hours and were conducted primarily in Korean, although some of my interlocutors mixed Korean and Japanese as we spoke. There was a diversity of age, occupation, and experiences among my interlocutors, although the gender balance favored women, reflecting the higher proportion of women emigrating from North Korea (72 percent, according to the Republic of Korea Ministry of Unification figures).

My participant observation in Japan took place in Osaka and Tokyo. I met and spoke with Zainichi returnees in restaurants and retail stores, in language institutes in which I studied Japanese alongside returnees, in returnees' homes and social groups, and at meetings of civic organizations. I became involved with activist groups by volunteering my services as a Korean-English translator and copy editor. Some returnees were initially reluctant to speak with me, perhaps skeptical of my motivations and fearful of possible reprisals for themselves or their family for talking of their irregular (undocumented) migrations. Other returnees were concerned that they might appear critical of either the North Korean or Japanese governments. I believe that the long-term nature of my research, my previous experience working with activist groups in South Korea, and my relationship with South Korean and Japanese civic groups went a long way to allaying such concerns.

I used two methods to structure interviews. The first was to construct a genealogy of each interviewee's family. I did this through a collaborative dialogue, during which I asked the interviewee questions designed to pull together the web of kin connections and fill in the details of major life experiences using a timeline reaching from 1900 to the present day. On the timeline we worked together to record the births, marriages, migrations, education, and employment history of every member of the interviewee's family that she or he could remember. The genealogy and timeline illustrated who is related to whom, whether the connection is by blood or by marriage, their marital status, when and where a person was born and died, when and where they migrated, their occupation in the country of origin, their occupation in the country in which they resettled, and the language(s) spoken by each person. The purpose of these exercises was to elicit a more comprehensive understanding of family relationships than a standard interview format might otherwise yield. I also anticipated that this exercise would historicize the movement of each family within one of four admittedly slippery periods that I characterize as colonial Korea (1910–45), postwar reconstruction Japan (1946–52), repatriation to the DPRK (1959–84), and return to Japan (2000–the present).

Some interlocutors recalled, with certainty, that their forebears had come to Japan from Cheju Island, off the southern coast of the Korean Peninsula. Others struggled to provide details on the lives of grandparents or great-grandparents. One respondent suggested that her grandfather had probably been a communist sympathizer fleeing from the South Korean government's violent purges of Cheju Island (1947–54). Another told me that her great-grandmother smuggled herself to Japan in a fishing boat prior to the outbreak of the Korean War. Often, however, it seemed that details of the first phase of migration from the Korean Peninsula to Japan had become murky with the passing years.

After almost a year in Japan, I moved to Geneva, Switzerland, to supplement returnees' life histories with archival evidence in the ICRC. The now declassified files yielded information on how the North Korean, South Korean, and Japanese governments negotiated the repatriation project. These data were critical for locating, describing, and understanding the context in which tens of thousands of people uprooted their lives and left for a country that was largely unknown to them.

References

Anderson, Benedict. (1983) 2006. *Imagined Communities: Reflections on the Origin and Spread of Nationalism*. New York: Verso.

Arendt, Hannah. 1973. *The Origins of Totalitarianism*. New York: Harcourt Brace & Company.

B AG 232 105-002. "Fundamental Conditions of Livelihood of Certain Koreans Residing in Japan," 27/02/1953–11/10/1957.

B AG 232 105-002. "Problème du rapatriement des Coréens du Japon, dossier I: Généralités." 27/02/1953–11/10/1957. Inoue, Masutarô. 1956. "Fundamental Conditions of Livelihood of Certain Koreans Residing in Japan." Japanese Red Cross Society, November 1956.

B AG 232 105-002. "Problème du rapatriement des Coréens du Japon, dossier I: Généralités." 27/02/1953–11/10/1957. Inoue, Masutarô. 1956. "The Repatriation Problem of Certain Koreans Residing in Japan." Japanese Red Cross Society, 1 October 1956.

B AG 232 105-006.01. Asahi Evening News, 24 October 1958, "Return-to-N. Korea move is launched in Japan." Généralités, 01/01/1958–15/12/1958.

B AG 232 105-006.03. "Copies pour information transmises par la Croix-Rouge Japonaise." 07/01/1958–01/11/1958. "Request on Collective Repatriation of Koreans from Japan," 8 October 1958.

B AG 232 105-006.03. "Copies pour information transmises par la Croix-Rouge Japonaise," 07/01/1958–01/11/1958. "Livelihood and Education after Repatriation Guaranteed Only the Attitude of Japanese Government Left unsettled." The General League of Koreans, 1 November 1958.

B AG 232 105 006-007. "Report of the Phyongyang Conference: held by Japanese and North Korean Red Cross Societies," (27 January–28 February 28, 1956). Postscript, 17 March 1956.

B AG 232 105-007.02. "Demandes écrites de particuliers ou d'associations de Coréens, réactions aux pourparlers entre le Japon et la République démocratique populaire de Corée concernant le rapatriament des Coréens vers la Corée-du-Nord." 29/01/1959–25/06/1959.

B AG 232 105-008.02. "Résolution de la Croix-Rouge Japonaise du 20 Janvier 1959 et dépliant intitulé: 'Korean repatriation question' publié par la Croix-Rouge Japonaise." 20/01/1959–03/03/1959. 14 February 1959.

B AG 232 105-015.01. "Extraits des procès-verbaux des séances du Comité, plénières, de la Présidence." 03/09/1959–28/12/1959, Annex 3.

B AG 232 105-015.05. "Copies de déclarations officielles, de notes, de télégrammes, pour information transmises par la Criox-Rouge Japonaise." 04/09/1959–26/12/1959.

B AG 232 105-019.01. "A Short Account on the Korean Question." 18/03/1960–31/12/1960.

B AG 232 105-019.01. "Monthly reports on the repatriation to North Korea," Immigration Bureau, Ministry of Justice. 18/03/1960–31/12/1960.

B AG 232 105-025. "An Analysis and Appraisal of the Problems of Koreans in Japan and the Role of the International Committee of the Red Cross and Other Agencies in Their Solution." Hallam C. Shorrock, Jr. 15 July 1959, Seoul, Korea.

B AG 232 105-028.02. "Rapports sur les convois." 17/01/1961–28/12/1964. 20 July 1961.

B AG 232 105-028.02. "Rapports sur les convois." 17/01/1961–28/12/1964. "Report regarding the 67th ships." 19 July 1961.

B AG 232 105-028.02 "Rapports sur les convois." 17/01/1961–28/12/1964. "Ship No. 52, Op. No.17, Room 2." 14 January 1962.

B AG 232 105-028.02. "Rapports sur les convois." 17/01/1961–28/12/1964. "Report on Repatriation Ship No. 91, "Norilsk." 9 April 1962.

B AG 232 105-028.04. "Problème du libre passage entre la Corée-du-Nord et le Japon." 05/06/1963–28/12/1964. *The People's Korea*, "'Free-Travel Movement' Winning Support from Abroad." 21 August 1963.

B AG 232 105-028.04. "Problème du libre passage entre la Corée-du-Nord et le Japon." 05/06/1963–28/12/1964. "Central Standing Committee of General Association of Korean Residents in Japan." 20 June 1963.

B AG 232 105-028.04. "Problème du libre passage entre la Corée-du-Nord et le Japon." 05/06/1963–28/12/1964 (file no. 2535).

B AG 232 105-028.04. "Problème du libre passage entre la Corée-du-Nord et le Japon." 05/06/1963–28/12/1964 (file no. 2798).

B AG 232 105-028.04. "Problème du libre passage entre la Corée-du-Nord et le Japon." 05/06/1963–28/12/1964. *Yomiuri Shimbun*, "Free Travel Between Japan, North Korea is Political Aim." 14 June 1964.

B AG 232 105-028.04. "Problème du libre passage entre la Corée-du-Nord et le Japon." 05/06/1963–28/12/1964. *The Mainichi*, "Special Consideration to be Studied on Visit to and from North Korea," Ministry of Justice. 17 December 1964.

B AG 232 105-030.01. "Monthly reports on the repatriation to North Korea." 31/03/1961–31/12/1964.

B AG 232 105-032.02. "Rapports sur les convois." 23/01/1965–23/12/1967. "Statistique des Coréens du Japon rapatriés."

B AG 232 105-033. "Problème du rapatriement des Coréens du Japon, dossier XXI." 14/11/1962–31/12/1967. *The Mainichi Daily News*, "N. Korean Repatriation Accord to be Suspended," 21 April 1967.

B AG 232 105-033. "Problème du rapatriement des Coréens du Japon, dossier XXI." 14/11/1962–31/12/1967. *The Japan Times*, "N. Korea Demands Japan Retain Repatriation Pact," 24 April 1967.

B AG 232 105-033. "Problème du rapatriement des Coréens du Japon, dossier XXI." 14/11/1962–31/12/1967. *The Unification of Fatherland*, 14 November 1962.

B AG 232 105-033. "Problème du rapatriement des Coréens du Japon, dossier XXI." 14/11/1962–31/12/1967. "Happy Life of Repatriates seen in figures." 19 May 1964.

B AG 232 105-033. "Problème du rapatriement des Coréens du Japon, dossier XXI." 14/11/1962–31/12/1967. "Monthly report on repatriation." 31 December 1967.

B AG 232 105-035. "Letter from DPRK Red Cross to the ICRC." 30 March 1965.

B AG 232 105-036. "Prolongation du rapatriement des Coréens du Japon en Corée du Nord. Proposition d'une nouvelle solution pour le rapatriement." 05/01/1968–19/03/1970.

B AG 232 105-046. "Pètition mise en place par Mme Fumiko Ikeda, représentante de 'The Association for Human Rights of Japanese Wives of North Korean Repatriates,' pour l'organisation d'une mission d'enquéte en Corée du Nord et pour la libre circulation au Japon des éspouses Japonaises de rapatriés Nord Coréens: Correspondance." 21/06/1974–13/01/1975. "Miserable Daily Life in North Korea, number 1."

B AG 232 105-046. "Pètition mise en place par Mme Fumiko Ikeda, représentante de 'The Association for Human Rights of Japanese Wives of North Korean Repatriates,' pour l'organisation d'une mission d'enquéte en Corée du Nord et pour la libre circulation au Japon des éspouses Japonaises de rapatriés Nord Coréens: Correspondance." 21/06/1974–13/01/1975. "North Korea: The False Promise, number 2."

Baldassar, Loretta. 2008. "Missing Kin and Longing to Be Together: Emotions and the Construction of Co-Presence in Transnational Relationships." *Journal of Intercultural Studies* 29 (2): 247–66.

Basch, Linda, Nina Glick Schiller, and Cristina Szanton Blanc. (1994) 2000. *Nations Unbound: Transnational Projects, Postcolonial Predicaments, and Deterritorialized Nation-States.* New York: Routledge.

Bauman, Zygmunt. 2004. *Wasted Lives: Modernity and Its Outcasts.* Cambridge, UK: Polity Press.

Bell, Markus. 2013a. "Manufacturing Kinship in A Nation Divided: An Ethnographic Study of North Korean Refugees in South Korea." *Asia Pacific Journal of Anthropology* 14 (3): 240–55.

Bell, Markus. 2013b. "We're So Happy to Have You Here (But We'd Rather You Hadn't Come): Exclusion, Solidarity and Network Building of North Korean Refugees." *Studia Ubb Philologia* 58 (1): 221–30.

Bell, Markus. 2014. "The Ties That Bind Us: Transnational Networks of North Koreans on the Move." *Resilience: International Policies, Practices and Discourses* 2 (2): 100–113.

Bell, Markus. 2016. "Making and Breaking Family: North Korea's Zainichi Returnees and 'The Gift.'" *Asian Anthropology* 15 (3): 260–76.

Bell, Markus. 2018. "Patriotic Revolutionaries and Imperial Sympathizers: Identity and Selfhood of Korean-Japanese Migrants from Japan to North Korea." *Cross-Currents: East Asian History and Culture Review* (E-Journal) 27: 1–25.

Bell, Markus. 2021. "Dye for My Grey Hair & Curry Powder for Cooking: Informal Politics of Exchange Between North Korea & Japan, 1959–1975." In *Popular Cul-*

ture and the Transformation of Japan-Korea Relations, edited by Stephen Epstein and Rumi Sakamoto, 34–47. New York: Routledge.

Bourdieu, Pierre. (1980) 1990. *The Logic of Practice.* Translated by R. Nice. Stanford, CA: Stanford University Press.

Brettell, Caroline. 2003. *Anthropology and Migration: Essays on Transnationalism, Ethnicity, and Identity.* Lanham, MD: Altamira Press.

Brubaker, Rogers. 1998. "Migrations of Ethnic Unmixing in the 'New Europe.'" *International Migration Review* 32 (4): 1047–65.

Brubaker, Rogers, and Frederick Cooper. 2000. "Beyond 'Identity.'" *Theory and Society* 29 (1): 1–47.

Buechler, Simone. 2004. "Sweating It in the Brazilian Garment Industry: Korean and Bolivian Immigrants and Global Economic Forces in São Paulo." *Latin American Perspectives* 31 (3): 99–119.

Buruma, Ian. 1994. *The Wages of Guilt: Memories of War in Germany and Japan.* New York: Farrar, Straus & Giroux.

Buyandelger, Manduhai. 2013. *Tragic Spirits: Shamanism, Memory, and Gender in Contemporary Mongolia.* Chicago: University of Chicago Press.

Buzo, Adrian. 1999. *The Guerilla Dynasty: Politics and Leadership in North Korea.* London: I.B. Tauris.

Caprio, Mark. 2009. *Japanese Assimilation Policies in Colonial Korea, 1910–1945.* Seattle: University of Washington Press.

Castles, Stephen, and Alastair Davidson. 2000. *Citizenship and Migration: Globalization and the Politics of Belonging.* Thousand Oaks, CA: Palgrave.

Castles, Stephen, and Mark Miller. 1998. *The Age of Migration,* 2nd ed. London: Palgrave.

Chamberlain, Mary. (1997) 2017. *Narratives of Exile and Return.* London: St. Martin's Press.

Chan, Tara Francis. 2018. "No Entry: How Japan's Shockingly Low Refugee Intake Is Shaped by the Paradox of Isolation, A Demographic Time Bomb, and the Fear of North Korea." *Business Insider,* 11 April. https://www.businessinsider.com.au/why-japan-accepts-so-few-refugees-2018-4?r=us&ir=t.

Chan, Yeeshan. 2011. *Abandoned Japanese in Postwar Manchuria: The Lives of War Orphans and Wives in Two Countries.* Japan Anthropology Workshop Series. New York: Routledge.

Chapman, David. 2004. "The Third Way and Beyond: Zainichi Korean Identity and the Politics of Belonging." *Japanese Studies* 24 (1): 29–44.

Chapman, David. 2008. *Zainichi Korean Identity and Ethnicity.* New York: Routledge.

Chung, Byung-Ho. 2008. "Between Defector and Migrant: Identities and Strategies of North Koreans in South Korea." *Korean Studies* 32: 1–27.

Climate Foresight. 2019. "Environmental Migrants: Up to 1 Billion by 2050." https://www.climateforesight.eu/migrations-inequalities/environmental-migrants-up-to-1-billion-by-2050/.

Collins, Robert. 2012. "Marked for Life: *Sŏngbun:* North Korea's Social Classification System." Committee for Human Rights in North Korea, Washington, DC.

Connerton, Paul. 1989. *How Societies Remember.* Cambridge, UK: Cambridge University Press

Connerton, Paul. 2008. "Seven Types of Forgetting." *Memory Studies* 1 (1): 59–71.

Conradson, David, and Deirdre McKay. 2007. "Translocal Subjectivitives: Mobility, Connection, Emotion." *Mobilities* 2 (2): 167–74.

Cook-Martin, David, and Anahi Viladrich. 2009. "The Problem with Similarity: Ethnic Affinity Migrants in Spain." *Journal of Ethnic and Migration Studies* 35 (1): 151–70.

Cronin, Michael. 2017. *Osaka Modern the City in the Japanese Imaginary.* Harvard East Asian Monographs, vol. 403. Cambridge, MA: Harvard University Press.

Cumings, Bruce. 2010. *The Korean War: A History.* New York: Modern Library.

Cupach, William R., and Tadasu Todd Imahori. 1993. "Identity Management Theory: Communication Competence in Intercultural Episodes and Relationships." In *Intercultural Communication Competence*, edited by R. L. Wiseman and J. Koester, 112–31. Newbury Park, CA: Sage.

Daniels, Inge. 2015. "Feeling at Home in Contemporary Japan: Space, Atmosphere and Intimacy." *Emotion, Space and Society* 15: 47–55.

de Carvalho, Daniela. 2003. *Migrants and Identity in Japan and Brazil: The Nikkeijin.* London: Routledge Curzon.

de Haas, Hein, Stephen Castles, and Mark Miller. 2020. *The Age of Migration: International Population Movements in the Modern World*, 6th ed. New York: Guilford Press.

"In first, five defectors in Japan sue North Korea for ¥500 million over rights abuses." 2018. Japan Times, 21 August 2018. https://www.japantimes.co.jp/news/2018/08/21/national/crime-legal/five-defectors-japan-sue-north-korea-%C2%A5500-million-rights-abuses/.

Democratic People's Republic of Korea (DPRK). 1959. *On the Question of 600,000 Koreans in Japan.* Pyongyang: Foreign Languages Publishing House.

di Leonardo, Micaela. 1987. "The Female World of Cards and Holidays: Women, Families, and the Work of Kinship." *Signs* 12 (3): 440–53.

Douglas, Mary. 1969. *Purity and Danger: An Analysis of Concepts of Pollution and Taboo.* New York: Routledge.

"Economic Challenge of Japan's Aging Crisis." 2019. *Japan Times*, 19 November 2019. https://www.japantimes.co.jp/opinion/2019/11/19/commentary/japan-commentary/economic-challenge-japans-aging-crisis/#.xw5rl5mzzqi.

Espiritu, Yen Le. 2003. *Home Bound: Filipino American Lives across Cultures, Communities, and Countries.* Los Angeles: University of California Press.

Fahy, Sandra. 2015. *Marching through Suffering: Loss and Survival in North Korea.* New York: Columbia University Press.

Ferguson, Kennan. 2007. "The Gift of Freedom." *Social Text* 91 (25, 2): 39–52.

Fox, Jon. 2007. "From National Inclusion to Economic Exclusion: Ethnic Hungarian Labour Migration to Hungary." *Nations and Nationalism* 13 (1): 77–96.

Freeman, Caren. 2011. *Making and Faking Kinship: Marriage and Labor Migration between China and South Korea.* Ithaca, NY: Cornell University Press.

Freeman, Carla. 2001. "Is Local:Global as Feminine:Masculine? Rethinking the Gender of Globalization." *Signs* 26 (4): 1007–37.

Gamlen, Alan. 2020. "COVID-19 and the Transformation of Migration and Mobility Globally—Migration and Mobility After the 2020 Pandemic: The End of An Age?" UN International Organization for Migration, Geneva. https://publications.iom.int/books/covid-19-and-transformation-migration-and-mobility-globally-migration-and-mobility-after-2020.

Glick Schiller, Nina, and Georges Fouron. 2001. *Georges Woke Up Laughing: Long-Distance Nationalism and the Search for Home.* Durham, NC: Duke University Press.

Glick Schiller, Nina, Linda Basch, and Cristina Szanton Blanc. 1999. "From Immigrant to Transmigrant: Theorizing Transnational Migration." In Pries, *Migration and Transnational Social Spaces,* 73–105.

Gmelch, George. 1980. "Return Migration." *Annual Review of Anthropology* 9: 135–59.

Gmelch, George. 1983. "Who Returns and Why: Return Migration Behavior in Two North Atlantic Societies." *Human Organization* 42 (1): 46–54.

Gmelch, George. 1992. *Double Passage: The Lives of Caribbean Migrants Abroad and Back Home.* Ann Arbor: University of Michigan Press.

Goffman, Erving. 1963. *Stigma: Notes on the Management of Spoiled Identity.* London: Penguin.

Goffman, Erving. 1967. *Interaction Ritual: Essays on Face-to-Face Behavior.* Garden City, NY: Anchor.

Goodkind, Daniel, and Loraine West. 2001. "The North Korean Famine and Its Demographic Impact." *Population and Development Review* 27 (2): 219–38.

"Gov't to End Repat Pact with N. Korea." *Japan Times,* 21 April 1967. Japan Times Archives.

Graeber, David. 2011. *Debt.* New York: First Melville House.

Greenhill, Kelly. 2011. *Weapons of Mass Migration.* Ithaca, NY: Cornell University Press.

Guarnizo, Luis Eduardo. 1997. "The Emergence of Transnational Social Formation and the Mirage of Return Migration Among Dominican Transmigrants." *Identities* 4: 281–322.

"Guidebook for Returnees." Japanese Red Cross Society (JRC). 1959 ICRC Archives.

Haggard, Stephan, and Marcus Noland. 2005. "Hunger and Human Rights: The Politics of Famine in North Korea." U.S. Committee for Human Rights in North Korea, Washington, DC.

Haggard, Stephan, and Marcus Noland. 2007. *Famine in North Korea: Markets, Aid, and Reform.* New York: Columbia University Press.

Haggard, Stephan, and Marcus Noland. 2011. "Witness to Transformation: Refugee Insights into North Korea." Peterson Institute for Economics, Washington, DC.

Haggard, Stephan, and Marcus Noland. 2012. "Gender in Transition: The Case of North Korea." Working Paper Series No.12-11, Peterson Institute for Economics, Washington, DC. https://piie.com/publications/wp/wp12-11.pdf.

Halbwachs, Maurice. 1992. *On Collective Memory.* Chicago: University of Chicago Press.

Hall, Stuart. 1996. "Minimal Selves." In Baker, Diawara, and Lindeborg, *Black British Cultural Studies, A Reader.* Chicago and London: The University of Chicago Press. 114–119.

Han, Ju Hui Judy. 2013. "Beyond Safe Haven." *Critical Asian Studies* 45 (4): 533–60.

Harrison, Jim. 1996. *After Ikkyū and Other Poems.* Berkeley, CA: Shambhala Publications.

Hashimoto, Akiko. 2004. "Culture, Power, and the Discourse of Filial Piety in Japan: The Disempowerment of Youth and Its Social Consequences." In Ikels, *Filial Piety,* 182–97.

Hirsch, Alan. 1992. "Nostalgia: A Neuropsychiatric Understanding." In *Advances in Consumer Research*, vol. 19, edited by John F. Sherry Jr. and Brian Sternthal, 390–95. Provo, UT: Association for Consumer Research.

Hobsbawn, Eric, and Terence Ranger, eds. (1983) 2003. *The Invention of Tradition*. Cambridge, UK: Cambridge University Press.

Hough, Jennifer, and Markus Bell. 2020. "North Koreans' Public Narratives and Conditional Inclusion in South Korea." *Critical Asian Studies* 52 (2): 161–81.

"I Believed North Korea's Propaganda." 2003. "Ich Habe Nordkoreas Propaganda Geglaubt." *AI-Journal*. http://www.amnesty.de/umleitung/2003/deu05/009?la ng=de&mimetype=text/html&destination=suche%3fwords%3dhiroshi%2bkato %26search_x%3d0%26search_y%3d0%26search%3dsuchen%26form_id%3dai_ search_form_block. Original in German.

Ikels, Charlotte. 2004. *Filial Piety*. 2004. Stanford, CA: Stanford University Press.

Inoue, Masutarō. 1960. "Repatriation to North Korea: Its Background and Points at Issue." Speech. Inoue, Meiji Club, Tokyo, 1 February 1960, 3. Located in the ICRC Library, Geneva.

International Crisis Group. 2011. "Strangers at Home: North Koreans in the South." Asia Report, 208. https://www.crisisgroup.org/asia/north-east-asia/korean-peni nsula/strangers-home-north-koreans-south.

International Monetary Fund (IMF). 2020. "Japan 2019 Article Iv Consultation-Press Release and Statement by the Executive Director for Japan." Report 20/39. https://www.imf.org/en/publications/cr/issues/2020/02/07/japan-2019-article- iv-consultation-press-release-staff-report-and-statement-by-the-executive-49032.

Jansen, Marius B. 2002. *The Making of Modern Japan*, 3rd ed. Cambridge, MA: Bel- knap Press.

"Japan Asks Red Cross Help." *New York Times*, 14 February 1959.

Jung, Hyang-jin. 2013. "Do They Mean What They Act? Surveillance, Theatricality, and Mind-Heart Among North Koreans." *Acta Koreana* 16 (1): 87–111.

Jung, Kyungja, and Bronwen Dalton. 2006. "Rhetoric Versus Reality for the Women of North Korea: Mothers of the Revolution." *Asian Survey* 46 (5): 741–60.

Jung, Kyungja, Bronwen Dalton, and Jacqueline Willis. 2018. "From Patriarchal So- cialism to Grassroots Capitalism: The Role of Female Entrepreneurs in the Tran- sition of North Korea." *Women's Studies International Forum* 68: 19–27.

Kashiwazaki, Chikako. 2000. "The Politics of Legal Status: The Equation of Nation- ality with Ethnonational Identity." In Ryang, *Koreans in Japan*, 13–31.

Kawashima, Takamine. 2009. "Kita Chōsen Kikoku Jigyō, Ima, Sono Shinjitsu O Kataru: Tessa Morris-Suzuki Shi No Kyogi Ni Tsuite," Hikari Sase! No. 4, 84–104.

Kearney, Michael. 1991. "Borders and Boundaries of State and Self at the End of Empire." *Journal of Historical Sociology* 4 (1): 52–74.

Kibria, Nazli. 1993. *Family Tightrope: The Changing Lives of Vietnamese Americans*. Princeton, NJ: Princeton University Press.

Kikuchi, Yoshiaki. 2009. "Kita Chōsen Kikoku Jigyō: 'Sodai Na Rachi' Ka 'Tsuihō' Ka,'" Tokyo, Chūkō Shinsho. In Kita Chōsen Kikokusha Mondai No Rekishi to Kadai, edited by Sakanaka Hidenori, Han Sok-Kyu and Kikuchi Yoshiaki, 197–318. Tokyo: Shinkansha.

Kim, Cheehyung Harrison. 2018. *Heroes and Toilers: Work as Life in Postwar North Korea, 1953–1961*. New York: Columbia University Press.

Kim, Mikyoung. 2013. "North Korean Refugees' Nostalgia: The Border People's Narratives." *Asian Politics & Policy* 5 (4): 523–42.

Kim, Si Joong. 2003. "The Economic Status and Role of Ethnic Koreans in China." In C. Fred Bergsten and Inbom Choi, eds. 2003. *The Korean Diaspora in the World Economy*. Washington, DC. Institute for International Economics, 101–27.

Kim, Suzy. 2010. "Revolutionary Mothers: Women in the North Korean Revolution, 1945–1950." *Comparative Studies in Society and History* 52 (4): 742–67.

Klekowski von Koppenfels, Amanda. 2009. "From Germans to Migrants: Aussiedler Migration to Germany." In Tsuda, *Diasporic Homecomings*.

"Korea Marchers Decry Tokyo Plan." *New York Times*, 15 February 1959.

Koo, Sunhee. 2016. "Reconciling Nations and Citizenship: Meaning, Creativity, and the Performance of a North Korean Troupe in South Korea." *Journal of Asian Studies* 75 (2): 387–409.

"Koreans in Protest: Stage Rally Against Japan's Repatriation Plan." *New York Times*, 22 February 1959.

Kowalski, Robert. 2011. "The Gift: Marcel Mauss and International Aid." *Journal of Comparative Social Welfare* 27 (3): 189–205.

Ikuno-ku Website. n.d. "Welcome to Ikuno-Ku, Osaka." https://www.city.osaka .lg.jp/contents/wdu020/ikuno/english/index.html.

Laidlaw, James. 2000. "A Free Gift Makes No Friends." *Journal of the Royal Anthropological Institute* 6 (4): 617–34.

Lankov, Andrei. 2006. "Bitter Taste of Paradise: North Korean Refugees in South Korea." *Journal of East Asian Studies* 6: 105–37.

Lankov, Andrei, and Seok-Hyang Kim. 2008. "North Korean Market Vendors: The Rise of Grassroots Capitalists in A Post-Stalinist Society." *Pacific Affairs* 81 (1): 53–72.

Leavitt, John. 1996. "Meaning and Feeling in the Anthropology of Emotions." *American Ethnologist* 23 (3): 514–39.

Lee, Changsoo. 1981a. "Koreans Under SCAP: An Era of Unrest and Repression." In Lee and De Vos, *Koreans in Japan*, 73–90.

Lee, Changsoo. 1981b. "The Period of Repatriation, 1945–1949." In Lee and De Vos, *Koreans in Japan*, 58–72.

Lee, Changsoo. 1981c. "The Politics of Repatriation." In Lee and De Vos, *Koreans in Japan*, 91–109.

Lee, Changsoo, and George A. De Vos. 1981. *Koreans in Japan: Ethnic Conflict and Accommodation*. Berkeley, CA: University of California Press.

Lee, Chung Min, and Jonathan D. Pollack. 1999. *Preparing for Korean Unification: Scenarios and Implications*. Santa Monica, CA: Rand.

Lee, Min Jin. 2017. *Pachinko*. New York, NY: Apollo.

"Letter to Our Compatriots in Japan, from the Enlarged Meeting of the Central Committee of the United Democratic Fatherland Front." 1958. 31 October. In Democratic People's Republic of Korea (DPRK). 1959. *On the Question of 600,000 Koreans in Japan*. Pyongyang: Foreign Languages Publishing House, 109-113.

Levin, Iris, and Ruth Fincher. 2010. "Tangible Transnational Links in the Houses of Italian Immigrants in Melbourne." *Global Networks* 10 (3): 401–23.

Levitt, Peggy. 2001. *The Transnational Villagers*. Los Angeles: University of California Press.

Light, Ivan, and Edna Bonacich. 1988. *Immigration Entrepreneurs: Koreans in Los Angeles 1965–1982*. Berkeley: University of California Press.

Lim, Jie-Hyun. 2010. "Victimhood Nationalism and History Reconciliation in East Asia." *History Compass* 8 (1): 1–10.

Lucht, Hans. 2012. *Darkness before Daybreak: African Migrants Living on the Margins in Southern Italy Today*. Los Angeles: University of California Press.

Malinowski, Bronislaw. (1922) 2014. *Argonauts of the Western Pacific; An Account of Native Enterprise and Adventure in the Archipelagoes of Melanesian New Guinea*. Oxford, UK: Oxford Benediction Classics.

Malkki, Liisa H. 1992. "National Geographic: The Rooting of Peoples and the Territorialization of National Identity Among Scholars and Refugees." *Cultural Anthropology* 7 (1): 24–44.

Malkki, Liisa. 1996. "Speechless Emissaries: Refugees, Humanitarianism, and Dehistoricization." *Cultural Anthropology* 11 (3): 377–404.

Marcus, George. 1995. "Ethnography in/of the World System: The Emergence of Multi-Sited Ethnography." *Annual Review of Anthropology* 24: 95–117.

Mauss, Marcel. (1925) 2002. *The Gift: The Form and Reason for Exchange in Archaic Societies*. Translated by W. D. Halls. London: Routledge.

McDonald, Hal. 2017. "The Art of Nostalgia: Nostalgia as an Aesthetic Form of Memory." *Psychology Today*, https://www.psychologytoday.com/us/blog/time-travelling-apollo/201710/the-art-nostalgia.

Merrill, John. 1980. "The Cheju-Do Rebellion." *Journal of Korean Studies* 2: 139–97.

Ministry of Foreign Affairs of Japan (MOFA-Japan). 2002. "The Position of the Government of Japan Regarding the Incident at the Japanese Consulate General in Shenyang, People's Republic of China." https://www.mofa.go.jp/region/asia-paci/china/shengyang.html.

Ministry of Foreign Affairs of South Korea (MOFA-ROK). 2019. "Figures Relating to Overseas Koreans." http://www.mofa.go.kr/www/wpge/m_21509/contents.do (in Korean).

Ministry of Foreign Affairs of the Republic of Korea [ROK, or South Korea] Ministry of Unification. 2018. "Settlement Support for North Korean Defectors." http://www.unikorea.go.kr/eng_unikorea/whatwedo/support/.

Miyoshi Jager, Sheila. 2013. *Brothers at War: The Unending Conflict in Korea*. London: Profile Books.

Morris-Suzuki, Tessa. 2007. *Exodus to North Korea: Shadows from Japan's Cold War*. Lanham, MD: Rowman & Littlefield.

Morris-Suzuki, Tessa. 2009. "The Forgotten Japanese in North Korea: Beyond the Politics of Abduction." *The Asia-Pacific Journal: Japan Focus* 7 (43:2): 1–19.

Nam, Keun Woo. 2012. "Rethinking the North Korean Repatriation Program: The Chang From An 'Aid Economy' to A 'Hostage Economy.'" *Korean Social Sciences Review* 2 (2): 219–51.

Narayan, Kirin. 2007. *My Family and Other Saints*. Chicago: University of Chicago Press.

Nayeri, Dina. 2017. "The Ungrateful Refugee: We Have No Debt to Repay." *The Guardian*, 4 April 2017. https://www.theguardian.com/world/2017/apr/04/dina-nayeri-ungrateful-refugee.

Nayeri, Dina. 2019. *The Ungrateful Refugee: What Immigrants Never Tell You*. Edinburgh, UK: Canongate Books.

Office of the United Nations High Commissioner for Human Rights (OHCHR). 2014 "Commission of Inquiry on Human Rights in the Democratic People's Republic of Korea." UN Office of the High Commissioner for Human Rights, Geneva. https://www.ohchr.org/en/hrbodies/hrc/coidprk/pages/commissionin quiryonhrindprk.aspx.

Ong, Aihwa. 2003. *Buddha Is Hiding: Refugees, Citizenship, and the New America.* Los Angeles: University of California Press.

Orr, James. 2001. *The Victim as Hero: Ideologies of Peace and National Identity in Postwar Japan.* Honolulu: University of Hawai'i Press.

Park, Hee-Jin. 2010. *"Jochiyihu Bukhan Yeosungeui Sagyungjehwaldong"* [Private Economic Activities of Women in North Korea After 7.1 Economic Measures], in Seongunsidai Bukhan Yeosungeui Salm. *Unification Studies* 14 (1): 93–125.

Park, Jung Jin. 2016. "North Korean Nation Building and Japanese Imperialism: People's Nation, People's Diplomacy, and Japanese Technicians." In *the Dismantling of Japan's Empire in East Asia: Deimperialization, Postwar Legitimation, and Imperial Afterlife*, edited by Barak Kushner and Sherzod Muminov, 119–219. London: Routledge.

Park, Kyeyoung. 1999. "I Am Floating in the Air: Creation of A Korean Transnational Space Among Korean-Latino American Remigrants." *Positions* 7 (3): 667–95.

Park, Kyung Ae. 1992–93. "Women and Revolution in North Korea." *Pacific Affairs* 65 (4): 527–45.

Park, Kyung Ae. 2011. "Economic Crisis, Women's Changing Economic Roles, and Their Implications for Women's Status in North Korea." *Pacific Review* 24 (2): 159–77.

Park, Yong-Ja. 2004. "Bukhaneui Yeosungnodong Jeongchaek (1953–1980): Nodonggyegup Hwawa Supyeongjeok, Sujikjeok Wuigyerul Jungshimeuro" [North Korea's Labor Policies (1953–1980s): Labor Classification and Horizontal and Vertical Hierarchy]. *North Korea Research Bulletin* 8 (2).

Pries, Ludger, ed. 1999. *Migration and Transnational Social Spaces.* Ashgate, UK: Aldershot.

Remennick, Larissa. 2002. "Transnational Community in the Making: Russian Jewish Immigrants of the 1990s in Israel." *Journal of Ethnic and Migration Studies* 28 (3): 515–30.

Remennick, Larissa. 2009. "Former Soviet Jews in Their New/Old Homeland: Between Integration and Separatism." In Tsuda, *Diasporic Homecomings*, 208–25.

Robinson, Courtland. 2010. "North Korea: Migration Patterns and Prospects." Nautilus Institute for Security and Sustainability, Berkeley, CA.

Robinson, Courtland. 2013. "The Curious Case of North Korea." *Forced Migration Review: States of Fragility* (43). Refugee Studies Centre, University of Oxford, Oxford, UK.

Robinson, Courtland, Myung Ken Lee, Kenneth Hill, and Gilbert Burnham. 1999. "Mortality in North Korean Households." *Lancet* 354 (9175): 291–95.

Rock, David, and Stefan Wolff, eds. 2002. *Coming Home to Germany? The Integration of Ethnic Germans From Central and Eastern Europe in the Federal Republic Since 1945.* New York: Berghahn.

Ryang, Sonia. 1997. *North Koreans in Japan: Language, Ideology, and Identity.* Boulder, Co: Westview Press.

Ryang, Sonia. 2000a. "Gender in Oblivion: Women in the Democratic People's Republic of Korea (North Korea)." *Journal of Asian and African Studies* 35 (3): 323–49.

Ryang, Sonia, ed. 2000b. *Koreans in Japan: Critical Voices from the Margin.* London: Routledge.

Ryang, Sonia. 2009. "Introduction: Between the Nations Diaspora and Koreans in Japan." In Ryang and Lie, *Diaspora without Homeland,* 1–20.

Ryang, Sonia, and John Lie, eds. 2009. *Diaspora Without Homeland: Being Korean in Japan.* Los Angeles: University of California Press.

Said, Edward. 2000. *Reflections on Exile and Other Literary and Cultural Essays.* London: Granta Books.

Schwekendiek, Daniel. 2009. "Regional Variations in Living Conditions During the North Korean Food Crisis of the 1990s." *Asia-Pacific Journal of Public Health* 22 (4): 460–76.

Scott, James. 1985. *Weapons of the Weak: Everyday Forms of Peasant Resistance.* New Haven, CT: Yale University.

Seol, Dong-Hoon, and John D. Skrentny. 2009. "Ethnic Return Migration and Hierarchical Nationhood." *Ethnicities* 9 (2): 47–174.

Shipper, Apichai. 2010. "Nationalisms of and Against Zainichi Koreans in Japan." *Asian Politics and Policy* 2 (1): 55–75.

Simmel, Georg. 1971. "The Stranger." In *Georg Simmel: on Individuality and Social Forms,* Edited by Donald Levine, 143–50. Chicago: University of Chicago Press.

Skrbiš, Zlatko. 2008. "Transnational Families: Theorising Migration, Emotions and Belonging." *Journal of Intercultural Studies* 29 (3): 231–46.

Smith, Hazel. 2015. *North Korea: Markets and Military Rule.* Cambridge, UK: Cambridge University Press.

Smith, Robert. 2006. *Mexicans in New York: Transnational Lives of New Immigrants.* Los Angeles: University of California Press.

Song, Jiyoung. 2013. "'Smuggled Refugees': The Social Construction of North Korean Migration." *International Migration* 51 (4): 158–73.

Song, Jiyoung, and Markus Bell. 2018. "North Korean Secondary Asylum in the UK." *Migration Studies* 6 (1): 1–20.

Sorensen, Clarke, and Sung-Chul Kim. 2004. "Filial Piety in Contemporary Urban Southeast Korea: Practices and Discourses." In Ikels, *Filial Piety,* 153–81.

Svašek, Maruška. 2010. "On the Move: Emotions and Human Mobility." *Journal of Ethnic and Migration Studies* 36 (6): 865–80.

Tai, Eika. 2004. "Korean Japanese." *Critical Asian Studies* 36 (3): 355–82.

Takenaka, Ayumi. 2009. "Ethnic Hierarchy and Its Impact on Ethnic Identities: A Comparative Analysis of Peruvian and Brazilian Return Migrants in Japan." In Tsuda, *Diasporic Homecomings,* 260–80.

Thapan, Meenakshi, ed. 2005. "Transnational Migration and the Politics of Identity." In *Women and Migration in Asia,* vol. 1, Thousand Oaks, CA: Sage.

"Japan, South Korea Sign Normalization Treaty, 4 Related Agreements." 1965. *Japan Times,* 23 June 1965. Japan Times Archives.

Toshihiro, Menju. 2019. "Japan's Historic Immigration Reform: A Work in Progress." *Nippon.Com: Your Doorway to Japan.* https://www.nippon.com/en/in-depth/a06004/japan%e2%80%99s-historic-immigration-reform-a-work-in-progress.html.

Tsuda, Takeyuki. 1998. "The Stigma of Ethnic Difference: The Structure of Prejudice and 'Discrimination' Toward Japan's New Immigrant Minority." *Society for Japanese Studies* 24 (2): 317–59.

Tsuda, Takeyuki. 2000. "Acting Brazilian in Japan: Ethnic Resistance Among Return Migrants." *Ethnology* 39 (1): 55–71.

Tsuda, Takeyuki. 2003. *Strangers in the Ethnic Homeland: Japanese Brazilian Return* Migration *in Transnational Perspective*. New York: Columbia University Press.

Tsuda, Takeyuki, ed. 2009. *Diasporic Homecomings: Ethnic Return* Migration *in Comparative Perspective*. Stanford, CA: Stanford University Press.

Tudor, Daniel, and James Pearson. 2015. *North Korea Confidential: Private Markets, Fashion Trends, Prison Camps, Dissenters and Defectors*. North Clarendon, VT: Tuttle.

Turner, Victor. 1967. *The Forest of Symbols*. Ithaca, NY: Cornell University Press.

UN Economic and Social Council (UN ECOSOC). 1998. "Guiding Principles on Internal Displacement." Geneva. https://undocs.org/E/CN.4/1998/53/Add.2.

UN International Organization for Migration (IOM). 2019a. "International Migration Law No. 34: Glossary on Migration." UN International Organization for Migration, Geneva. https://publications.iom.int/books/international-migration-law-ndeg34-glossary-migration.

UN International Organization for Migration (IOM). 2019b. *World Migration Report.* UN International Organization for Migration, Geneva. https://www.un.org/sites/un2.un.org/files/wmr_2020.pdf.

UN Office of the High Commissioner for Human Rights (UNHCR). 1951. "Convention and Protocol Relating to the Status of Refugees." UN Office of the High Commissioner for Human Rights, Geneva. https://www.unhcr.org/3b66c2aa10.

UN Office of the High Commissioner for Human Rights (UNHCR). 2018. *Global Trends: Forced Displacement in 2018*. Geneva: UN Office of the High Commissioner for Human Rights. https://www.unhcr.org/5d08d7ee7.pdf.

UN Office of the High Commissioner for Human Rights (UNHCR). 2019. "2019 UNHCR Donor Ranking." UN Office of the High Commissioner for Human Rights, Geneva. https://www.unhcr.org/en-au/partners/donors/5baa00b24/2019-unhcr-donor-ranking.html.

UN Office of the High Commissioner for Human Rights (UNHCR). 2021. "Syria Refugee Crisis Explained." UN Office of the High Commissioner for Human Rights, Geneva. https://www.unrefugees.org/news/syria-refugee-crisis-explained/.

van Gennep, Arnold. (1909) 1960. *The Rites of Passage*. Translated by Monika B. Vizedom and Gabrielle L. Caffee. Chicago: University of Chicago Press.

Vollset, Stein Emil, Emily Goren, Chun-Wei Yuan, Jackie Cao, Amanda E. Smith, Thomas Hsiao, Catherine Bisignano, et al. 2020. "Fertility, Mortality, Migration, and Population Scenarios For 195 Countries and Territories From 2017 to 2100: A Forecasting Analysis for the Global Burden of Disease Study." *The Lancet*, doi: https://doi.org/10.1016/s0140-6736(20)30677-2.

Walkerdine, Valerie. 2006. "Workers in the New Economy: Transformation as Border Crossing." *Ethos* 34 (1): 10–41.

Whittaker, Elvi. 1992. "The Birth of the Anthropological Self and Its Career." *Journal of the Society for Psychological Anthropology* 20 (2): 191–219.

Wilson, Thomas. 2017. "UN Urges Japan to Take in More Refugees After It Takes in 3 in 6 Months." *Business Insider*, 17 November, 2017. https://www.businessinsider.com/japan-urged-to-accept-more-refugees-into-the-country-2017-11?ir=t.

Wolman, Andrew. 2011. "North Korean Escapees' Right to Enter South Korea: An International Law Perspective." *Yonsei Law Journal* 2 (2): 141–59.

Wolman, Andrew. 2012. "North Korean Asylum Seekers and Dual Nationality." *International Journal of Refugee Law* 24: 793–814.

World Bank. 2018. "Climate Change Could Force Over 140 Million to Migrate Within Countries by 2050." World Bank, Washington, DC. https://www.worldbank.org/en/news/press-release/2018/03/19/climate-change-could-force-over-140-million-to-migrate-within-countries-by-2050-world-bank-report.

Wright, Brendan. 2015. "Politicidal Violence and the Problematics of Localized Memory at Civilian Massacre Sites: The Cheju 4.3 Peace Park and the Kŏch'ang Incident Memorial Park." *Cross-Currents: East Asian History and Culture Review*, 4 (1): 151–80.

Yang, Yŏnghŭi, Dir. 2005. "디어 평양 *Dear Pyongyang*." Ansan: Cheon, Inc.

Yang, Yŏnghŭi, Dir. 2009. "*Itoshiki Sona* 愛しきソナ" [*Sona, The Other Myself*]. Tokyo: Wahaha Hompo.

Yomiuri, Shimbun, and Kaji Onose. 1964. "Free Travel Between Japan, North Korea Is Political Aim." 14 June 1964.

Yoon, In-Jin. 2012. "Migration and the Korean Diaspora: A Comparative Description of Five Cases." *Journal of Ethnic and Migration Studies* 38 (3): 413–35.

Index

www.ingramcontent.com/pod-product-compliance
Lightning Source LLC
Chambersburg PA
CBHW070622030426
42337CB00020B/3884